DIGITAL TRANSFORMATION

IMPLEMENTATION HANDBOOK

SOUMITRA PODDAR
RAJAN K PRASAD

Blue Hill Publications
www.bluehillpublications.in

Blue Hill Publications Pvt. Ltd.

#301, Yogshila Sahusadan, Road No. 4,
Sri K.V. Colony, Saichak,
Beur, Patna, Bihar.
Pincode – 800002
First published by Blue Hill Publications 2022

Website: www.bluehillpublications.in
Mob.: +91-79030-80600

ISBN: 978-93-94741-43-0

This book is dedicated to
the cause of vocational and community engagement
with society in general and the underserved in particular,
to enable them in harnessing the potential of digital transformation.

Launched on the 75th Independence Anniversary of India,
it looks forward to the growth in next 25 years of growth
enabled by digital technologies.

ABOUT THE AUTHORS

Soumitra Poddar

Founder, Strategic Services Consulting

Soumitra Poddar is an alumnus of IIT Kharagpur and has worked as a technology consultant with PwC and IBM for 30+ years. He has extensive technology implementation and transformation experience across APAC, EU, and North Americas markets, and has engaged in clients in FMCG, Oil and Gas, TMT, and Public Services verticals.

Soumitra is the Founder/Partner at Strategic Services, an advisory firm focused on data and technology implementation projects. He works closely with startups and provides mentorship to scale new ventures. Soumitra is a Visiting Faculty at the Vinod Gupta School of Management (VGSoM) at IIT Kharagpur, and at the Indian Institute of Social Welfare and Business Management (IISWBM).

For more details, connect with him on LinkedIn:

https://www.linkedin.com/in/soumitra-poddar-48567914

Rajan K Prasad

Managing Partner, SynSys Consulting

Rajan K Prasad is a management consultant with industry experience of more than 35 years across diverse functions. An engineer/MBA by training, he has managed the implementation of innovative computer-based solutions in information management and decision support systems for logistics, human resource, administration, and facilities management in integrated operations of Steel Authority of India Limited (SAIL) and other CPSEs.

A unique performance enhancement program, PeP, designed and delivered by him has been helping many production shops achieve their targets through techno-managerial interventions. A corporate trainer, coach, and mentor by passion, he enjoys reading, writing and editing.

For more details, connect with him on LinkedIn:

https://in.linkedin.com/in/rajankprasad

FOREWORD

Digital Transformation entails the adoption of digital technology to transform services or businesses by replacing non-digital or manual technology/processes with newer digital ones. Digital disruption is here to stay, and smart business leaders will have to invest in digital technologies to stay relevant in the emerging world.

The four identified pillars of **focus** in digital transformation are, 1. Product, 2. Process, 3. People, and 4. Perspective. Organizations that transform their business digitally are more likely to benefit and accrue double-digit growth and are less likely to lose out on potential revenue.

To beat technology disruption, organizations have to look at the identified **tools of transformation** that include:

- Biz automation, to drive efficiency
- Mobility, to achieve access anytime and anywhere
- Emerging technologies & analytics for real time Information, decision, and support
- Cloud, for on demand tech elasticity, scalability, computational power
- Extensibility, for integrated and connected systems.
- Skilling, for reskilling, upskilling, and continued skilling

The concept of Industry 4.0, which till recently was a larger discussion point only in forums and events, is now considered a commitment to a new industrial revolution. Today we are looking at an active collaboration of big data, data analytics, Robotic Process Automation (RPA), simulation, Augmented Reality (AR), Cloud, Artificial Intelligence (AI), Internet of Things (IoT), process digitization, and a cyber security umbrella across the business value chain. This is helping in moving towards digital from analog systems, to individualized products from mass production, and from paper-based processes to smart factories.

Digital transformation shall continually impact the industry, economy, society, and its citizens at large. It will help create innovative business models, enhancing production processes, increasing productivity, improving quality, driving economies of scale to meet global competitiveness challenges and in improving market access & reach.

In the current times of great adversity and constraints, the Indian industry, especially the SMEs, have understood that accepting technology is the only way to grow, expand to remain competitive in both national and global markets.

India and Digital Transformation

The Government of India has set an ambitious goal of becoming a US$ 5 trillion economy by 2024-25. It considers the SMEs as the major catalyst for triggering the larger and incremental industrial growth.

India's journey to embrace technology for digital transformation has come a long way, and over the last couple of decades, the country has leapfrogged in adoption of technology. It witnessed huge mobile penetration in the first decade of this millennium and that created the base for the adoption of new wave of emerging technologies in the disruptive second decade. The Government has laid a sound foundation with its flagship programs like Digital India, Make in India, Smart Cities, Jan Dhan Yojana, Start-up India, Skill India, Atmanirbhar Bharat etc. Every stakeholder in the ecosystem has their own share of efforts and achievements vis-à-vis creation of the largest rural broadband network, largest global program on citizen digital identity (UIDAI), largest direct benefit transfer (DBT) program, largest citizen engagement program (MyGov) and the largest COVID monitoring platform (COWIN). With this sound foundation in place, India could weather the COVID storm most effectively/ efficiently despite being a large nation with huge population density.

Various studies have highlighted the potential of a positive impact of emerging technologies like AI, IoT, big data on economic growth. These technologies will help to address critical societal issues, improve citizen experience and reform & redesign Government service delivery through intelligent systems. Enhanced Government-Industry collaboration is essential to create and drive such digital transformation programs through effective governance structures to tap the huge opportunities they bring to emerging economies like India.

Skilling for Digital Transformation

The programs around emerging technologies would require attention on skilling, reskilling and capacity building, work organization and redesign, standardization and inter-operability, regulatory framework, cyber security, and public safety. A programmatic approach is what is the need of the hour to move forward in this direction. Industry - government collaboration would be the key to success here also.

Skilling is a very important component to have a digitally transformed India. Ministry of Skill Development & Entrepreneurship (MSDE) is working at a great pace towards removal of disconnect between demand and supply of skilled manpower, building the vocational and technical training framework, skill up-gradation, building of new skills and innovative thinking for ever changing job scenarios. Directorate General of Training (DGT) is working very closely with the industry to drive changes in the curriculums of institutions governed by them, like Industrial Training Institutes (ITI) and National Skill Training Institutes (NSTI) to fulfill the objectives of Skill India.

New curriculums like drone technology and IoT are being added to include emerging technologies to skill and up-skill resources needed for the future by the industry. The ministry has catalyzed up-skilling & re-skilling of the industry resources through its functional arms - National Skill Development Agency (NSDA), National Skill Development Council, NASSCOM (Future Skills program), National Small Industries Corporation skill training centers. Ministry of MSME is also ensuring skilling efforts to the SME clusters through their tool rooms spread across the country.

Industry is collaborating with the Government by executing industry-oriented curriculums in institutions. Joint diploma and certification courses offered enable enhanced employability of students. This in turn would provide the appropriate qualified resource to the industry, which in turn is also spending a large percentage of its CSR funding toward skilling for the new tomorrow.

This book presents a 360-degree view of the processes, technologies, and challenges encountered in the path of Digital Transformation and brings out solutions through illustrative use cases. It is quite a comprehensive resource for organizations, institutions, and individuals engaged in the impending technological revolution that is changing its course exponentially and giving everybody a run for their money.

(Tulsidharan Viswanathan)
Co-founder, VITTI Research Foundation,
Government Affairs, Cyber Security and Emerging Technology Evangelist.

TABLE OF CONTENTS

EXECUTIVE SUMMAR

Our world today is increasingly going digital, and so a digital technologies, from smart phones and GPS systems to AI and Digital Twins in Industry 4.0 have rendered the business world of today unrecognisable from that of the early 2000's. Having an online presence is now a strategic resource for firms; for consumers, markets are increasingly becoming digital; and supply chain systems have undergone redesign to accrue value out of these new changes. According to recent statistics, over 91% of companies across the globe have either already adopted a digital-first business strategy, or plan to do so in the forthcoming future. Be it a new startup or an incumbent firm, companies which can leverage digital technologies have the potential to disrupt the business models of yesteryears. As such, digital transformation has come about as a critical strategic action for companies which aspire to remain relevant in today's disruptive era, and to grow or sustain their competitive advantage.

Despite the unanimous prioritisation, over 70% of companies fail to achieve their desired digital transformations results. Even more successful firms like GE, Ford, and Procter & Gamble have suffered from digital transformation failures. Despite the alarming statistics, the fact hasn't changed that such strategic actions are critical for the future of companies across almost every industry. The world today is no longer where the real value of a business is just about numbers on the balance sheet or the physical assets. Data has come about as the new oil, and digital assets have come about as the new currency of market differentiation. Even Enterprise Resource Planning (ERP) systems, which formerly drew on structured data, now make use of analytical capabilities to help firms sustain their competitive advantage. Competitive differentiation for firms can also emerge from coupling digital capabilities with powerful technological infrastructure. The fusion of business and technology has the potential to be the next big move for businesses ushering in the new order - a hybrid approach to business as lines blur between functions, markets, and workplaces.

As the second fastest growing digital economy in the world, India is on the path to becoming a $5 trillion digital economy by 2025. With more than 1.2 billion telecommunication subscribers and more than 830 million internet subscribers, India hosts the second largest telecommunication market in the

a. With the BharatNet project linking villages across the country with re optic network, it holds the potential to bring high speed internet access to the population. The path-breaking digital initiatives of the Government of India holds tremendous potential to spur entrepreneurship, increase India's global competitiveness, and meet the nation's goal of 'Growth for All'. The three-pronged strategy thrust - a digital backbone for the country, platforms and portals to improve access to government services, and open "stacks" to work as a catalyst for developing ecosystems.

The National Strategy for Artificial Intelligence (NSAI) has highlighted the potential of Artificial Intelligence (AI) in boosting India's annual growth rate by 1.3 percentage points by 2035 and has identified priority sectors for the deployment of AI with Government's support. Promotion of research, skilling, and re-skilling of the workforce, facilitating adoption of AI solutions, and development of guidelines for 'Responsible AI' are the key focus areas of Government of India's digitization plans. Creation of the Unified Payments Interface (UPI), an underlying infrastructure for payments has catalysed India's digital payments revolution. There has been a structural shift, and as of 2022, there has been a quantum jump in the number of transactions which are completed online. The movement has been fuelled by Information Technology, which has grown from a backend support to being the backbone of the nation's innovation and progress. Today, IT shapes the way we work, learn, shop, and live.

The Covid-19 pandemic has furthermore accelerated the adoption of digital technologies and has resulted in an irreversible shift of companies having to adapt to remote working styles during the pandemic restrictions. Two years and two lockdowns later, the concept of a hybrid workplace has become the new reality. Companies across industries, from energy to real estate to banking, are attempting to integrate the old and new world learnings to build a robust hybrid approach. Driven by agile management, companies are placing the enterprise in a better stead from a continuity perspective in case of black swan events like the pandemic. They are increasingly realising that people, processes, and technologies need to work in an integrated way.

Companies across industries are increasingly using digital transformation exercises to drive business transformation. For example, platform firms have resorted to using an omni-channel approach, which allows companies to work with large ecosystems outside their traditional partners (e.g. Uber, Rapido, Flipkart, Swiggy, and Dunzo) to fulfil orders. During the pandemic, Spencer's, the pan-India retail chain, faced a significant drop in footfall across its 162 stores. In the pre-pandemic phase,

98% of sales for Spencer's originated from stores, while a mere 2% came from other channels. Post the pandemic, non-store sales have reached a robust 15% of total sales, signalling over a 7-fold increase. In the BFSI sector, Edelweiss Asset Management, driven by technology adoption practices, came out on top as the fastest growing mutual fund of 2021.

In the era of changing user tastes and behaviours disrupting businesses, firms are adopting digitization strategies. However, firms need to be cognizant of the social and economic risks arising out of digitization practices. To mitigate the risks associated with such technologies, 'Responsible AI' has been promulgated as the strategic approach. A Responsible AI program is the comprehensive set of policies, standards, roles, processes, tools, training, and other elements that are put in place across an organisation to ensure that all AI systems are designed, developed, deployed, and used in a responsible manner. New disruptive technologies like 'Voice AI' have the capacity to reduce immense pressure on the system by increasing efficiency, reducing time, and customising service offerings like healthcare needs, safety and critical support, entertainment, education and training, etc.

Understanding consumer behaviour, choices, and preferences is critical to businesses, and being able to use such data in a productive manner is important for firms. There is now a driving imperative for IT to shift from managing data storage to unleashing the power of data to improve customer offerings and customer services, as well as increasing productivity and efficiency of business processes. It benefits not only in curation of appropriate products, but also in raising manpower productivity by 25-30%, as organisations are able to better predict the kind of product or service they should be offering to customers.

However, with data gaining significance as a strategic resource, ransomware has become a big threat, and data protection is an important component of IT planning and architecture. Data is collected across edge, core, and cloud. The objective of all the data managers and data innovators today is to get access to data in real-time and understand the context of the data.

Common Pitfalls with Digital Transformation in Organisations

- **Not engaging with people:** Successful digital transformations require buy-in from employees and stakeholders. Getting highly engaged employees requires changing the perception of the people by making them aware of exactly how to use the new solution to their advantage.

- **Not being clear on the goal:** When goals are confusing or lack clarity, projects fail. The leaders need to have clarity about the objectives and the process of implementation to drive the project in successful ways.
- **Starting with technology:** The buzz surrounding emerging technologies has potential to cloud the decision making process. Instead of focussing on the technology, decision-makers need to focus on the goal of the digital transformation process to fulfil business requirements.
- **Not approaching it the right way:** The best practices are known as best practices for a reason: they help achieve results smoothly and efficiently, and are grounded in evidence. Reinventing the wheel while attempting digital transformation leads to employees turning against the project early on, stakeholders lacking confidence in the benefits, and capital investment being wasted
- **Not being able to measure success:** A vital element of any successful project is both about measuring the success as well as knowing when to stop. Ideas and ambitions are great, but unless there are metrics, both to achieve them and for knowing when to stop, there are chances of losing sight of the value one adds through the digital transformation initiatives.

ABOUT THE BOOK

The Handbook on Implementation of Digital Transformation for Enterprises is meant for business management professionals to get a comprehensive overview about the digital transformation journey. By drawing from case studies, the handbook presents insights about the digital transformation process in a stepwise manner. From presenting the key concepts of digital technologies in today's world, to reviewing the best implementation practices, the book highlights the approaches, techniques, challenges, and opportunities to empower implementers to overcome the pitfalls which are ubiquitous to the digital transformation process.

Chapter 1

INTRODUCTION

1.1. The Framework

Over the past few years, the world has moved toward a tipping point where enterprises are leveraging technology holistically to transform their business models. The digital transformation has moved inwards from the front or edge of the organization to deep into the core. At the same time, technologies such as AI, automation, Internet of Things (IoT), Mobility, and Robotics have reached a level of maturity that can be leveraged at scale to drive real impact on business outcomes. Organizations across all industries are seeking to become technology, platform, and experience companies. This evolution marks the emergence of Cognitive Enterprises, which are brought to life by imagining market-making platforms, shaping of Intelligent Workflows, and a deeper focus on people experience and humanity.

The COVID crisis has had its impact on these Cognitive Enterprises. It has accelerated the digital transformation journey, reinforced the importance of applying exponential technologies to produce more efficient, effective, and flexible processes; and has clarified the case for leveraging hybrid cloud infrastructures to deliver adaptive consumption models and services. We have seen that the three main building blocks of the Cognitive Enterprise have been stretched by the new reality. These three, namely Market-making Business Platforms, Intelligent Workflows, and Enterprise Experience centred around Humanity, have opened new vistas beyond conventional growth strategies for organizations.

As the impact of the COVID epidemic surged in 2020 -2022, political, administrative, and business leaders came to a common solution: Digital transformation! Due to travel restrictions and nationwide lockdowns, people were compelled to turn to online shopping, e-learning, and social media to maintain a semblance of normality. Tech companies, educational institutions, and other organizations resorted to extensive use of digital technology to collaborate and operate remotely, seamlessly, and without considerable drop in effectiveness.

Although the outbreak of COVID-19 brought to the traditional business its biggest challenge yet, the bitter truth is that those who do not go digital will soon become obsolete. Even before the pandemic had shown its real colors, 80% of the 4000 business leaders from different parts of the world had placed digital transformation as one of their top priorities in 2020 according to the Dell's Digital Transformation Index 2020. The World Economic Forum suggests that by 2025, the value of digital transformation would reach $100 trillion for society and industry combined together.

More than eight out of ten (82 percent) leaders expect that humans and machines will work as integrated teams within their organization within five years (26 percent say their workforce and machines are already successfully working this way). Ninety percent of highly mature agencies agreed that they were already seeing the benefits of digital initiatives launched during the pandemic, compared to 55% of low-maturity organizations. Also, 79% of government executives in India say that in five years, all governmental agencies will have extensive digital capabilities.

1.2. Digital Transformation: From the Past to the Present

The term Digital Transformation may have started dominating the industry now, evidenced by tenfold increase in search on Google over the past five years; it's hardly a new concept. The seminal paper, "A Mathematical Theory of Communication," by Claude E. Shannon in 1948 sowed the roots of digitization which paved the path for digital transformation, the way we know it.

Microchip came in the 1950s itself, transmission of the first message over ARPANET in the 1960s laid foundations of the internet, home computer took birth the 1970s, World-Wide-Web emerged in the 1980s and in the 1990s it became the norm of modernization of business. The retail industry stuck to conventional modes of selling mostly with cash till 2000, yet their advertising and marketing campaigns incorporated digital elements.

With the advent of smart devices and social media platforms, customer expectations grew dramatically and a drastic change occurred in how consumers and businesses communicate with one another. Now e-Commerce is the new normal and companies are operating digital-first exploiting technology and SaaS creating lean, agile operations that react instantly to changes in the competitive environment, freeing employees from the drudgery of manual admin to focus on strategic thinking.

In the case of India, the digital economy is expected to grow to $800 billion by 2030 on the back of rising internet penetration and increasing income according to Finance Minister Nirmala Sitharaman at an IIT Bombay event. Recently, the Indian technology industry crossed the $200-billion revenue mark, touching $227 billion in revenue during FY22, according to Nasscom Strategic Review 2022 . It is expected that various factors, such as increasing spending on marketing and advertising activities by enterprises, changing landscape of customer intelligence to drive the market, and proliferation of customer channels are expected to drive the adoption of digital transformation technologies and services.

Figure 1.1: Timeline of Technology Innovation

However, the Digital Transformation imperatives are making Industry 4.0 move towards a stage where businesses begin to allow customers to customize the product and its delivery. And that will be the rise of Industry 5.0 that would be focused on return of human hands and minds into the industrial framework. With real time data coming from the field, the manufacturers are using advanced technologies to make man and machine reconcile and find ways to work together to improve the means and efficiency of production. Rather than becoming entirely computerized, they're maturing towards collaborative working with optimal use of technology in consonance with man-machine interaction.

Key Trends of the Future of Digital Transformation Industry

- Growing spending on Digital Transformation.
- Shift from B2B towards B2B2C will gain prominence.
- The Internet of Things (IoT) will have significant opportunities.
- Artificial Intelligence (AI) and Machine Learning will revolutionize manufacturing.
- Skill loss in IT and other sectors will be filled by AI.
- XaaS (Everything as Service) will dominate the In-House solutions.
- DT won't be just about technology, it will be about people.
- Cybersecurity will become a key to competitive advantage.

1.3. Digital Transformation in Action

Organizations have been able to identify certain concrete action areas that have made them move from Transition phase to Transformation phase in the ever challenging Digital Ecosystem. They include Creating new business blueprints, Orchestrating compelling changes, Escalating the bet, Embedding exponential technologies, Driving value from data these strategies can be identified and analyzed for implantation in any business. Let us take a peek into these components under the three Building Blocks of creating Cognitive Enterprises, Deploying through hybrid multi-cloud, Elevating human-technology partnerships, Cultivating smart leadership culture, and Performing with purposeful agility.

Although different business verticals adopt their industry specific strategies while overcoming the unique challenges faced by them, yet the main components of digital transformation can be categorized under the three building blocks of creating cognitive enterprises.

1. **Market-making Business Platforms and Ecosystems**
2. **Intelligent Workflows**
3. **Enterprise Experience and Humanity**

However, leaders in every industry are today confronting the most daunting challenge of their lifetimes by having to make decisions as to how to respond to the new market ecosystem created by platforms and the changing customer expectations that come with them. They have to respond to the need for making big and bold bets on how the future will unfold.

The conventional marketing concept of producing, promoting, and meeting the demand by selling has been forced to give way to market-making business platforms. In order to establish these platforms organizations need to instil new rigor and focus to move beyond experimentation, to sidestep cognitive chaos, and to balance stability with agility. These platforms have given rise to a completely new genre of organizations and they are the Virtual Enterprises that we see across all businesses.

1.3.1. Virtual Enterprises Characteristics

These Virtual Enterprises are characterized by some typical attributes and it is important to have a look at them.

- **Purpose:** The Virtual Enterprise takes full advantage of the flexibility and nimbleness promised by hybrid cloud architectures. It enables the openness of the enterprise to connect with business partners as well as access the full potential of leading open technologies to drive innovation. The Virtual Enterprise is therefore underpinned by robust networks and secure technology infrastructure, with right workloads within right overarching architecture and plug compatible with the world around. The dual demands of adaptability and resilience are therefore prerequisites of the journey to become a Virtual Enterprise — a journey on which many organizations have now embarked.
- **Openness:** Openness is the defining characteristic of the Virtual Enterprise. We see organizations recognizing the power of combining platforms to seize new markets, as well as recognizing that the scale of the impact that is required demands this alignment

with other substantive players. By optimizing platform economics, open connectivity, and frictionless engagement, the Virtual Enterprise enables all participants across market-making platforms and ecosystems. Most importantly, openness animates the stretching of the business platforms that are being envisioned to encompass wider ecosystems.

- **Acceleration:** The openness of Virtual Enterprise accelerates access to new sources of product and service innovation. These innovations are led by the It takes a scientific discovery approach, constantly experimenting, relying on predictive and prospective analysis fueled by the massive amount of data it can access from itself and its ecosystem partners. More and more industries are seeing the value that used to be the preserve of R&D-led industries (for example, pharmaceuticals) as they look forward rather than backward and mine the information in their value chains to spark creativity.
- **Agility:** Agility creates the backbone of the value chains that bind the ecosystem participants. As the reach of the workflows is extended, the power of applied technologies such as extreme automation, AI, IoT, and others is multiplied to unlock efficiency and differentiation thereby rendering the platforms ever more attractive. Virtualization adds new opportunities for networks, connectivity, and skills engagement to bring the workflows to life and drive agility in the organization.
- **Boosting Collaboration:** With an open cloud-based AI environment, forward looking companies are developing leading digital solutions and deploy innovative technologies to enable performance and sustainability for the global industry. This helps in accelerating customers' move to the cloud, where customers' teams can collaborate freely across boundaries—breaking down traditional data silos. A leading oilfield service company is providing access to the company's cutting edge exploration and production (E&P) solutions and applications, where the DELFI environment enables energy companies to create new data-driven workflows and adopt game-changing technologies like AI, analytics, and automation. Customers and partners worldwide are able to integrate their data platforms with the industry standard for energy data.
- **Accelerating Science and Data-Led Innovation:** The Future Enterprise is fundamentally one that looks forward and outward. It

does not seek to innovate or drive decisions based on history and internal information, but through a combination of predictive and prospective analysis based on massive access to data and new kinds of crowd and swarm intelligence. The Virtual Enterprise is also more rigorous, pursuing a deeper scientific discovery approach to innovation. And with COVID vaccines currently being developed and tested in months instead of years, scientific discovery is the concept du jour. What if we could apply a similar accelerant to business innovation? Experimentation, simulation, and testing of hypotheses have long formed the core of scientific discovery. For the Enterprise, access to exponential technologies such as AI, IoT, and quantum computing enables analogous processes for business — faster than ever before — and across many different industries.

As AI and machine learning enable ever better pattern recognition, workflow optimization solutions become clearer and more powerful, further perpetuating golden workflow threads throughout the enterprise, its platforms, and its ecosystems. Cross-industry partnerships and consortia can also be amplified by smart application of scientific methods to drive ecosystem-wide innovations.

Data-led innovation operates at multiple levels in the Virtual Enterprise. It can be at the base level of insights driven from a particular analysis of customer data that prompts the reshaping of a service proposition. It can be within the context of a workflow, where continual monitoring and mining of the activities and performance within a process can highlight areas for improvement and prompt automated or human intervention.

Science and discovery drive innovation across industries and constitute $52 trillion of the $88 trillion world economy. Businesses that rely on science and discovery-based Information include enterprises in Aerospace and defence, Chemicals, Automotive, Commercial transportation, B2B tech hardware, Energy and utilities, Life sciences, Healthcare services, Medical devices, Industrial goods, IT services, Software, Banking, Financial markets, Insurance, Consumer staples, Discretionary consumer goods, E-commerce, Retail, etc.

- **Sustainability and Impact:** The Virtual Enterprise reinforces the extent of connectedness around the world and the impact of humans on each other and on the planet. It aligns purpose and intent with wider societal impacts. With sustainability and stakeholder capitalism taking hold of the C-suite, the new ecosystem business models are helping provide solutions to the biggest challenges of our time around climate, health, security, and equality. This plays an increasing part, also, in bringing the desired change in the way that customers, partners, and employees feel about engaging with the organization.

1.3.2 Barriers to Successful Digital Business

Adoption of Digital Business processes suffers from certain barriers that impede the implementation and though these are more prominent in the sectors which are labour intensive, yet they exist in all sectors.

- Lack of a digital vision and strategy
- Lack of workforce readiness
- Technology constraints
- Time and money constraints
- Law and regulations

1.4. Government's Role in Digital Transformation

Governments are now working on making digitization friendly policies by taking initiatives like enhancing connectivity, promoting electronic payments, encouraging remote working, developing E-learning platforms, and easing access to digital services and tools. While promoting E-commerce and E-payments have been on the priority list of all the governments, quite innovative actions are being taken in different areas to support digitization. These include concrete actions like granting of temporary access to spectrum in the 5.9 GHz band in the United States, creation of a toolkit for tele-working by France, subsidizing training of SMEs and free access to online training platforms by China, the Digital Solidarity portal by Italy where small firms can access digital services of large companies free of cost, and the Fintech initiative of Mexico to alleviate liquidity problems of entrepreneurs in digitization field.

Governments all over the world have undergone significant digital advancement trying to keep pace with technological developments. Significant progress was made in the direction of providing digitized services to their people, but that remained mostly at the front-end level and the tougher issues of fundamentally reengineering the government operations, processes, and systems remained getting postponed. The administrative superstructure became wired but the systems didn't get digitally transformed.

The pandemic, COVID-19 became a historic pivot point for digital transformation of many governments vaulting them headfirst into the next stage of digitization. For the first time in modern history have the governments across the globe rolled out so many large-scale innovative solutions like tele-health, work from home, virtual courts, and virtual education etc. in such a short time and on such a massive scale. But the journey hasn't been smooth. The demand for services kept coming in surges and the infrastructure couldn't accommodate and support. Instances of websites crashing, call centres getting overburdened, tele-health being delayed, and virtual learning falling short of the expectations were a common sight. It has brought to light the underlying frailty of digital foundations of many governments.

The pressure faced by legacy IT systems during the pandemic brought out the need for modernization at the top of the agenda for most of the governments. The need for meeting the citizen's demands for services and their expectations, ensuring delivery of benefits of government's schemes to the beneficiaries, rising to requirements of innovation, and adhering to compliance with statutory regulations have been the key drivers for the impetus being given to digitization. The stark difference in customers' experiences with the corporate world and with government agencies has been a major factor in raising citizens' expectations from governments. In 2019, 80% of US federal agencies scored "poor" or "very poor" on Forrester's US Federal Customer Experience Index, compared with only 14% of brands in the private sector.

1.4.1. Beginning Digital to Being Digital

Now, governments are taking advantage of the current momentum and building upon the lessons learned over the past two years. They are pushing forward on the path to becoming a truly digital enterprise that is better able to thrive in a fast-changing and uncertain world. However, being truly digital requires a fundamental change in how governments think about service delivery and the underlying back-end systems that support such services. The journey to digitization starts from "Beginning Digital" and moving through "Doing Digital" and "Becoming Digital" it reaches "Being Digital". Governments are at different stages in their journey and some trailblazers have already emerged in this field.

The governments, that have reached the "being digital" stage, consistently use digital to achieve better mission outcomes. "Being digital" is characterized by the level of digitization in two fields: service delivery and government operations. For example, Estonia, a small Baltic state has become the world's most advanced digital society. It is one of the first countries in the world to declare internet access a basic human right way back in 2000 and the first to give its citizens blockchain-backed mobile IDs. It has been able to build the world's first paperless government: e-Estonia. Today 99 percent of all Estonian state services can be accessed online, 98 percent of Estonian citizens have an electronic ID card that can be used for digital signature, and more than 45 percent of the population use internet voting.

It uses an AI-powered matching engine to find suitable jobs for the unemployed. It has been found that after six months of joining, around 72% of the candidates selected through the AI-aided system were still with their jobs, compared to 58% of those selected through traditional systems. Thus, Estonia has given an entirely different outlook on what a truly human-centric society entails for digital citizens.

1.5. Digital Transformation in Indian Industry and Government

As the second fastest digitizing economy in the world, India is on the path to becoming a $5 trillion digital economy by 2025 turning aspirations of 1.3 billion Indians. Fuelled by IT, which has grown from a backend support into being the backbone of Indian innovation and progress, India has shown to have a strong ecosystem of over 50,000 startups out of which 10,000 came up amidst the challenge of the pandemic. The Digital India program is a flagship programme of the Government of India with a vision to transform India into a digitally empowered society and knowledge economy. The Vision is to provide a facility of seamless digital payment to all citizens of India in a convenient, easy, affordable, quick and secured manner.

The three key vision areas of Digital India are:

- Digital infrastructure as a utility to every citizen.
- Governance and services on demand.
- Digital empowerment of citizens.

In order to achieve these visions, Government of India focused its efforts on availability of high speed internet as a core utility for delivery of services, cradle to grave digital identity that is unique, lifelong, online and authenticable, citizen participation in digital & financial space, shareable private space on a public cloud, easy access to common service center, and safe and secure cyberspace.

1.5.1. Atmanirbhar Bharat Abhiyan (Self-Reliant India Campaign): The fight against COVID-19 pandemic triggered a need in India for re-inventing itself to make the country and its citizens independent and self-reliant in all senses. The Atmanirbhar Bharat Abhiyaan or Self-reliant India campaign, the vision of new India, envisages five pillars – Economy, Infrastructure, System, Vibrant Demography, and Demand. Special economic and comprehensive package equivalent to 10% of India's GDP has been allocated to this program year after year since 2020 itself.

Government has identified structural reforms and enablers across seven sectors of MNREGA, Health and Education, Business during COVID, Decriminalisation of Company Act, Ease of doing business, Policy related to Public Sector Units, State government and resources related to it. Several bold reforms such as Supply Chain Reforms for Agriculture, Rational Tax Systems, Simple & Clear Laws, Capable Human Resource and Strong Financial System have been taken up by the government.

1.5.2. DigiLocker: DigiLocker is an Indian digitization online service provided by the Ministry of Electronics and Information Technology, Government of India under its Digital India initiative. DigiLocker or digital locker provides access to authentic virtual documents. It is a digital document wallet where you can store your documents such as driving licence, PAN card, Voter ID, policy documents, etc. You can upload the documents and keep these safe when you sign up for a DigiLocker account.

1.5.3. Startup India: Startup India is a flagship initiative of the Government of India, intended to build a strong ecosystem that is conducive for the growth of startup businesses, to drive sustainable economic growth and generate large scale employment opportunities. The Government through this initiative aims to empower startups to grow through innovation and design and to transform India into a country of job creators instead of job seekers. These programs have catalyzed the startup culture, with many entrepreneurs availing the benefits of starting their own business in India and startups getting recognized through the Startup India initiative.

Startups are using digital technologies and processes for developing platforms to scale business resulting in India replacing the UK in having the third highest number of unicorns in the world. As many as 44 unicorns have been identified in India between 2020 and 2021, which have created wealth for India. The Indian unicorn club in 2021 included Flipkart Moglix, BharatPe, CoinDCX, upGrad, Groww, BlackBuck, Droom, OfBusiness, Meesho, Chargebee, CRED, Digit, Gupshup, Infra.

1.5.4. Embedding Digitization in MSME: The Union Government has projected doubling the Indian economy to US $5trillion in the next five years. To achieve this goal, generation of employment opportunities for the young is imperative, and the rise of the Micro Small Medium Enterprise (MSME) sector has the potential to serve as a key enabler of the same. The sector is receiving special mention across for its contribution to the gross domestic product of the country and is contributing to the development of entrepreneurship among people and professionals especially in the rural and semi-urban areas. With more than 6 Crore MSMEs functional in the country at present, their importance in nation building and economic revival cannot be overemphasized.

While the requirements to bring MSME to digital platforms has always been there the pandemic has only accelerated the need more. Worldwide, the pandemic has been viewed as a change catalyst for the MSME sector. It has enabled rapid transition and adoption of digital payments in this sector that has reached a much wider population across different strata of society.

What began as a means to avoid currency notes for fear of infection during the first wave became a major awakening to the speed and convenience of using digital platforms instead. This is not without any hiccups. In India, there are still connection drop issues with failed payments in many areas that are geographically remotely located. However, while there may be occasional reservations when it comes to more expensive purchases and payments, the fact is that Indian customers now tend to insist on digital payment in case of smaller spend and are often avoiding vendors who do not offer it.Furthermore, the government has an objective to enhance MSME share in exports and its contribution to GDP ensuring that the sector gets further strengthened.

1.6. Role of Leadership in Digitization

Corporate Enterprises including MSME have embarked upon the Digital Transformation journey with the goal of achieving the industry best performance metrics for agility, quality, productivity, profitability, customer experience, environment and social responsibility through data insights. This goal or objective can be reached by establishing a lean and agile business process driven by digitally enabled customer centric ecosystems with 100% data literate employees at its core. Eventually, this would culminate into organizations becoming a data-driven end-to-end connected organization.

The best companies combine digital activity with strong leadership to use technology and turn transition into transformation. This is what is termed as Digital Maturity. Companies vary in their digital maturity, and those that are more mature outperform those that are not. Organizations that enable digital payments have been on a mission to empower home grown brands for quite some time now and are now using performance marketing to create a real impact in this genre. Not only this, these organizations also work to bring high intent customers to their partners and reduce their cost of acquiring customers by 5 times.

Leading digital change requires managers to have a vision of how to transform their company for a digital world. It is widely agreed that support from senior leadership is necessary for the successful adoption of artificial intelligence within large organizations. While this could perhaps be said of any relatively new technology, AI stands to have a bigger business impact than most in achieving Digital Transformation. It is widely perceived that if Artificial Intelligence (AI) is the engine of the Fourth Industrial Revolution, data is the new oil, just like fossil oil of the 18th century. As with oil, data is now shaping the world and thus termed as the 'New oil of the Digital Economy and the new currency of the digital world'.

Oil drove the evolution of automobiles and development of infrastructure like roads and bridges as well as air travel that broke down the global barriers for travel and trade. Similarly, the value in the data that is already there is breaking barriers of scale and geography. Today retailers have access to massive amounts of 'big data' that is external to their organizations, ranging from demographics to industry category.

In the context of the Internet of Things, the quantum of data starts to paint a different picture - a much bigger picture. Whereas oil is a finite resource whose value is tied mostly to its scarcity, IoT has the potential to make data virtually an unlimited resource.

While having a robust framework in place can speed up the digitisation process, it isn't enough. The biggest challenge to achieving widespread transformation is reluctance from the employees to accept new technologies or policies. The company's size is a huge factor too; the larger the size, the harder it can be to convince the workforce to accept the change.

In the process of implementing digital transformation in a company, the leadership has the responsibility to foster enthusiasm among the employees for the transformation opportunities. The leaders have to have customer-focused business objectives, to integrate conventional management and communication techniques using digital tools to make them more transparent and efficient, and to get teams to see that technology can reduce their workload and help add more value to the company.

Given the hurdles that businesses face and the inexorable race to move everything online and make available in real-time, 24/7, leaders are at least united in the belief that they need to transform.

1.7. Broad scope of a Digital Transformation (DT) project

The job entails extensive use of Industry 4.0 technologies such as Industrial Internet of Things, Machine Learning, Artificial Intelligence, Computer Vision, Data & Video Analytics, Digital Twins, Augmented/Virtual Reality, Cloud Computing, Robotics, 3D Printing, Cybersecurity etc. In terms of the infrastructural capabilities, Data Storage and Management, Internet & Network Stability / Speed / Connectivity, Wi-Fi, 5G etc. would be the cornerstones.

However, leaders are struggling with the pace of change in the area of Digital Transformation. Change management and upskilling/re-skilling are potentially the major challenges of the process.

A company engaged in implementing Digital Transformation would need to identify and engage with Startups/MSMEs with missionary zeal as well as acquire the required resources and capabilities to:

- Be a Co-Pilot in the Digital Transformation Journey of the organization/client.
- Comprehend OT Data and Conceptualize Pain Areas specific to the business/industry.
- Formulate/Identify the optimal digital solutions and hand-hold implementation in the organization.

- Train the workforce on Emerging Technologies towards 100% data-literate employees.

1.8. The Road Ahead

The new digital world there will be stronger human-machine partnerships through application of machine learning and AI to customer data to predict and understand customer behavior like never before. As companies take a customer-first approach it will eventually result in stronger human-human relationships.

In order to keep pace with the challenge of Digital Transformation, the organizations will have to focus on the following key areas.

- Gain employee buy-in.
- Make customer experience a boardroom concern.
- Align compensation, training and KPIs to digital goals and strategy.
- Task senior leaders with spearheading digital change. Appoint a chief AI officer.
- Put policies and tech in place to support a fully remote, flexible workforce.
- Teach employees coding and understanding software development.
- Automate everything and encourage customers to self-serve.

Businesses will have to have a mid-term plan to achieve the following milestones within a span of next 5 years.

- Have effective cyber-security defences in place
- Deliver product offering as a service
- Complete transition to a software-defined business
- Strong R&D initiatives to drive the organization forward
- Use AI to pre-empt customer demands
- Delivering hyper-connected customer experiences with VR

Businesses intend to meet these priorities by escalating their investments in emerging technologies as well as in the underlying infrastructure and computing power. The proportion of companies investing in advanced AI is expected to more than triple within five years and the number of companies investing in Virtual / Artificial Reality is also expected to triple.

Business leaders have a consensus that in order to become a contender in the next era, they'll have to meet the targets of Digital Transformation. They are aware of the challenges they have to face in the form of an endemic ad hoc approach to digital transformation that fails to combine the latest and greatest in technology with a change in culture and mindset.

Chapter 2

BUSINESS BLUEPRINT FOR DT DEPLOYMENT

2.1. Introduction

A business blueprint is the step-by-step way to identify the business's needs, goals, and strategic plan. Having a business blueprint is essential because it provides the framework for the business during the process of its development. It is a helpful tool in determining what business model would work best for a specific business. Companies that have not developed a blueprint beforehand may find it challenging to identify where to start and how to move forward.

Business blueprint provides structure and guidance at the organizational level, helps in increasing business and staff efficiency, ensures transparency in the decision-making process, and assists in identifying new opportunities for growth beyond the current scope of the business model. It helps in defining all the critical success factors and key performance indicators.

2.2. Need for Business Blueprint

A business blueprint in its essence is a genuine, realistic and conclusive detailing of scope, specifications and complete solution design of the business processes leading to fulfilment of objectives, desired business outcomes and envisioned goals. It requires mapping business processes, enlisting all important information in the simplest way possible and devising the best way to grow and scale.

It gives a detailed description of a company's business processes e.g. Materials Management, Sales and Distribution, integration with Finance modules, Production Planning and Human Resources etc. The typical template of a business blueprint focuses on understanding, authenticating and documenting project scope, specifications.

Creating a business blueprint is an important objective in itself because it forces managers to think things through and look at the components of the business from different perspectives, thereby allowing them to find possible flaws and deal with them as early as possible. It is not a one-time project, and it should be updated on a regular basis. The process involves identifying development needs which could result in the need for a form, report, interface, enhancement or workflow.

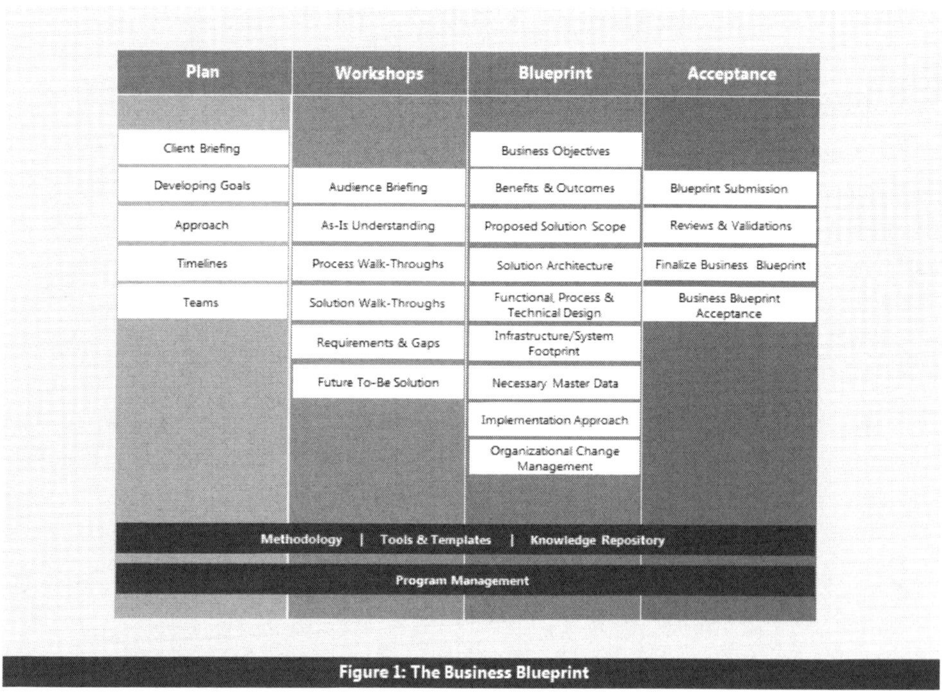

Figure 2.1: The Business Blueprint ***(cf: SAP Blogs)***

2.3. Steps for Developing a Business Blueprint

Business blueprinting is an iterative process that has to be tailored to the specific needs of a company to ensure that the business achieves the success it desires. However, from a broad perspective, all the business blueprints have ten key steps.

1. Taking Inventory of the Current Business Process: Taking inventory of the current business processes helps in identifying new opportunities for growth and success in the future. The activities in this step include identifying what is working, what is not working, the key facilitators of the company's business strategy, and the constraints being faced by the organisation.

2. Developing a Workflow Chart: After taking the inventory, the next step is to develop the workflow in terms of interdependence of various processes, requirement and utilization of resources, impact of individual components in the value chain, and availability of alternatives to the current processes.

Documenting this information and making it accessible to various teams helps in dissemination and validation of the information on details of the overall business process. It is a critical step in the blueprinting project because it helps in gaining buy-in from everyone in the company by providing context on what will change and what value will be gained from such change.

3. Creating Vision of the Organisation: The company has to develop a vision as to where do the stakeholders see the company in a year and what about it in the next five years. The direction in which the business has to move has to be charted out. This exercise aims to uncover the business goals and help assess the best route to get there.

Most importantly, this exercise helps in identifying the key performance indicators that would help in measuring success of the business blueprinting initiative.

4. Drawing Out the Blueprint: The drawing board of a business blueprint is the crucible of brainstorming sessions with the key personnel in which it is articulated as to who is responsible for each aspect of the business. The specific stages of handoffs between various business units are identified and formulated so that everyone in the organization easily knows and understands their role in the company's success.

5. Outlining Project Estimates: Like any change management initiative, the company needs to understand what it will cost to make the necessary changes in the business processes. The project estimates should outline the required resources, the technology solutions needed, and the money and time investment. The initial steps of documenting the project scope helps in making the whole organization see the business value of blueprinting and understand the need for investment for deriving returns in the future.

6. Getting Feedback on the Blueprint: A business blueprint is a typical project that requires a continuous feedback loop amongst key stakeholders. Gaining perspective from everyone ensures the blueprint makes sense and reflects reality, while also helping teams become flexible to the needs of future changes. This feedback loop also helps in establishing stakeholder support in refining who is in charge of what and ensures the blueprint is executed as documented.

7. Creating an Implementation Plan: Success of the entire exercise of blueprinting depends on the implementation plan which is almost as important as the entire business blueprint itself. If what is blueprinted cannot be executed, the complete project gets jeopardised. The implementation plan should elaborate the steps needed to implement the blueprint, the employee training required to be done, and the measures of success.

8. Doing a Trial Run: For successful implementation of any change project, it is sensible to test the blueprint on a small scale and assess the possible areas of concern that may arise with implementation of the whole blueprint. Trial runs help teams gain clear understanding of the plan that has been mapped out and also develop improved processes that fit the business' needs better than what has been initially planned.

9. Implementing Changes Quickly and Efficiently: On completion of the trial run the insights gained from the experiment must be used to set improvement targets with appropriate linkages to the previously defined measures of success. Information regarding the changes has to be communicated to the right people to ensure that people never lose sight of company goals while working out the intricacies of the new business processes.

10. Making continuous improvement a practice: No change is permanent and changes keep occurring in the business environment more as a rule than exception. It is essential to ensure that the business blueprint of a company continues to drive improvement in consonance with the changes in the external as well as internal environment. A business blueprint needs to be evaluated on a regular basis in terms of performance of the new business processes and wherever necessary additional improvements ought to be brought in to promote efficiency and further success.

2.4. Digital Transformation and Business Blueprint

While creation of a business blueprint is necessary at every stage of business development and growth, it assumes utmost importance in the process of Digital Transformation. As Digital Transformation aims at utilizing modern technology to create new - or modify existing - business processes, culture, and customer experiences, it involves re-imagining of business in the digital age equipping organizations with the tools necessary to keep up with competitors and to meet changing market requirements. This type of transformation transcends traditional roles like sales, marketing, and customer service, and is primarily concerned with how organizations think about, and engage with, customers. With the incorporation of new technology, organizations have the opportunity to re-examine how they carry out business. It has the potential to open doors for significant growth and to allow businesses to greatly increase their customer experience as well as branch out into industries that were never before possible.

The digitization process of organisations started in the 1990s when companies started realizing the power of data and began effectively using that data to create change in their business practices. The progress has been in distinct phases till now. It started with collecting, storing, and using internal data to generate information that was easily accessed by employees. It was the phase of Systems of Record (SOR). Enterprise Resources Planning (ERP) is one of such systems that may include CRM (Customer Relations Management) for a customer-facing company, HRMS (Human Resource Management System) for an employee-focused company, and Electronic Health Record (EHR) system for a healthcare organization. It basically creates a record and specialized data that a company can use to support the decision making process by providing processed relevant data through the MIS (Management Information System) at the click of a button.

With time it emerged that just having SOR in place wasn't able to magically modernize an organization and bring in the desired productivity change that businesses aspired to. The major limitation was restricted accessibility of data that was stored in silos and was available to only some of the departments. A need was felt to break out of the silos so that the information is dispersed and everyone is kept informed, and systems of collaboration emerged. Systems of collaboration (SOC) tap the data collected by the SOR, but more importantly, they allow for a flow of knowledge between employees across the organisation. Teams can pull out this knowledge and collaborate with each other to improve the overall performance of the company.

However, companies have realized they need systems to compile and digest the wealth of information already available with the previous systems. Advances in database optimization technology have allowed Systems of Engagement (SOE) to collect and source this data much faster and provide actionable business insights at a rapid pace. This has led to a switch from being product-focused to delivering service-focused business. This has resulted in improved customer experience and their engagement and has served as a catalyst for the next step in the evolution.

Now, by threading systems of productivity and outcomes together, organisations can create efficiencies for the teams, customers, and the company as a whole — without adding to the existing workload of their people. A truly unified digitization takes advantage of everything technology has to offer to the business world, for mapping out the workflows for the entire company quickly, and the decision makers can focus on creating the all-important end-user experiences. These can be called Systems of Outcomes (SOO).

However, SOR (System of Records) remains the central plank of any organization's digitization and any innovative technology has to rely on it to be effective. Although Digital Transformation is not the same thing as Enterprise Resource Planning (ERP), but it is essentially the platform on which the digital transformation initiative is launched. ERP systems are used by organizations looking to manage their business functions within a centralized and integrated system. It brings together customer management, human resources, business intelligence, financial management, inventory, and supply chain capabilities into one system.

2.5. Enterprise Resource Planning

Enterprise Resource Planning (ERP) covers the techniques and the methods employed for the integrated management of businesses as a whole from the viewpoint of the efficient use of the management resources, to improve the efficiency of an enterprise.

It facilitates company-wide integrated information systems, covering all functional areas by assisting in aggregating logistics and finance data and mapping business processes across finance, manufacturing, customer relationship management (CRM), supply chain business processes, analytics, and electronic commerce for enterprises both small and medium and large sized companies.

The benefits of ERP address the top business priorities and they cover all aspects of the business.

- **Streamlining Business Processes:** The foremost requirement of assessing "leading practices" and "documenting" the process definitions ensures that Standard Operating Procedures (SOPs) are put in place across core and support processes for all operations and locations.

The integration of data and information with appropriate validations facilitates in transitioning from a state of "people dependency" to being "largely process driven". This ensures removal of slack, unreliability, and redundancy from the system.

- **Improve Customer Experience:** It provides access to a complete view of customer needs by tying all customer-facing applications together with a single customer database. Customer Experience solutions help the organisation migrate away from highly customized legacy systems to create an excellent e-commerce experience for customers.

The company can provide customers with easy and intuitive channels for selecting their products, services, and preferences. ERP systems map the customer journey to specific channels and touch-points to help ensure every interaction and outcome is appropriate at all times. It helps in deriving the real-time data insights that the company needs to provide a differentiated customer experience that delivers the right offer at the right time, in the right channel, to the right customer.

- **Attract New Customers:** ERP systems enable companies to engage with customers where and how they prefer – online or offline, mobile, social, or chat – and deliver consistent experiences through all the touch points. They make it possible to deliver differentiated and contextual experiences, whether the company is selling to consumers or organizations.

Closing of deals becomes faster by taking advantage of collaboration technology such as video conferencing and social collaboration platforms. It lets companies harness new technologies, such as machine learning and the IoT, to gain intelligence and efficiency in customer acquisition processes.

Insights from a variety of sources, including online and offline transactions, marketing activities, service interactions, social media, and even data from devices based on Internet of Things (IoT) technology can be leveraged for a complete view of the customer.

- **Enable Growth (Revenue, Market Share):** Companies equipped with ERP are prepared to adapt their business models by scaling quickly and flexibly in ways that meet new requirements as the company grows. They are in a position to respond quickly to opportunities, with 360-degree visibility and a comprehensive view of business operations, by securing a single point of truth across the business.

Such companies are able to explore and find new opportunities to expand their business with variations of existing products, new products, or new markets. They can set a strong foundation of agile finance processes to help ensure the effectiveness of a new product, pricing scheme, or revenue strategy.

- **Increase Profits and Reduce Costs:** By practicing strategic sourcing the company is able to improve profits by lowering costs associated with finding and qualifying suppliers through the use of advanced collaboration tools and commerce networks. There is considerable improvement in the supply chain with visibility across every step of the process by tracking customer demands, asset use, and inventory levels.

Similarly, manpower utilization improves as team members can be utilized efficiently resulting in reducing staff overhead by scheduling talent effectively and matching available resources to the business needs.

In essence, these new technologies help in cutting the cost of IT ownership with integrated software solutions hosted on Cloud.

- **Improved Employee Experience:** Employee engagement increases with the increase in openness regarding the objectives, processes, and performance of the company. It helps in motivating them to perform at their best through ongoing dialogue with managers and a process of continuous coaching and feedback can be put in place.

Effective talent management and collaboration transforms the new-hire experience and helps them ramp up quickly, as well as accelerates employee development and career progression.

A learning culture gets built in through increased collaboration and knowledge sharing between employees, managers, and experts. Management can listen, understand, and respond to employee needs and experience gaps to ensure employees' resilience and productivity.

- **Minimize Business or Compliance Risk:** ERP facilitates establishment of basic policies, compliances, and controls across core business processes that support operations and audit teams. It also manages access governance for business-critical and strategic financial applications to help ensure that right people have access to them while unnecessary access without oversight is contained.

As such, it can screen business partners, if engaging in cross-border trade, to avoid doing business with sanctioned or denied and restricted parties. Careful management of imports, exports, and free trade agreements is made possible to improve compliance for cross-border trade as well as to reduce taxes and tariff. The organisation can remain compliant as the business expands by choosing technology vendors who meet the mandatory requirements, such as labour, tax, and environment legislation.

One of the latest additions to the list in the Indian context is Goods and Service Tax (GST) .Typical ERP systems associate HSN/SAC codes with your goods and services and record the GSTINs for contacts at the time of creation. The next time you generate a transaction, the corresponding information is auto-populated. From place of supply to GST levied on goods and services, display all relevant details in your bills and invoices so your transactions meet the Government mandates. Create e-Way bills from within your ERP software and automatically detects transactions that require e-Way bills and helps you capture the e-Way bill information in your invoices and transport copies.

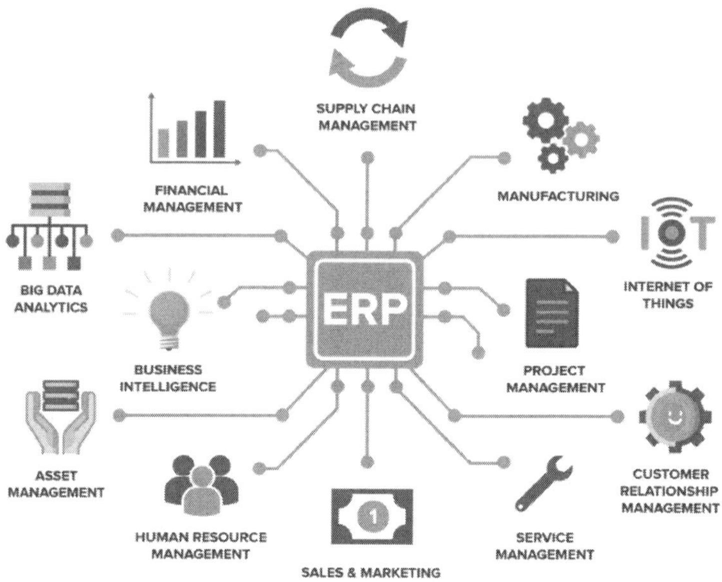

Figure 2.2: The ERP Ecosystem

2.6. ERP & Digitization

Over the years, businesses across sectors have been struggling with some common issues, including:

- Dealing with out of stock situations and order delays.
- Duplication of work killing productive hours of your key people.
- Matching performance figures from different sources and different functions of the organisation.
- Unreliable reports from different systems leading to hours of reconciliation.
- Managing multiple software in business giving rise to serious issues like managing complex hardware structure, compatibility issues and vendor dealings

The more progressive a business wants to be, the more real-time reporting tools are needed. A single integrated system like ERP eliminates the workload of employees caused due to multiple standalone systems and also enables a consolidated digital way of working. It provides customer insights using analytics to provide relevant cross-selling and up-selling opportunities.

Thus, futuristic companies are taking steps to simplify systems and save major resource time. They are assessing if:

- Existing "IT system" is effectively "leveraged" to manage business processes and is moving towards.
- Transforming business process framework from "Detective Control" driven to "Preventive controls" driven
- Focusing and investing in one system that is scalable. This eliminates duplication and synchronization issues, using fully integrated software to get end to end real-time reports and trigger action notifications.
- Removing standalone software and invest in single business solution for consistent information and efficiency.

2.6.1. Benefits of ERP

- End to End Accounting and Logistics Transactions
- Online Payment acceptance
- Authorisation Controls based on roles in Organisation
- Connected Banking
- Monitor stock levels
- Real Time Reports and Insights
- Tamper-proof Audit Trails
- Scalable E-Invoicing
- Automate Workflows
- Multi User Access
- One Click GST Filing

2.6.2. ERP Implementation Strategy

An enterprise resources planning (ERP) system may be key to improve business productivity and efficiency by automating processes and providing a centralized source of data for all teams at a company. But implementation of ERP in any organisation can be complex and sometimes challenging, largely because it affects people and business processes across the entire organization from accounting to human resources to procurement to engineering to sales and marketing. It basically brings a new system of working where multiple groups work with a single source of information that everyone can access on a real-time basis allowing teams to make better decisions, faster.

Driving this change requires strong project management and backing from senior leadership. To develop the new system, the organization needs a committed project team that represents all users of the ERP platform. This would ensure that the software will support the needs and business processes of all departments across the company.

2.6.3. Phases of ERP Implementation in Organizations

ERP implementation in any organisation is a multi-phase project that includes redesigning businesses processes to take advantage of the new system's capabilities, configuring the software, migrating the organization's data from legacy systems, training users, and making them use the new system. The process typically takes a few months and can take up to a year at large organizations. It's usually managed by a project team that includes stakeholders from all functional groups in the company.

- **Phase 1 (Discovery and Planning):** The first step in implementation of ERP in an organisation is identifying the need, ascertaining the scale, and deciding the overall project boundaries. Planning and designing of the implementation process in terms of details of how to go about the implementation with time schedules, deadlines etc for the project are done. Roles and responsibilities of the key personnel are identified and assigned.
- **Phase 2 (Package Evaluation and Selection):** The most important phase of the ERP implementation is package evaluation, because the package that one selects will decide the success or the failure of the project. An ERP system involves a huge investment and major organisational interventions. Hence, once a package is purchased, it is not an easy task to switch to another one.

Thus, it is a 'do-it-right-the-first-time' proposition. The objective is to find a package that is flexible enough to meet the company's needs. It may not be a perfect fit but it ought to be a 'good fit'. It is always better to form a selection committee for the evaluation of the packages. This committee should comprise people from the various departments like the functional experts etc.

- **Phase 3 (Project Formulation and Chartering):** With the selection of the package and the implementation partner or vendor, it is important to define the roles, responsibilities and the key milestones associated with the project. The Project Charter outlines the governing principles and approach to executing the project and provides additional guidance on:
    - Scope and objectives
    - Critical success factors / constraints surrounding execution
    - Approach to service delivery and project protocols
    - Project team roles and responsibilities
    - Project timeline, key milestones and budget
    - Project governance structure, the primary stakeholders, and individuals / groups impacted in the course of service delivery
- **Phase 4 (Implementation Team Formation):** ERP Project implementation typically involves two ERP Project Teams: one from the organization and the other from the consultant/vendor.
- The **ERP Project Team from the Organisation** side must have a Senior Management Executive as the Project Owner/ Sponsor, a dedicated Project Manager, and a group of Subject Matter Experts from each function. There should also be a person responsible for Change Management in the ERP Project Team, who could be the Project Manager or the Project Owner or any other individual identified for the specific task.
- From the **ERP Software Consultant/Vendor** side, there has to be an Account Manager who would manage customer relations, a Project Manager who would be responsible for the day to day activities, and a group of Technical and Functional Experts to coordinate with the Subject Matter Experts.

It is important that both teams work in close coordination with each other and have a very clear understanding of their roles and responsibilities for smooth, successful, and on-time completion of ERP implementation.

- **Phase 5 (GAP Analysis):** This is the process through which the companies create a complete model of where they are now, and in which direction they will opt to move in future. The model helps the company to anticipate and cover any functional gaps and what emerges is a document that enumerates the business requirements.
- **Phase 6 (Business Process Reengineering):** Business process reengineering is one of the most important parts of an ERP project but it is not a simple exercise. It enables organisations to gain a better understanding of how their business currently operates and how the processes could be improved for better results. It works in two ways. Firstly, it allows companies to redesign their organisational structure and secondly, it allows companies to improve their decision making process through better data dissemination. If undertaken correctly it can reduce cycle time and thereby the cost by allowing businesses to get rid of the activities that are unproductive, redundant, and ineffective. It can also help companies to improve the quality of their work by reducing fragmentation and establishing clear ownership for each process.

However, it is important to realise that business process reengineering should happen before the ERP project starts so as to make sure the chosen system can support the new processes.

- **Phase 7 (Software Configuration):** With the business requirement document prepared and business reengineering aspects mutually agreed between the vendor and the client, it is the time for the subject-matter expert and his team of developers to work on software customization. This team configures the product for the specific company based on preset options within the software. They also customize the software by adding new features to the application. Finally, the ERP software is integrated with those existing systems that the business wants to retain, or anticipates it will need in future.
- **Phase 8 (Testing):** In this phase the system is to be tested first in a disintegrated mode and then in integrated mode. Test cases are developed and real life scenarios along with exceptional occurrences are created to test the transactions and functionalities of different modules. The objective of the tests is to find the weakest link so that it can be rectified before integration and before going live.

- **Phase 9 (Data Migration):** ERP data migration is the process of transferring data from its original sources to the ERP system's database. It often involves moving data from a variety of different systems, formats and storage types into a single, common structure.

The data migration process is critical for ensuring that the data in the new ERP system is accurate and complete, which is vital because the business in future would rely on that historical data. Well-planned data migration can help keep the entire ERP implementation project on time and on budget. It's also an opportunity to winnow out obsolete and redundant data lurking in the organization's older systems.

People may be tempted to hoard data, importing every piece from the old systems into the ERP system in the belief that it may be needed one day. But not all historical data is useful and doesn't need to be immediately accessible. In fact, importing every historical data item can be counter-productive, slowing system performance and making it harder for users to find the information they really need.

- **Phase 10 (End-User Training):** While the process of implementation is going on, the company trains its employees to implement the ERP system and later run it in their regular business activities. Employees should become self-sufficient to manage the software after the vendors and consultants have left.

In this phase the actual users of the system are identified and trained on HOW to use the system. This training is very important because the success of the ERP system lies in the hands of the End-users.

- **Phase 11 (Going Live):** This is the stage when the work of data conversion has been completed, databases are up and running, the configuration is complete and testing has been done. The system is officially proclaimed to be "LIVE" and transactions can start as per the cut off date. Once the ERP system is live, the old system is removed and the new system is used for doing business.

- **Phase 12 (Post Implementation Support):** Once the implementation is over, the vendor and the hired consultants would generally leave and in order to reap the fruit of the ERP system it is very important that the system has wide acceptance.

There should be enough employees who are trained to handle problems that may crop up from time to time and also be able to identify as well as address the need for further enhancements. The system must be updated with the change in technology.

2.7. ERP Implementation Challenges and Risks

In order to realize the benefits of the new system, people often have to change the way they work, often replacing longstanding manual and legacy processes, procedures, norms and standards of performance. As ERP implementation involves people as well as technology and thus, in addition to technical obstacles, it may face people-related challenges, such as resistance to change and getting users and functional groups to change their ways in order to work with the new solution. ERP implementation is a change management process and thus backing from top leaders and executives is essential to overcome these challenges.

Some of the common challenges faced by organisations going for ERP implementation are as below.

- **Project Management:** ERP implementations entail multiple phases and each phase brings critical tasks to be accomplished for the project to stay on track. Participation from all the groups involved in developing and using the system is an incredibly challenging task, because each department juggles its ERP project responsibilities with multiple other priorities.

  It requires strong and meticulous project and people management that should ensure setting realistic expectations, timeframes and milestones, along with timely two-way communication which is critical to success of the project. Additionally, successful ERP implementations require.

- **Project Planning:** ERP projects are infamous for sailing past budgets after the implementation kicks off. Organizations often underestimate the time and budget required for implementation of the project. Moreover, businesses have a tendency to add capabilities or features to the system that weren't part of the original plan. This is called scope creep and it adds to time and budget overruns.

  Another common flaw is underestimating staffing needs both in terms of numbers and the individuals being selected on the internal team for the ERP project during initial phases. Many times people who can be easily spared from regular work, without impacting on their main business activity, are put on these teams. Organisations should realise that such people cannot bring onto the table the insights of the business that key persons with core skill set and authority can bring out. The people on these teams should focus on identifying alternative ways and simplifying the processes as much as possible before committing to the ERP implementation partner.

- **Data Integration:** This process requires finding all the historical and current data which may be spread far and wide across the organization, buried in accounting systems, department-specific applications, spreadsheets and perhaps on paper. Collecting, collating, and corroborating this distributed information may be much more challenging than expected.
- **Data quality:** Data Migration to the ERP system generally involves a serious data hygiene exercise, because multiple departments often have duplicate versions of the same information in their systems. Also, the information may be stored in different formats and ensuring data quality can become a sizable project on its own, involving validating the data, cleaning out duplicates and adding missing values before migrating data to the ERP system.
- **Change management:** An ERP implementation typically involves overhauling business processes to take maximum advantage of the possible efficiency and productivity improvements with the new solution. It is much more than just switching to a new software system. This requires a shift in mindset and a change in everyday work processes for many employees, which presents typical change management challenges.

  Resistance to change can be a formidable roadblock and getting buy-in from leadership and stakeholders across departments very early in the implementation process is crucial to a successful implementation. All the stakeholders, especially end users on the front lines, should be kept informed about the features and advantages of the new ERP throughout the implementation process. Proper training and collaborative interactions help in overcoming this challenge.
- **Continuous improvement:** Implementation of ERP in an organisation is not a one-off effort that is complete when the new system goes live. The solution must continue to evolve to support new business demands and technology. The project team has to continue to manage the project after deployment, fixing issues and supporting new requirements as they come up.

Periodic assessment of the efficacy of the ERP system whether it is still meeting the organization's requirements is necessary to ascertain need for up-gradation or replacement. The traditional on-premises systems are more difficult to upgrade than the new age cloud-based systems, which automatically make new features and innovations available to users.

Chapter 3

CLOUD COMPUTING

3.1. Introduction

Cloud computing is the on-demand delivery of IT resources over the Internet with a pay-as-you-go-pricing model. Instead of buying, owning, and maintaining physical data centres and servers, end users can access technology services, such as computing power, storage and databases, on an as-needed basis from a cloud provider. The cloud providers are third-party organizations that make dynamic provisioning of IT capabilities (hardware, software, or services) over a network.

Cloud computing is a computing model and not a technology. In this model of computing, all the servers, networks, applications and other elements related to data centres are made available to IT end users via the Internet, in a way that allows IT to buy only the type and amount of computing services that they need.

The cloud model differs from traditional outsourcing in terms that customers don't hand over their own IT resources to be managed. Instead, they plug into the "cloud" for infrastructure services, platform (operating system) services, or software services, treating the "cloud" much as they would treat an internal data centre or computer system providing the same functions.

Organizations of every type, size, and industry are using the cloud for a wide variety of use cases, such as data backup, disaster recovery, email, virtual desktops, software development and testing, big data analytics, and customer-facing web applications. For example, healthcare companies are using the cloud to develop more personalized treatments for patients, BFSI companies are using the cloud to power real-time fraud detection and prevention, while video-game makers are using the cloud to deliver online games to millions of players around the world.

3.2. Cloud Computing Evolution Timeline

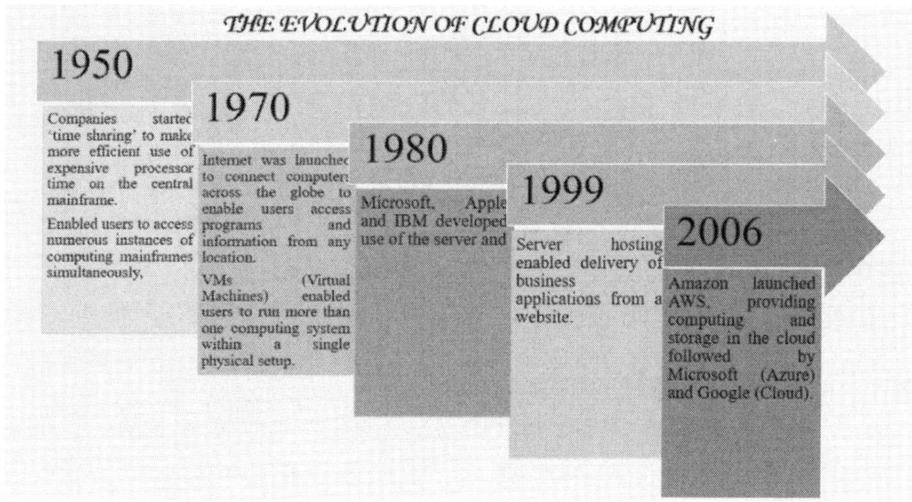

Figure 3.1: Cloud Computing Evolution Timeline

3.3. Characteristics and Advantages of Cloud Computing

Digital technologies are transforming industrial production processes from design and engineering up to manufacturing are helping organisations harness the full potential of Industry 4.0 in terms of greater flexibility in processes, improved productivity, higher quality production, and increased revenue.

As the proliferation of digital technologies continues to disrupt market segments and industries, adopting cloud platforms can help organizations transform to meet changing business conditions and cater to the evolving customer needs.

The more production-related initiatives a company undertakes, the more it needs to share data across sites. Meanwhile, cloud technologies continue to get faster and more powerful. Thus companies will increasingly deploy machine data and analytics to the cloud, thereby enabling more data-driven services for production systems.

Cloud computing can help organisations lower costs, reduce business risks, improve operational efficiency, become more agile, innovate faster, create new revenue streams, and reinvent customer and employee experience.

An overview of the cloud computing architecture is provided in Figure 3.2.

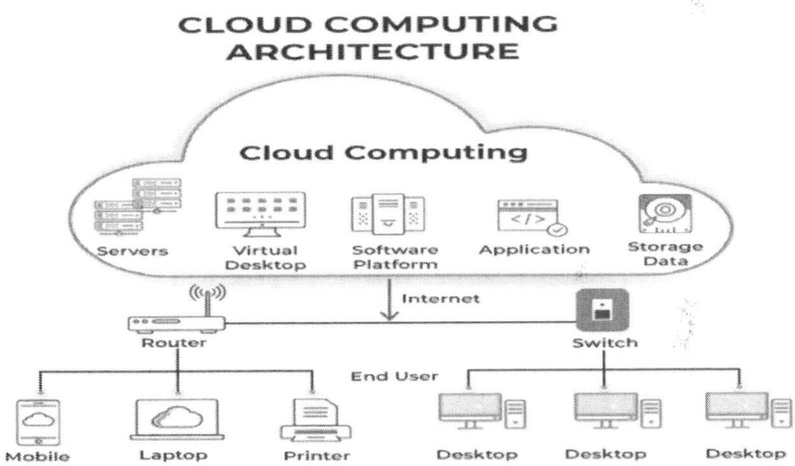

Figure 3.2: Cloud Computing Architecture

3.3.1. Agility: The cloud gives the end users easy access to a broad range of technologies so that they can innovate faster and build nearly anything that they can imagine. Users can quickly spin up resources as they need them – from infrastructure services, such as compute, storage, and databases, to Internet of Things, machine learning, data lakes and analytics, and much more.

They can deploy technology services in a matter of minutes, and get from idea to implementation several orders of magnitude faster than before. This gives them the freedom to experiment, test new ideas to differentiate customer experiences, and transform their business.

3.3.2. Scalability and Flexibility in Capacity: Cloud computing offers a set of flexible facilities that can be turned off, scaled up or trimmed down as per the circumstances of the user. IT users don't have to over-provision resources up front to handle peak levels of business activity in the future. Instead, they provision the amount of cloud resources that they actually need. Suppose a promotion of sales is very popular, in that case IT capacity can be immediately and quickly added to it for the avoidance of crashing servers and losing sales. When those sales are done or events are over, the capacity can be shrunk to contain costs. When scaling up and down, users are altering the power of an instance, perhaps using one with a greater CPU power, and are simply adding or removing the number of instances they are using.

There is workload resilience because the cloud service providers (CSPs) often implement redundant resources to ensure resilient storage and to keep users' important workloads running, often across multiple global regions. This offers a significant advantage compared to on-premise solutions from a cost perspective alone.

3.3.3. Cost Management: Using cloud infrastructure reduces capital costs as organizations don't have to invest massive amounts of money buying and maintaining hardware, equipment, facilities, utilities or building large data centers to accommodate their growing IT needs with the growing businesses. This allows them to trade capital expenses for variable expenses. Additionally, companies don't need large IT teams to handle data center operations because they can rely on the expertise of their cloud providers' teams. The variable costs are also lower in cloud computing because cloud resources are measured at a granular level, enabling users to pay only for the resources and workloads they use. There is no standby cost.

With many cloud services, users pay only for what they use. This is the concept of utility-based metering. For instance, if a user has taken only one server, running for two hours, and then has shut it down, it pays for only two hours of computing resources.

Moreover, as the cloud providers are working with very large infrastructures and resources that are optimized and shared between different organizations, the end users benefit from exceptionally low compute storage and network costs compared to traditional hosting. The variable expenses are much lower than what IT users would incur doing it by themselves because of the economies of scale.

Cloud computing also cuts costs related to downtime. In practice, downtime rarely happens because of the in-built redundancy and cross hot-standby provisions. Thus companies don't have to spend time and money fixing issues related to or arising out of the downtime.

3.3.4. Global Deployment, Data Accessibility, and Workload Mobility: Cloud computing offers another advantage of working from anywhere across the globe, as long as there is an internet connection available. Storing information in the cloud means that users can access it from anywhere with any device with just an internet connection and they don't have to carry around USB drives, an external hard drive or multiple CDs to access their data. Corporate data can be accessed via smartphones and other mobile devices, enabling remote employees to stay up to date with co-workers and customers without limitation of the device used.

Also, users of cloud services can expand to new geographic regions and deploy globally in minutes. Most of the cloud service providers have infrastructure all over the world, so the users can deploy their applications in multiple physical locations with just a few clicks.

End users can spin up computing resources such as server time, storage and network for almost any type of workload on demand. They can provision these capabilities themselves in self-service mode thereby eliminating the traditional need for IT administrators to provision and manage computing resources.

3.3.5. Business Continuity and Disaster Recovery (BCDR): One of the major concerns of an organization using IT is loss of data. Storing data in the cloud guarantees that users can access their data not just anytime but even when their devices, e.g., laptops, tabs, smartphones etc are inoperative or have been hacked. It also offers greater security to sensitive data in case of loss of some equipment as the user can even remotely wipe out data from the lost machines to avoid it getting in the wrong hands. With cloud-based services, organizations can quickly recover their data in the event of emergencies, such as natural disasters or power outages. This ensures business continuity and helps in recovery of data and information making them available even if the business suffers damage or disruption

3.3.6. Migration Flexibility, Multi-Tenancy and Resource Pooling: Organizations can move certain workloads to or from the cloud, or to different cloud platforms as desired for cost optimization or to use new services as they emerge. With resource pooling, cloud providers service numerous customers from the same physical resources. The concept of multi-tenancy lets numerous customers share the same physical infrastructures or the same applications yet retain privacy and security over their own data.

The CSPs optimize their resource pools by putting applications in closer proximity to end users as it reduces latency and improves the user experience.

3.3.7. Automated Updates on Software: In cloud computing, the CSPs regularly upgrade and update the software including the updates on security. So, the users do not need to agonize regarding getting obsolete and spend their crucial time on maintaining and upgrading the system.

3.3.8. Better Control on Documents and Enhanced Collaboration: Before cloud came into being, employees needed to send files in and out as email attachments for being worked on by a single user at a time. Due to this organisations ended up with a mess of contrary titles, non-compatible formats, and out of date file content. Moving to cloud computing has facilitated central file storage. This has brought in enhanced collaboration by authorizing diverse groups of people to virtually meet and exchange information with the help of shared storage. Such capability helps in improving the customer service and product development and also reducing the marketing time.

3.4. Cloud Computing Models

Cloud computing is basically a process of delivering computing services and as is the case with any service sector product, there are different models with their own typical combination of services delivered, their advantages, and their limitations.

There are three basic models of cloud computing and each model represents a different part of the cloud computing stack. The cloud computing stack consists of layers of cloud computing services, servers, platforms, and components, which can leverage several different clouds forming a single application stack.

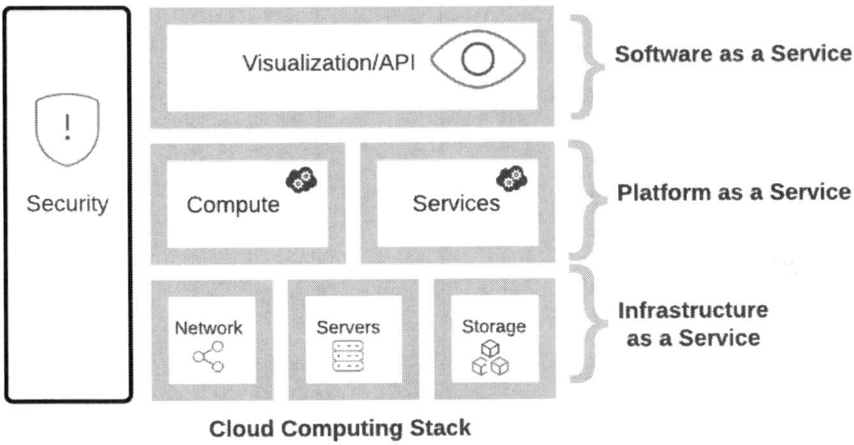

Figure 3.3: Cloud Computing Stack

3.4.1. Infrastructure as a Service (IaaS)

IaaS contains the basic building blocks for cloud IT and typically provides access to networking features, computers (virtual or on dedicated hardware), and data storage space. The CSPs provide grids or clusters or virtual servers, networks, storage and systems software designed to augment or replace the functions of an entire data centre. Users are also provided application programming interfaces (APIs) that let them migrate workloads to a virtual machine (VM). They have an allocated storage capacity and can start, stop, access and configure the VM and storage as desired. IaaS providers offer small, medium, large, extra-large, as well as memory or compute-optimized instances enabling customization of instances for various workload needs generally on a pay-as-you-go model.

The IaaS cloud model is closest to a remote data centre for business users and it provides the user with the highest level of flexibility and management control over their IT resources and is most similar to existing IT resources that many IT departments and developers are familiar with today.

Examples of IaaS include Amazon's Elastic Compute Cloud [EC2] and Simple Storage Service under Amazon Web Services (AWS). Diadem Technologies is amongst India's leading cloud service providers that provides cloud, dedicated and hybrid hosting solutions to clients across the globe.

3.4.2. Platform as a Service (PaaS)

Platform-as-a-service removes the need for organizations to manage the underlying infrastructure (usually hardware and operating systems) and allows them to focus on the deployment and management of their applications. In this model the CSPs provide virtualized servers on which users can run existing applications or develop new ones without having to worry about maintaining the operating systems, server hardware, load balancing or computing capacity. Users access the development tools hosted on the infrastructures of cloud providers over the internet using APIs, web portals or gateway software. PaaS is used for general software development, and many PaaS providers host the software after it has been developed. This helps the user organisation to be more efficient as they don't need to worry about resource procurement, capacity planning, software maintenance, patching, or any of the other undifferentiated heavy lifting involved in running their application. PaaS is available on an on-demand and pay-as-you-go model.

Examples of PaaS include Microsoft's Azure and Salesforce's Lightning Platform, AWS Elastic Beanstalk of Amazon and Google App Engine.

3.4.3. Software as a Service (SaaS)

The most widely known and widely used model of cloud computing, SaaS, provides all the functions of a sophisticated traditional application, but through a Web browser, not a locally-installed application. In most cases, people referring to Software as a Service (SaaS) are referring to end-user applications that are often called web services. It is a complete product that is run and managed by the service provider. In this model, while users gain access to application software and databases, they don't have to worry about the underlying infrastructure, the servers, storage, application development and related common concerns of IT. Their main concern is how to use the particular service available under SaaS on-demand or by subscription.

Examples of SaaS include Microsoft 365 for productivity and email services, Google's Gmail and Apps, instant messaging from AOL, Yahoo and Google, and VoIP from Vonage and Skype.

3.5. Cloud Computing Deployment Models

Cloud deployment is the process of deploying an application through one or more hosting models i.e. IaaS, PaaS, SaaS to leverage the cloud. This includes architecting, planning, implementing and operating workloads on cloud. There are three typical cloud models for different levels of management and security: 1. Public, 2. Private, and 3. Hybrid.

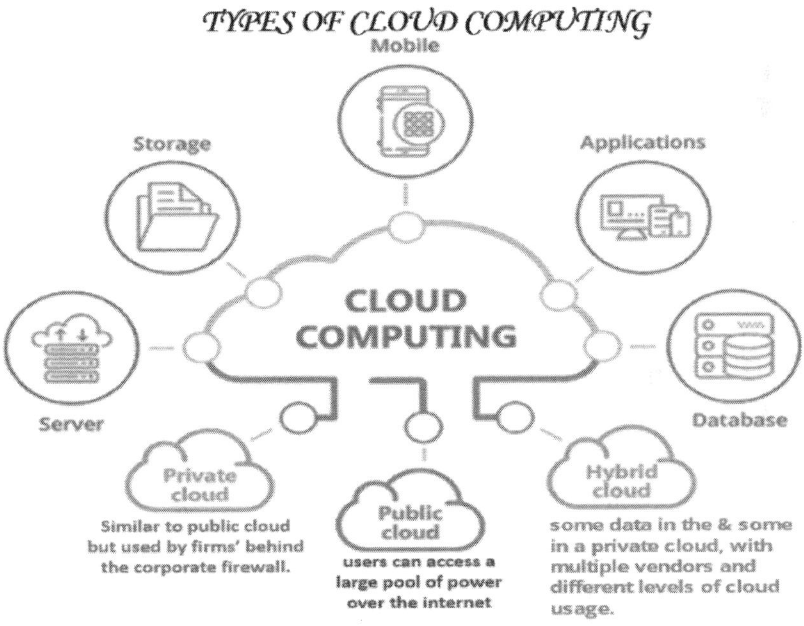

Figure 3.4: Cloud Computing Types

3.5.1. Public Cloud

A public cloud model is where a vendor makes available use of shared infrastructure, including computing storage and network resources that can be provisioned on demand and typically accessed over the internet for public usage. The set of hardware, networking, storage, services, applications, and interfaces owned and operated by a third party for use by other companies or individuals is the public cloud. The consumer never gets to see the hardware used, nor knows the exact location of their data. However, they may specify the geographical region to optimize speed of performance and reduce latency depending on where users are located.

Cloud Service Providers create a highly scalable data center that hides the details of the underlying infrastructure from the consumer. Public clouds are viable because they offer many options for computing, storage, and a rich set of other services. Applications in the cloud are either created in the cloud or are migrated from an existing infrastructure to take advantage of the benefits of cloud computing.

3.5.2. Private Cloud

The set of hardware, networking, storage, services, applications, and interfaces owned and operated by an organization for the use of its employees, partners, or customers is the private cloud. This can be created and managed by a third party for the exclusive use of one enterprise. The private cloud is a highly controlled environment not open for public consumption. Thus, it sits behind a firewall, giving the company using it greater and more direct control of its data. As a result, the hardware is usually held on premises.

This differs from a typical on-premises server file approach in the sense that the cloud principles of virtualization and resource management tools are applied to create a pool of shared compute, storage, and network resources. With this approach, greater capital expenditure is required to acquire the host and the data center. Additional resources are needed for the day-to-day operations and maintenance of this equipment.

On-premises deployment does not provide many of the benefits of cloud computing but is sometimes sought for its ability to provide dedicated resources.

3.5.3. Hybrid Cloud

The hybrid cloud makes use of both public and private clouds. This model may be used for seasonal burst traffic or disaster recovery.

A hybrid model is established when a network link is configured between the private cloud to the services within the public cloud, essentially extending the logical internal network. This takes the benefits given from both the public and private models and allows the users to architect their services in the most appropriate model. **Hybrid clouds** are normally short-term configurations, either for testing purposes or for augmenting computing power in peak load seasons. They are often seen as a transitional state for enterprises before moving their service to the public cloud entirely.

However, beyond the three standard cloud deployment categories, two more types of deployments can be seen in practice: Community Cloud, and Multi-Cloud.

3.5.4. Community Cloud

This deployment model supports multiple organizations sharing computing resources that are part of a community. Examples include universities cooperating in certain areas of research, or police departments within a county or state sharing computing resources. Access to a community cloud environment is typically restricted to the members of the community.

3.5.5. Multi-Cloud

"Multi-cloud" means multiple public clouds. A company that uses a multi-cloud deployment incorporates multiple public clouds from more than one cloud provider. Instead of using one vendor for cloud hosting, storage, and the full application stack, users in a multi-cloud configuration use several vendors. They can leverage multiple IaaS vendors, or can incorporate different vendors for different services i.e. IaaS, PaaS, and SaaS. Multi-cloud can be purely for the purpose of redundancy and system backup.

Each cloud deployment model satisfies different organizational needs, so it's important to choose a model that will satisfy the needs of the organization. Perhaps even more important is the fact that each cloud deployment model has a different value proposition and different costs associated with it. Therefore, in many cases, choice of a cloud deployment model may simply come down to money. In any case, to be able to make an informed decision, one needs to be aware of the characteristics of each environment so as to optimize the resources.

3.6. Cloud Migration Journey

Cloud Migration Journey is the process of migrating business operations from a legacy on-premises infrastructure to a cloud-based one or from one cloud provider to another. It entails moving data, recreating computing resources, such as bare-metal servers or virtual machines (VM), and transitioning entire applications to a cloud infrastructure. The journey can be complex, costly, and carries substantial risk.

A cloud journey is not just a technical change, it is a business decision. It involves changes in the entire IT framework, multiple business departments, and critical business processes. Translating business goals into a migration plan is time consuming, but advanced planning is the key to a successful migration.

Stages of a Cloud Journey

1. Making the Business Case
2. Identify the Right Applications
3. Select a Cloud Service Provider
4. Initial Adoption
5. Full Migration
6. Post-Migration

3.6.1. Making the Business Case: Identifying the Business Objectives for Migration to the Cloud

A company should start by evaluating the business implications of adopting a cloud infrastructure. Decision-makers must understand how the cloud differs from a traditional IT setup. They must be able to assess the benefits, risks, compliance, security, and data control implications on the organization as a whole and its IT activities in particular. Determine what systems and apps should be first to migrate, and what are the costs and the total cost of ownership (TCO) of the expected cloud deployment.

Common business objectives for migrating to the cloud can include:

- Avoiding maintenance costs that come with data centers,
- Achieving increased scalability,
- Improving resiliency with better failover capabilities,
- Increasing remote collaboration.

Here it is important to gain consensus from the entire team about the business objectives to ensure that the purpose is clear to everyone. For example, for the case of UPPC (Uttar Pradesh Power Corporation Ltd), the priority areas included increasing billing efficiency and enhancing customer satisfaction by focusing on reducing daily operational challenges. BookMyShow & iQuippo commenced cloud service usage for zero downtime deployments and for conducting large financial transactions.

3.6.2. Cloud Readiness Assessment: Identifying the Right Applications

Cloud readiness assessment is an essential step that can provide a solid footing before moving forward with plans. A cloud readiness assessment is the process where the existing applications and data are examined to determine if they can be moved to the cloud with minimal impact on operational continuity. The assessment is necessary to help gain a good grasp of what should be done to ensure a seamless cloud migration. Each application has its own unique design, which may or may not fit a cloud environment. If the application is suitable for the cloud, they can be just "lifted and shifted" to the cloud. Otherwise, there might be a need to make some changes.

Assessing cloud readiness also involves assessing potential of the team and identifying skill gaps, scrutinizing current IT infrastructure, identifying security requirements, and assessing operational readiness of the organisation. For example, for the case of UPPCL, cloud service assessments highlighted the need of a centralized billing and metering system, as well as a self-service information and transactional tool for internal and external users. The cloud service as such would help users understand natural language queries keyed-in by the user and provide the information requested or process a transaction on behalf of the user.

3.6.3. Selecting a Cloud Service Provider

There is a wide range of cloud service providers, each offering a distinct architecture with a unique set of capabilities, licensing, and support. Some of the considerations for selecting a CSP include:

- Suitability of the architecture of the cloud to the design of the organisation's workloads in terms of requirements of modifications in the existing systems.

- Cloud implementation support from the provider in terms of their capabilities and services on offer regarding support needed before, during, and after the migration process. They should be included in the service level agreements (SLAs).
- Licensing requirements and use of the existing licenses on the cloud.

For example, for the case of the Bihar School Examination Board, the requirement was of scaling operations from a minimal set of users to thousands at any given time. As such, they migrated their operations to AWS Cloud, paying attention to the cost, scalability, & security of the system. Similarly, iQuippo dealt with large scale financial transactions; it required a robust and secure DevOps compliant cloud service infrastructure architecture, and as such, chose AWS by Amazon as the cloud service provider.

3.6.4. Piloting and Initial Adoption

Initially, less business-critical applications such as office productivity, accounting, human resources, and customer relations management (CRM), may be migrated, preferably in SaaS mode. Business-critical solutions, such as warehousing, production, and enterprise resource planning (ERP) that are typically tightly integrated with core business systems may require adopting PaaS and IaaS solutions. This requires pilots and proofs of concept, test and development environments, batch processing, and data archival before transitioning operations to a new, cloud-based solution.

The important aspect of developing the strategy to migrate needs to be addressed with regard to the existing applications. Decision needs to be taken regarding the applications that can be considered for:

- **Retire**: the applications that are not needed in the future are got rid of.
- **Retain**: the applications that are to be kept exactly as is till re-evaluation in future.
- **Re-host**: the applications are migrated as is into the Cloud environment -"Lift and Shift".
- **Re-platform**: some of the applications are migrated after making some changes to take advantage of some of the special capabilities of the cloud – "Lift, Reshape, and Shift".

- **Re-architect**: it is redesigning / refactoring the application in a more cloud-native manner creating a server-less version of the legacy application.
- **Re-purchase**: abandoning the existing software and migrating to a cloud-first application.

At this stage itself, the organisation should develop a cloud governance strategy detailing which business tasks are performed where, the access policies, and monitoring and security tools that span both on-premises and cloud environments.

3.6.5. Full Migration

Execution of migration to cloud is a transitional activity where the main challenge is carrying out the migration with minimal disruption to normal operation, at the lowest cost, and over the shortest period of time.

If the data becomes inaccessible to users during migration as the system is synchronized and updated after the initial migration takes place, there is risk of impacting the business operations. Every workload element individually migrated should be proven to work in the new environment before migrating another element.

Ways have to be found out to synchronize changes that are made to the source data while the migration is ongoing. This is especially important for mission-critical applications that cannot sustain a long period of downtime. Test your plan, and then start executing it. Create a backup and recovery strategy, and use it if or when issues occur.

3.6.6. Post-Migration

The cloud journey doesn't get completed with migration. It is the time to compare pre- and post-migration performance of the system. Cloud performance has to be monitored in accordance with the service level agreements (SLAs) and the organisation's performance goals. Customer issues that arise from the new cloud environment, unexpected changes, and synchronization issues may require fine tuning the applications and infrastructure.

Some important actions that need to be taken post-migration are:

- **Closure**: Immediately after migration, it's crucial to do a clean-up including shutdown and removal of any redundant systems, severing of superfluous network connectivity, and switching to production status of relevant applications on the cloud platform. These actions are extremely important from an operations standpoint. The cost of running those extra resources is one thing, but those systems are easily forgotten over time. When they co-exist, they only cause operational confusion and security issues. Action should be taken to do a controlled but prioritized decommissioning of such systems and connectivity.
- **Security Review**: In the coexistence phase during migration, security policies have to allow traffic and system access between applications on both environments. Those policies need to be reviewed immediately after decommissioning of the "legacy" side of the application. While it can be a tedious process, any security breaches will end up consuming even more time, so it's best dealt with as soon as possible. The security review shouldn't be limited to just the legacy workloads. Security for cloud platforms is very different from traditional platforms, and migration provides an opportunity to review the capabilities available and take advantage where possible.
- **Evaluation**: Once the platform is stable, evaluation of what was gained from the whole exercise has to be done with an eye on measuring the parameters on a "like for like" basis. Evaluation and documenting before and after the migration is important as it keeps the team on their goals and any decisions made.
- **Cost Reviews**: Sizing of machines is one area where organisations err on the side of caution and oversize as in the early days of migration, applications tend to live in both environments, thereby increasing the running costs in the short term. Once the migration is complete, the focus has to be on optimizing for costs. A review should be done on a regular basis to determine how resources can be optimally utilized to reduce the costs. Small and manageable improvements can be made over time to gain efficiencies and it should become part of an ongoing process to improve applications.
- **Centre of Excellence**: The migration team goes through many highs and lows during the process. It develops a lot of skill and knowledge that is priceless, and it would be a disaster if that team disbands

completely after migration and goes back to their routine jobs. Technical members of the team generally continue with the new platform, but other members who have precious knowledge of the whole journey should also not be ignored. Preserving that knowledge and experience by keeping the team as part of "Centre of Excellence" where they meet on a regular basis for strategic discussions and decisions going forward would benefit the organisation.

As a practical approach, the following practices can be adopted.

- Getting the key buy-in from businesses on the expected downtime and informing them on the progress, milestones achieved and the key risk and issues throughout the migration process is critical.
- The testing of both pre- and post-migration metrics on key process chains needs to be done for validation as an important step.
- Data migration and checks and balances need to be signed off during the cloud adoption process.
- Issues and resolutions should always be documented. This helps with root cause analysis as the logs can then be referred.
- The availability and back-ups of key technical and functional resources needs to be ensured for archival purposes.

In order to achieve its goals of the cloud journey, a company goes through the five milestones of Discovery, Review, Documenting Findings, Setting Milestones, and Remediation.

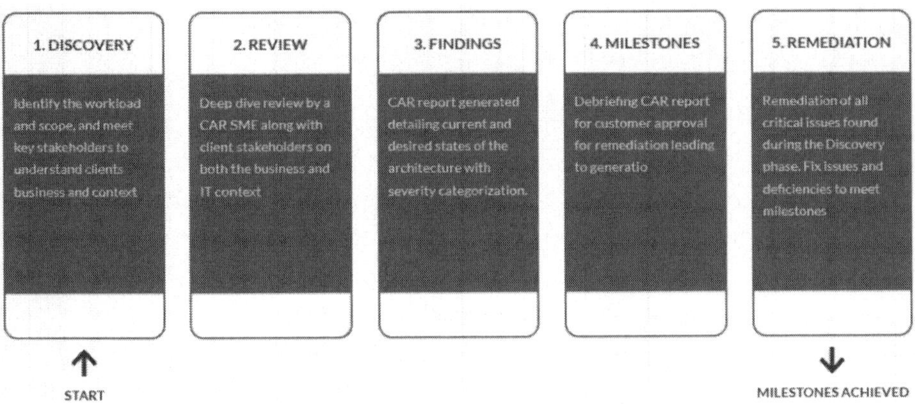

Figure 3.5: Cloud Computing Practicalities

3.7. Cloud Migration Challenges

The use of cloud technology has exploded over the last couple of years, and it's no surprise because operating on the cloud has numerous benefits for businesses of all sizes. The global cloud computing market is expected to hit $623 billion by 2023 at a Compound Annual Growth Rate (CAGR) of 18 percent.

Even with such significant growth, many enterprises are yet to realize the full potential of a cloud data environment because migration is often a huge challenge. Uncertainty over financial costs, security, and internal resistance to change are among the issues of major concern. For this reason, businesses need to develop a meticulous plan and to carry out meticulous execution for a safe and successful migration.

Some of the common challenges that have to be overcome in a cloud migration project include:

- **Interoperability:** Some existing applications require adjustment, or even complete refactoring, to interact with a cloud environment. Whether to move an application's dependencies, such as databases, to the cloud as-is, or transition to equivalent cloud-based services is a challenge.
- **Availability:** Cloud migration process may require business systems to be temporarily offline. Migrations can also result in unplanned downtime. By developing a cloud-compatible disaster recovery plan, to avoid downtime that can impact business operations and customers, this risk can be surmounted.
- **Data Mobility:** Although cloud vendors give some freedom for customers to download the stored data, the risk with using someone else's application is often that the users can't get all their data out of it in a way that's usable in a different vendor's software.
- **Cloud Expertise**—Traditional IT teams may not be familiar with cloud environments. Knowledge of on-premises data centres and management of physical servers does not translate directly to the public cloud.
- **Data Security and Integrity:** Cloud migrations can result in data loss or corruption, and may also open the door to attackers. Identifying security and compliance issues that may arise during the migration process, and in the target cloud environment, is important and the security strategy would have to be adapted to the cloud.

With cloud monitoring and management software being excessively flexible, a customer's ability to know for sure who's looking at what data and using it, especially from within their own organizations, is limited.

Ensuring compliance with security and privacy regulations for data stored in the cloud raises myriad issues for companies. The volume of data at stake is massive. Users have a tendency to upload more data than they can reasonably use, adding to security complexity and compliance costs. Access is another issue. The cloud enables and encourages more people to access data. And then there is the increasing number of devices supported by cloud platforms, which can become a security risk.

Despite this, it is seen that many companies under-invest in cloud security services. When confronted with a cloud breach, organizations tend to bolster security only in that area of weakness. But that tack can be costly and generally offers a lower-level safeguard than if higher levels of security had been integrated with system architecture at the time of design.

From a practitioner perspective, the following are key for dealing with technical challenges associated with cloud computing.

- The Roll Back Strategy needs to be clearly understood and documented in case of failures for data uploads or migrations.
- Disaster Recovery (DR) needs to be tested and validated for data replication
- Scope creep for applications including the cutover plan needs to be managed and controlled.
- Communications on risks and issues needs to be done periodically to the stakeholders as per the project plan
- The cloud licenses need to be understood and controlled by the business stakeholders.

3.8. Implementation Strategy: Cloud Architecture Review Framework

It is critical to have the right understanding of the state of the workload and get an insightful understanding of architectural best practices. Company business should always have the optimal mix of infra, solutions and spends. Only then will they be able to take home the dividends of the cloud's promise - of agility, scalability, responsiveness and business impact. Simply put it is vital for businesses to align their workloads – measure and improve, based on the business and technical objectives. To get a handle on all of this, teams need a well architected and optimised cloud environment.

The Cloud Architecture Review Framework describes the key concepts, design Principles, and architectural best practices for designing and running workloads in the cloud. By answering a set of foundational questions, the company learns how well its IT architecture aligns with cloud best practices and is provided guidance for making Improvements. The framework helps businesses to decide, build and deploy infrastructure faster on the cloud. While doing so it helps in lowering and mitigating risks.

This framework delivers insights that enable informed decisions and as the cycle progresses teams end up learning and making best practices as part of their customer driven culture.

In the course of its cloud journey, the company should follow the five pillars of the process of cloud migration to improve their efficiency by using Cloud: Operational Excellence, Security, Reliability, Performance Efficiency, and Cost Optimization.

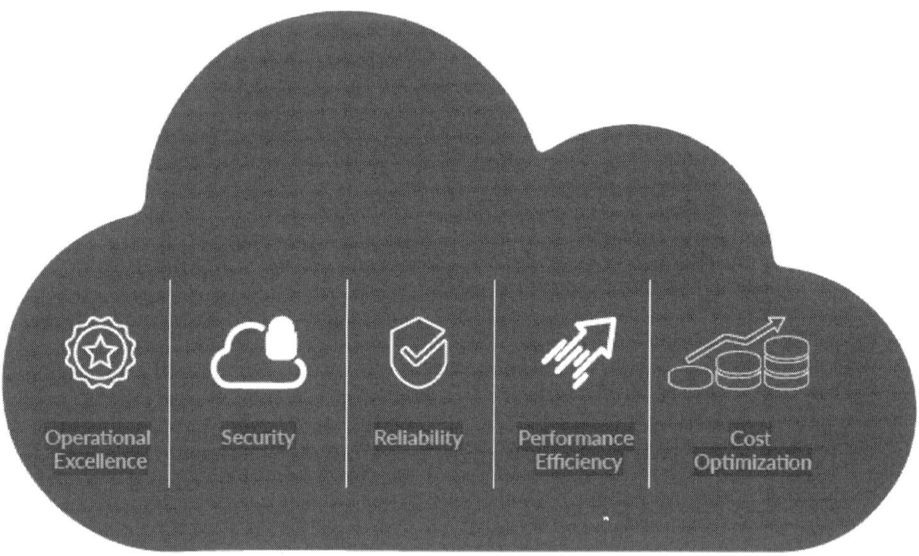

Figure 3.6: Cloud Computing Framework

3.9. Cloud Migration Timeline

Companies move to the cloud at different rates. An application migration timeline includes planning the migration, training staff, and modifying applications to facilitate deep cloud integration. Each organization will accomplish these steps at its own pace. A medium project involving migrating on a SaaS model may take 2-4 months while it can take 6-24 months to set up more complex server setups and configure cloud-native services in case of PaaS and IaaS models.

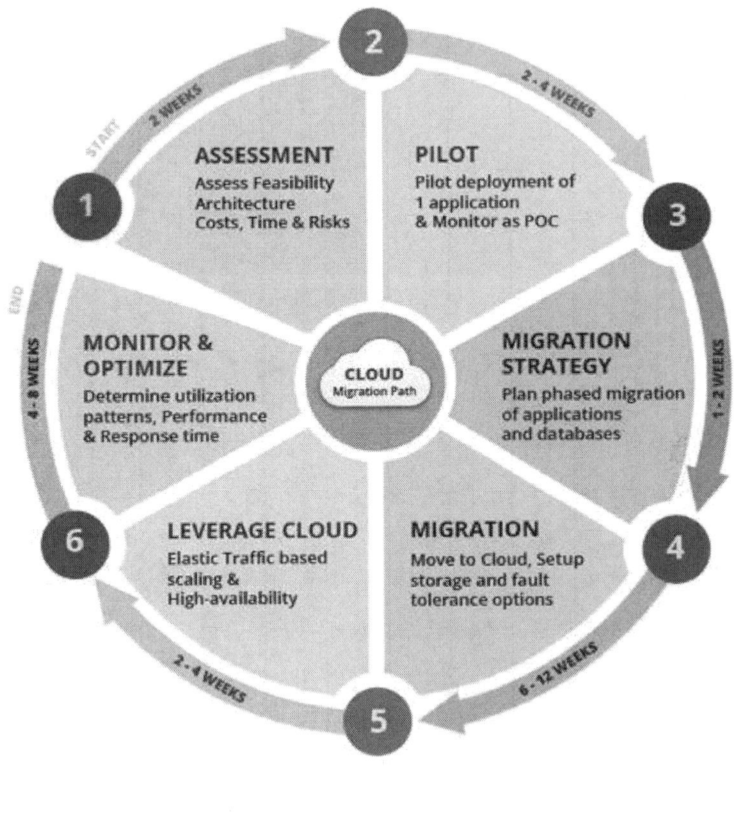

Figure 3.7: Cloud Computing Process

As we see in our cases, cloud migration periods vary significantly. For example, UPPCL's cloud-migration exercise took over a period of 8 weeks , while BSEB took 12 weeks to achieve similar targets. On the other hand, iQuippo required around 6 months to achieve full cloud-migration. As one can see, cloud migration timelines are not constant for companies across industries, but varies according to the complexity of the firm requirements, the challenges it faces in the early-phases, as well as the time it takes for firms to create alliances with cloud service providers.

Chapter 4

API, IOT, & CONNECTED SYSTEMS

4.1. Introduction

An organisation's digital ecosystem is the group of interconnected information technology resources that function as a unit. From the internal perspective of an enterprise, such digital ecosystems are made up of suppliers, customers, trading partners, applications, third-party data service providers and all respective technologies. As such, interoperability is the key to the ecosystem's success. From a supply-chain perspective, firms that originally functioned in separate markets are also coming together in digital ecosystems to support the development of new products and services, and transforming the world of business by creating linear paths between suppliers and customers, thus creating new business opportunities. From a customer perspective, similarly, there has been an exponential rise in the development and adoption of technologies such as IoT, AI, chatbots, voice assistants, and smart phones.

Modern digital banking apps are one example of such a digital ecosystem. The ecosystems created through these apps integrate all services and applications into one place, including expense managers, digital wallets, online banking and digital passbooks. Similarly, digital real-estate ecosystems provide potential homebuyers with tax, electric and heating cost estimations, catalogue of realtors, information and service providers, and strong, trustworthy financial advice. The healthcare industry too benefits from digital ecosystems; it incorporates data from each touch-point in a patient's journey, including scheduling appointments, receiving appointment reminders, storing test results and recording prescriptions. Many healthcare organizations are now exploring the integration of artificial intelligence (AI) and machine learning (ML) into their systems as a way to improve customer experiences and decision-making processes.

As such, the exponential growth in digital ecosystems has forced the need for companies to expand their digital potential in order to stay connected with all of these modern technology touch-points. However, the sheer existence of a significant number of resources, such as infrastructure, programmes, software, and developers does not demonstrate the digital prowess. Furthermore, such technologies are extremely fast-paced, and as such, organizations face difficulties in integrating them to achieve desired performance goals. As such, the success of a digital ecosystem depends upon its effective management; it involves the use of insights (data), and effective management of digital services both within the organization and beyond its boundaries. The role of effective IT integration is critical, and with the exponential growth in connected technologies, enterprises have increased their focus on such processes since the very beginning of large data processing capabilities.

When an organization incorporates digital transformation in its strategies, it is essential that its digital ecosystem is properly established and is managed effectively to improve the performance. Furthermore, no matter where a company is in its digital journey process, the ecosystem necessitates enterprises to give relevant information to the appropriate people at the right time in order to be alive and competitive in contemporary digital technology-driven business settings. A well managed digital ecosystem allows an organization to focus its energies on facilitating business value addition by removing frustrations typical to information flow characteristic to the legacy B2B services due to limitations of processing capabilities, restrictions on data availability, and compartmentalisation of information.

4.2. Application Programming Interface (API)

Application programming interfaces, or APIs, simplify software development and innovation by enabling applications to exchange data and functionality easily and securely. They enable companies to open up their applications' data and functionality to external third-party developers, business partners, and internal departments within their companies. This allows services and products to communicate with each other and leverage each other's data and functionality through a documented interface.

APIs allow the world to access data by binding the business systems, data, and processes together, thereby, acting as a governing authority between business data, systems, processes, and the UI. In order to access a particular application or a server system, businesses with agility need structuring of APIs to integrate with numerous outside applications easily. APIs also prove to be extremely useful in scenarios that require dealing with legacy systems, as APIs prove to be effective in securely utilizing the functionalities without having to bother about system re-configurability on the other end. Therefore, businesses now can modernize their systems and utilize the benefits of digital transformation without having to replace legacy systems.

An API is a set of defined rules that explain how computers or applications communicate with one another. APIs sit between an application and the web server, acting as an intermediary layer that processes data transfer between systems. Thus, APIs enable business systems to securely connect with various endpoint devices or applications at any given time. Developers don't need to worry about various aspects of data and information exchange between systems. They simply use the interface to communicate with other products and services. API use has surged over the past decade, to the degree that many of the most popular web applications today would not be possible without APIs.

The API works in a five step process:

1. **Request**: The client application initiates an API call to retrieve information.
2. **Validation**: The request is processed to the web server via the API's Uniform Resource Identifier (URI).
3. **Forwarding**: The API sends the call to the external program or web server.
4. **Retrieval**: The server sends a response to the API with the requested information.
5. **Response**: The API transfers the data to the initial requesting application.

While the data transfer will differ depending on the web service being used, this process of requests and response all happens through an API. Whereas a UI (user interface) is designed for use by humans, APIs are designed for use by a computer or application.

APIs offer security by design because their position as middleman facilitates the abstraction of functionality between two systems. The API endpoint decouples the consuming application from the infrastructure providing the service.

4.2.1. Taxonomy of Common APIs

As API allows businesses to make their resources accessible while maintaining security and control, it has opened many new vistas in modern business. Some popular examples of APIs that have become all pervasive in business world and day-to-day life of people include:

- **Third-party Payment Processing:** The ecommerce websites use the ubiquitous third-party payment processing platforms like Razorpay, Paytm, UPI, GPay, RuPay etc and all of it works through APIs. It lets people pay for products online without exposing sensitive data or granting access to unauthorized individuals.
- **Universal Logins:** Another popular use of API usage is enabling people to log in to websites by using their Facebook, Google, or LinkedIn profile login details. It gives websites a tool to leverage an API from the popular services to quickly authenticate the user, freeing them from the hassle of setting up a new user profile for their services.
- **Travel and Hotel Bookings:** Travel and hotel booking sites aggregate the available services, filtering and sorting them as per customers' requirements and then giving them options to choose from. These applications use APIs to provide users the latest information about availability from airlines and hotels, dramatically reducing the time and hassles required for planning a trip.
- **Google Maps:** The online business of delivery at the doorsteps or the cab services are using the API services of Google Maps that itself utilizes other APIs to provide users with directions and optimized routes as well as location of services.

- **Social Sites like Twitter, Facebook, LinkedIn:** The data available with these sites includes details of the user, a unique ID, messages, timestamps, locations etc. Users across various sectors of business access this data through APIs only.
- **Online Business Platforms like Amazon, Flipkart, JioMart, Uber, Zomato:** These websites depend heavily on the data available to them through APIs regarding their users, customers, and service providers.

4.2.2. API Protocol Journey

During the early development of computing machines, the systems were distributed and stand-alone having decentralized computing processes. However, in very early stages itself the need for integration and transfer of data was felt, mainly in military logistics, inspiring development of concepts like Electronic Data Interchange (EDI) and Remote Procedure Calls (RPC) that provided communication protocol for systems.

With the surge of business-level systems and the World Wide Web in the 1990s there came in greater demand for distributed systems and client-server topologies. The Object-Oriented Programming (OOPs) ushered integration between various systems through Common Object Request Broker Architecture (CORBA) that allowed communication between systems and software written in different languages and running on different machines, i.e. the data exchange became independent of operating systems, programming languages, and hardware platforms. With increase in the need for further integration of data various proprietary EAI's (Enterprise Application Integration) were developed that basically served as translators enabling use of diverse platforms and systems.

Earlier in the times of mainframe computers, software was nothing more than a collection of discrete subroutines performing specific sets of functions and interacting through interfaces that were a cluster of commands launched/triggered from a terminal. But in today's hyper-connected digital world, software functions as a real-world application that interacts with people over the Internet, and this interface has evolved into what is now identified as an API.

The proliferation of internet increased the use of web APIs necessitating development of protocols to provide users with a set of defined rules that specifies the accepted data types and commands so as to standardize information exchange. Some of them are:

- **SOAP** (Simple Object Access Protocol)
- **XML-RPC** (Extensible Markup Language – Remote Procedure Call)
- **JSON-RPC** (JavaScript Object Notation – Remote Procedure Call)
- **REST** (Representational State Transfer) - A set of web API architecture principles, which unlike a protocol doesn't have official standards but adheres to certain architectural constraints.

The Internet has made use of web services a routine activity for users. Web services are components that can be accessed via web address and through a network it exposes an application's data and functionality. Thus every web service, in effect, is an API. However, not every API is a web service.

In its initial stages, API referred to interface connecting applications that may have been created with a low-level programming language, such as COBOL, C, Javascript etc. The modern API adheres to REST principles and the JSON format and is typically built for HTTP, resulting in developer-friendly interfaces that are easily accessible and widely understood by applications written in Java, Ruby, Python, and many other languages.

4.2.3. The API Architecture

The mainstream enterprise's borders are shifting across industries, as companies offer their on-premises data and application capabilities to partners, web, applications, smart devices, and cloud. APIs are at the heart of the whole new open enterprise, allowing businesses to utilize their current data assets across multiple touch-points. Enterprises are deploying their API strategy in an integrated manner facilitating faster go-to-market and increased visibility of the APIs across organizations.

An API architecture is an indispensable need for enterprise level API enablement and for the organisations which are looking for performance, scalability and reliability. The process of developing a software interface that discloses backend data and application capabilities for implementation in new applications is referred to as API architecture. With an API-first architecture in place, organizations can build modular and reusable application ecosystems. Thus, API architecture has become an important and relevant element in the process of digital transformation.

Even the most flexible and simple API approaches also require solutions to certain practical challenges such as service provider supervising security, regulating traffic volumes, orchestrating the conventional components to deliver the requested service and desired results. Other than this there are also regular challenges regarding what functionality an organization is to set up externally and to whom, and how to keep internal record systems unaffected from any external activities.

The API platform should be a robust, secure, and scalable platform that enables systematic maintenance using processes and tools specially designed to manage E2E requirements of API Lifecycle. There are two common architectural approaches while establishing API structure: Service-oriented Architecture (SOA), and Microservices architecture.

- **SOA** is a software design structure where features are split up and implemented with web services, making the functional building blocks accessible through standard communication protocols. It has been a vital evolutionary step in application development and developers often use functions from legacy systems as service interfaces.
- Micro services Architecture is more common in Cloud Computing age. In it developers divide an application into smaller, independent components and then work on one component independent of the others of separate services making it easier to test, maintain, and deploy at a granular level, with shorter iteration cycles and more efficient use of cloud computing resources and scale up business.

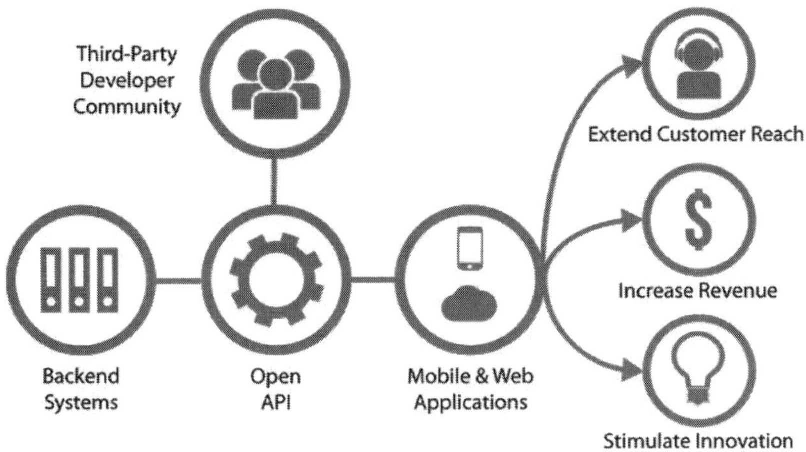

Figure – 4.1: A typical API structure

4.2.4. Types of API Integration

Cloud-based or Web APIs: Cloud based APIs are interfaces that are accessed using the HTTP protocol as the basis of all information exchanges online, however they differ in their privacy policies, terms and conditions, and security measures.

Open APIs: Open APIs have minimal restrictions and permit wide data availability with complete transparency making them useful for third-party users, such as vendors and software developers, who need to access information externally. They are also known as external or public APIs.

Internal APIs: Internal APIs are intended to hide data from external parties and they only allow departments within a company to share information, programs, and resources. There are intensive security measures, access limits, audit trails, and a standard interface linking systems securely.

Partner APIs: Partner APIs allow data access to third-party businesses but with control on admittance, limitations on specific information, and better protection. It helps in enhancing communications and supply chain management while keeping the company information secure and protected.

Composite APIs: Composite APIs allow access to multiple software applications in one call through different endpoints in one session. It helps in reducing the server load time and improving functionality and performance and is used extensively in microservice infrastructure.

4.2.5. Benefits of embracing API Integration

API integration has earned support from many businesses, from startups to large enterprises, because of its ability to aggregate a wide range of applications. Application integration gives organizations a competitive edge over other companies in their industry directly through heightened productivity.

Successful integration throughout a company provides several advantages by facilitating **Process Automation, Reduced Human Error,** and **Improved Communication and Reporting.** All of these lead to an overall increase in operational efficiency, which improves functionality, performance, and bottom line of the business.

Some of the advantages businesses can get by API integration include:

- **Promotes Digital Transformation**: Enterprises can future proof revenues and growth by Digital Transformation using API first strategy. While the idea of a digital transformation may seem formidable, removing outdated systems can significantly improve functionality. Many organizations implement robotics, artificial intelligence (AI), and the internet of things (IoT) but negate the process of connecting the systems. With API integration platforms, companies can optimize their current operations and promote business expansion through advanced connectivity.

- **Fuels Innovation**: An API platform doesn't just enable API solutions, it allows businesses to create new components according to existing applications. This capability opens up countless opportunities to implement new functions and features within a company.
- **Enhances Cloud-Based Applications:** As technology evolves, many companies are switching to cloud-based systems that allow users to access data from anywhere at any time. Therefore, cloud computing API solutions enhance the functionality of these services by maximizing connectivity and workflow. It helps them explore and implement new business combinations beyond boundaries of the organisation and the industry.
- **Optimizes Enterprise Productivity:** Integration of API platforms simplifies the maintenance, system management, and diversification of the digital services allowing IT managers to conduct the procedures that result in enhanced and optimized processes and enhanced enterprise productivity.
- **Secure Data Management:** Achieving complete system integration throughout a large enterprise is nearly impossible when done manually. API integration platforms meet this challenge by acting as a centralized database in which all other APIs report to. This method increases transparency throughout the network, simplifying data management, and compliance procedures.
- **Mitigation of Disintermediation**: An API strategy may even be able to lessen the threat of disintermediation. By offering APIs to bring business activities as near to the customer as feasible, the danger of a third party filling the gap and cutting the supplier out is reduced.
- **Timely and Efficient compliance of regulations:** API integration platforms provide interconnectivity between various systems which may have differing compliance schedules and submission

requirements. This helps in ensuring timely raising of tickets for adherence to the dates and also provides consolidated and collated information for compliance of the regulations.

- **Robust Infrastructure:** An Integrated API system provides a strong foundation for integrating all of a company's systems in which all the existing and concurrent data can be translated and transmitted throughout the platform. This helps developers in updating older API platforms, reducing expenses, and ensuring successful integration of the business process resulting in delivery of services in user-friendly collaborative manner.
- **Opportunities for New Revenue Streams:** Organizations can unlock the value of their digital resources and uncover new ways to build business by monetizing APIs. Functionality, when delivered through an API, can be billed to users for usage (or use a revenue-sharing model to pay them). This offers an innovative new solution to clients and consumers that may generate new income streams, and firms can respond much more swiftly to both new possibilities and challenges.
- **Reduced cost and faster Go–To-Market:** Reduced development time and faster go to market strategy is another benefit of API-driven architecture. Developers know that most of the functionality they'll need to incorporate to an app is already available in other places. They've learnt to save time and money by relying on cost-effective APIs from third-party platforms rather than recreating the wheel or using APIs they have already built. Adopting and utilising APIs allows developers to focus on providing the unique features of their apps faster, saving time and money for organisations. The ability to deliver efficiently and cost-effectively is critical in a world where technology is constantly altering workforces, consumer expectations, and even whole sectors.

With enhanced speed of data exchange and secured transactions an Integrated API system provides a superior customer experience through improved services and customized products. This not only makes it possible for new businesses to go to the market, but also to monetize the APIs for new revenue streams.

Figure 4.2: API Ecosystem

4.2.6. Strategies for Implementing API Integration

Strategies for API integration are about a lot more than implementing the REST concepts correctly. It encompasses the wider perspective of APIs and can be observed from several viewpoints. A Unified platform to manage the end-to-end API lifecycle is an enterprise-grade platform and provides components to enable and manage the digital enterprise of today and the future.

By implementing an API solution, businesses can focus on expansion efforts without worrying about manually collaborating system data. As the company grows and more interfaces are introduced, an API integration platform can ensure information is updated accurately and shared throughout the organization.

It is not only about technology when it comes to creating a successful API strategy. Enterprises must identify the basis of their API initiative in terms of strategy, monetization plan, target audience, goals, and so on. They ought to then examine and select an ideal solution to carry out the API lifecycle. No product launch is possible without a well-defined Go-to-Market strategy and APIs are no different. They require support and assistance in order to reach their greatest potential.

The typical API platform provides the following, integrated features in one enterprise package

- **API Gateway:** API Gateway acts as an entry point for applications to access data, business logic, or functionality from any backend services, such as workloads running on private or public clouds, web application, or real-time communication applications. The API Gateway enforces governance and mediation of APIs via policies.
- **API Manager:** The API Manager is the control plane to manage the end-to-end lifecycle of APIs. It provides management control to onboard APIs, publish / unpublish APIs, versioning of APIs, decommissioning of APIs and access point for other core features of the platform.
- **API Monitoring:** API Monitoring provides Real time monitoring of APIs. It can be configured to alert in case there are any anomalies in the API endpoints.
- **Management and Analytics Dashboard:** This is the management GUI (Graphical User Interface) that provides an enterprise-wide, real-time and historical view of all the APIs and critical metrics, a monitoring mechanism to ensure the liveliness and health of the APIs.
- **Developer Engine:** Developer Engine is the Low Code platform to rapidly design, develop, test and deploy APIs. It provides Functions, developer-focused CLI and remote data source (databases/web services) connectors to integrate and build business logic.
- **Internal/External Marketplace:** The API marketplace or Developer portal is used to on-board new developers. It generates API documentation, provides efficient discovery of APIs, seamless integration and controlled distribution of APIs.

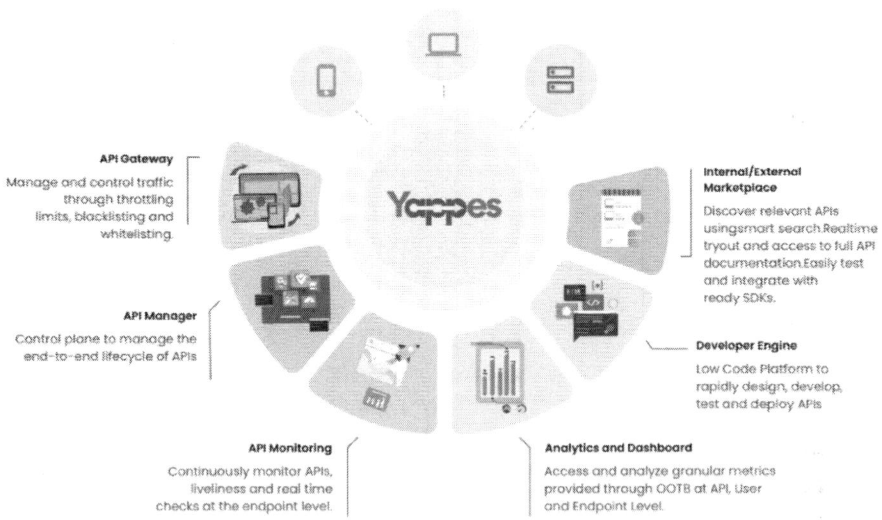

Figure – 4.3 API Integration (a typical example)

4.2.7 Checklist for selection of API Platform for implementation in an enterprise:

- The developer engine needs to be focused on rapidly building, testing and deploying APIs.
- It should provide downloadable and installable libraries for multiple programming languages (Nodejs, PHP and Python).
- There should be hassle-free and seamless onboarding of existing APIs. It should not require rewriting the code.
- It should provide an API marketplace (developer portal) for efficient discovery, seamless integration and controlled distribution of APIs.
- It should work as API Gateway to orchestrate micro services, and provide governance and mediation of APIs.
- It should have an effective management and analytics dashboard to provide an enterprise view of all the APIs and critical metrics.
- It should incorporate a monitoring mechanism to ensure the liveliness and health of the APIs.

- It should have multi-dimensional security features such as authorization, authentication, message signature, RBAC, onboarding of customers / partners / vendors etc.
- It should be sector and cloud agnostic, and be deployable on public or private cloud or on-premises infrastructures.
- It should have transparent API Version Management**.** As the app functionality and or features change over time, the API provider should make changes to the APIs as well and in the current architecture.
- It should have Automatic API Documentation so as to enable developers in different teams to easily understand and consume APIs in their software.
- The API Analytics should ensure availability of details like how many requests were made to each API, when, how many requests were serviced in a specific time interval, how many requests were left out, etc.
- It should provide for API Monitoring by checking the network availability of API servers so as to avoid unexpected service failures.

4.3. Internet of Things (IoT)

The requirement for speed and agility has never been stronger for organizations that want to be disruptors rather than being disrupted by rivals. Adopting API-driven initiatives is the only way to obtain such digital capabilities. APIs are now vital for enterprises to drive agile innovation, swiftly respond to market changes, outperform rivals, create new income streams, and establish profitable collaborations.

One of the most upcoming and path-breaking usage of API Integration is the emergence of Internet of Things (IoT). A network of physical objects i.e. devices —"things"—that are connected to each other and exchanging data among themselves and other systems over the internet is called Internet of Things. These devices ranging from ordinary household objects to sophisticated industrial tools are embedded with sensors, software, and other technologies for this purpose.

Such smart devices that are capable of machine-to-machine (M2M) communications were already existing before they got the IoT label due to the entry of the internet and their integration through APIs. These APIs are the logical connectors that allow applications to communicate with different manufacturer's IoT devices and enable them to transmit data to various applications that control the device and serve as a function interface.

The internet of things is also a natural extension of supervisory control and data acquisition (SCADA), a category of software application programs for process control that gathers data in real time from remote locations to control equipment and conditions. SCADA systems include hardware and software components. The hardware gathers and feeds data into a computer that has SCADA software installed, where it is then processed and presented in a timely manner. The evolution of SCADA is such that late-generation SCADA systems developed into first-generation IoT systems.

4.3.1. Importance of Internet of Things (IoT)

IoT has become one of the most important technological advances of the 21st century with people being able to connect everyday objects—kitchen appliances, cars, thermostats, baby monitors—to the internet via embedded devices. Now there is seamless communication possible between people, processes, and things. Low-cost computing, the cloud, big data, analytics, and mobile technologies have enabled physical things (devices) to share and collect data with minimal human intervention.

In the IoT environment the physical world meets the digital world, and they cooperate. The digital systems can record, monitor, and adjust each interaction between connected things.

4.3.2. Reasons for the Growth of IoT

- **Access to Low-cost, Low-power Sensor Technologies:** Affordable and reliable sensors are making IoT technology possible for more manufacturers.
- **Connectivity.** A host of network protocols for the internet has made it easy to connect sensors to the cloud and to other "things" for efficient data transfer. It is the age of Hyperconnectivity.
- **Cloud Computing Platforms.** The increase in the availability of cloud platforms enables both businesses and consumers to access the infrastructure they need to scale up without actually having to manage it all.

- **Machine Learning and Data Analytics.** With advances in machine learning and analytics, along with access to varied and vast amounts of data stored in the cloud, businesses can gather insights faster and more easily. The emergence of these allied technologies continues to push the boundaries of IoT and the data produced by IoT also feeds these technologies.
- **Conversational Artificial Intelligence (AI).** Advances in neural networks have brought natural-language processing (NLP) to IoT devices (such as digital personal assistants Alexa, Cortana, and Siri) and made them appealing, affordable, and viable for home use.

4.3.3. Applications of IoT

IoT devices have extensive applications in consumer, commercial, industrial, military, and infrastructure spaces.

4.3.3.1 Consumer Applications of IoT: The IoT applications that are created for consumer use like connected vehicles, home automation, wearable technology, connected health, and appliances with remote monitoring capabilities.

- **Smart Homes:** IoT is used today to monitor and control lighting, heating and air conditioning, media, camera and security systems providing long term benefits like energy savings by automatically turning off lights and electronics when not in use and making the residents aware of usage. The devices can also be operated by applications on smart phones.
- **Senior Care:** Another key consumer application is to provide assistance to elderly individuals and to those with disabilities. These systems use assistive technology to accommodate an owner's specific disabilities. Voice control can assist users with sight and mobility limitations while alert systems can be connected directly to cochlear implants worn by hearing-impaired users. They can also be equipped with additional safety features. These features can include sensors that monitor for medical emergencies such as falls or seizures.

A very important feature of this system can be a 'Panic Button' option set with each of the Devices. A very easy press of a soft touch button can relay help messages to the respondent numbers in a matter of few seconds. The frequency, content or the designated recipients of Panic Messages can be customized as desired. The Message includes the identity of the sender as well as the zone from where the panic message is generated. This system integrated with the CCTV networks can give us a precise camera zone and a feed of the specific area.

- **Fitness Monitoring:** The fitness monitors worn by new-age health conscious netizens provide data about heart beat, blood pressure, physical activities etc. Such smart technology applications can provide users with more freedom and a higher quality of life.
- **Real Estate and Home Automation:** IoT devices can be used to monitor and control the mechanical, electrical and electronic systems used in various types of buildings (e.g., public and private, industrial, institutions, or residential), by integration of the Internet with building energy management systems in order to create energy-efficient and IOT-driven "smart buildings". It is a possible means of real-time monitoring for reducing energy consumption, management and control of common services, and monitoring occupant behaviors.

4.3.3.2 Commercial Applications of IoT: When applied to business and corporate settings the IoT is known as Enterprise IoT (EIoT). Generally, enterprises are looking for IoT solutions that can help in four areas: energy use, asset tracking, security, and the customer experience.

- **Digital Supply Chain Management:** This is one of the most pervasive examples of use of IoT. Process visibility during Warehouse and Store Management is the biggest challenge for implementation and monitoring of set processes. For example, an organisation can set SOPs for 'Put-Away' and 'Pick-Up' cycles but due to lack of monitoring across the process, the implementation is never in control. The IOT system provides visibility across the process for better management along with integration to existing ERP Systems.
- **Yard Management:** It is emerging as one of the most sought after IoT Solutions for big industries. This module helps industries improve the process from Entry to Exit of carrier vehicles by quick processing of documentation, warehouse coordination, driver monitoring etc. The average waiting time reduction is more than 32%

during yard operations. As such, Fleet and In-Transit Logistics Management is emerging as a critical area of supply chain, going beyond GPS tracking

- **Process Digitisation:** Production and Assembly lines can be digitised for seamless (streamlined) movement of goods and improving the workstation efficiency. Each workstation would have a User Interface like a Tab (smart device), which would contain the tasks to be accomplished and other related information. After completion of each task, the workman or the supervisor can tick (check) the designated box. This would automatically update the central ERP system and would help everybody to be on the same page to understand the progress. Such a system would help plan and execute the entire production process to a far greater efficiency. The cloud monitoring of P/A Line minimises human interaction and intervention. With enormous flexibility of data analytics and process formulation, BLE (Bluetooth Low Energy) platform can be a boon in multi-fold improvement in the Production Management
- **Task assignment & monitoring:** Task assignment and monitoring is a very effective management tool to keep track of the tasks allocated to individuals. The alerts and update features help increase the visibility without being engaged all the time with delegated jobs.
- **Scrap management:** Scrap management is probably one of the biggest pain areas of organisations for various reasons. The losses and the risk of losing proprietary knowledge are immense. This system allows digital processes to be compulsorily followed without personal exposure to analyse scrap and prevent loss. The unique and non-renewable ID generation for each critical scrap eliminates the risk of mal-practices
- **Asset tracking and resource optimisation:** In the industries, teams can locate and track the assets inside the warehouse / storage facility or the Production arena through a network of Gateways. A virtual mesh shall be created which would earmark the location hubs inside the arena. In this system, assets are tagged with a unique digital ID supported by a buzzer and / or a beacon light. To locate a particular Fixture, the team is first guided to a predefined location hub, from where the Buzzer / Light System would get activated to help precisely locate the Fixture. The tracking can be done through any smart device having necessary system ware. To further enhance the

utility, team can integrate pre-fed data for each fixture like timelines, utility, user guidelines, integration schedule etc. It can generate the necessary alerts for defined parameters. Using this it can also map the efficiency and time utility of specific assets and set the necessary changes, if desired. Going ahead, it can integrate the pre-fed work schedule and task specific instructions on each asset. This might help each operator execute the job in a better way.

- **Wearable Health and Safety Equipments:** The health monitoring wristbands provide features like pulse, heart rate, SpO2 etc., along with related alerts. The parameters depict the stress level for each individual. Some of the add-on features include monitoring of any one or a group of personnel for their movement, keeping an eye on specific areas, unreasonable assembly of personnel etc. The system is extremely flexible and can be moulded to deliver numerous requirements. Safety helmets provide tracking, fall-impact alerts, and audio communication over Wi-Fi, fan & torch etc.
- **Remote Monitoring:** Teams can set up the Temperature and Gas Leakage Sensors at the designated locations, which would continuously monitor these parameters for us. Team can then set the desired ALARMS for critical situations like High Temperature, Gas Leakage levels etc. With an automated system like this working 24*7, we can avoid the human risks and fatal situations
- **Predictive Maintenance:** All the manufacturing industries are quickly moving to the predictive maintenance of machinery from the earlier models of preventive maintenance. As per an IBM study, predictive maintenance can reduce the maintenance costs up to 72%. The IoT can predict the need for maintenance before a breakdown takes place by capturing, collating, processing, and analysing the data of various parameters regarding health of the critical components in equipment and initiate action for triggering preventive maintenance schedules.
- **GPS monitoring during Transit:** This would include the GPS Tracking of vehicles, which are en-route to deliver the finished goods to their destination. The system would also have features like Intelligent Route Mapping, Route Deviation Alarms, Stoppage Report, Speed Alerts and host of other routine reports. In case the company owns any vehicles (in-house fleet) used for transport, an added module of Fleet Management can be integrated with the GPS

system. Furthermore, a combination of Inertial Sensors like temperature, pressure, and humidity monitoring can help tracking of material during transit.

4.3.3.3 Application of IoT in Industries: Industrial IoT (IIoT) devices acquire and analyze data from connected equipment, operational technology (OT), locations, and people to monitor devices, regulate and control industrial systems. Industrial Internet of Things (IIoT) data is growing at an accelerating rate, now estimated by IDC and other analysts to be beyond 35% growth year over year. Currently, data is in the range of 44 zettabytes in volume. Industrial IoT can vastly improve connectivity, efficiency, scalability, time savings, and cost savings for all types of industrial organizations. Some organizations are already experiencing the benefits of IIoT through cost savings from predictive maintenance, improved safety, and increased operational efficiencies. IIoT networks of intelligent devices allow industrial organizations to break open data silos and connect all their people, data, and processes from the factory floor to the executive offices. Business leaders can use IIoT data to get a full and accurate view of how their enterprise is doing, which helps them to make better decisions leveraging the full product portfolio.

- **Data Management & Storage:** Industry 4.0, the Fourth Industrial Revolution involves harnessing technology to automate industry and manufacturing using Digital twin, which helps to build digital models of Industry assets, processes, or products. In manufacturing engineering, changes to production are often tested on real systems. But this testing means that the team needs to halt ongoing production. If errors occur, you must eliminate them before restarting production with the changed configuration.

These downtimes are expensive and significantly decrease the flexibility of production. Digital system mapping would solve both problems. In production, changes can be tested on a digital image of the system before modifying the real system. It could end up finding the majority of problems in the virtual environment and help with prior resolution, which would reduce downtime of the main system. Originally, the digital twin was conceived to virtualize expensive tests in industry to reduce development costs through virtual testing.

- **Manufacturing:** The IoT can connect various manufacturing devices equipped with sensing, identification, processing, communication, actuation, and networking capabilities. Network control and management of the process parameters, equipment, assets, and situations allow IoT to be used for industrial applications and smart manufacturing. IoT intelligent systems enable rapid manufacturing and optimization of new products, and rapid response to product demands. Digital control systems to automate process controls, operator tools and service information systems to optimize plant safety and security are within the purview of the IIoT. Industrial asset management to maximize reliability can be done using the predictive maintenance, statistical measurement, and evaluation using IIoT. Industrial management systems can be integrated with smart grids, enabling energy optimization. Measurements, automated controls, plant optimization, health and safety management, and other functions are provided by networked sensors.
- **Agriculture:** There are numerous IoT applications in farming such as collecting data on temperature, rainfall, humidity, wind speed, pest infestation, and soil content. This data can be used to automate farming techniques, take informed decisions to improve quality and quantity, minimize risk and waste, and reduce the effort required to manage crops. Farmers can now monitor soil temperature and moisture from afar, and even apply IoT-acquired data to precision fertilization programs. The overall goal is that data from sensors, coupled with the farmer's knowledge and intuition about his or her farm, can help increase farm productivity, and also help reduce costs.
- **Maritime:** IoT devices are in use monitoring the environments and systems of boats and yachts. Many pleasure boats are left unattended for days in summer, and months in winter so such devices provide valuable early alerts of boat flooding, fire, and deep discharge of batteries. The use of global internet data networks combined with long-life batteries, and microelectronics allows the engine rooms, bilge, and batteries to be constantly monitored and reported to a connected Android or Apple applications.
- **Infrastructure and Construction applications:** Monitoring and controlling operations of sustainable urban and rural infrastructures like bridges, railway tracks and on- and offshore wind-farms is a key

application of the IoT. Usage of IoT devices for monitoring and operating infrastructure is likely to improve incident management and emergency response coordination, coordination, uptime and service-quality as well reduce costs of operation in all.

4.3.3.4 Internet of Medical Things (IoMT): IoMT is an application of the IoT for medical and health related purposes, data collection and analysis for research, and monitoring. IoT devices can be used to enable remote health monitoring and emergency notification systems. These health monitoring devices can range from blood pressure and heart rate monitors to advanced devices capable of monitoring specialized implants, such as pacemakers, Fitbit electronic wristbands, or advanced hearing aids. Smart beds can detect when they are occupied and when a patient is attempting to get up. It can also adjust itself to ensure appropriate pressure and support is applied to the patient without the manual interaction of nurses.

The application of the IoT in healthcare plays a fundamental role in managing chronic diseases and in disease prevention and control. Remote monitoring is made possible through the connection of powerful wireless solutions. The connectivity enables health practitioners to capture patient's real-time data and apply complex algorithms in health data analysis.

4.3.3.5 Administrative and Governance Applications of APIs & IoTs in India: The Government of India has been playing an important role in supporting the data ecosystem and building bridges between businesses and the citizens for a variety of reasons. In order to bring a paradigm shift in the people in favour of digitisation and yet have popular appeal, it has taken many initiatives. The fourth Industrial revolution rides on digital technology and the government's technology plan is designed to build platforms that offer tools and seed ecosystems that will take full advantage of these over the next decade.

- **Digital Platforms for Service Delivery:** The government is deploying its vision by building open, scalable digital public platforms such as Aadhaar, DigiLocker and UPI. These are also platforms around which private players have created ecosystems of solutions. In India, the Fintech growth is built on the strength of these platforms, as evident from 38 billion transactions worth almost Rs.72 trillion handled by UPI in 2020-21. Another digital transformation is the planned healthcare registry and platform, Ayushman Bharat Mission which envisages accessing and sharing health records digitally.GOI is also developing open network protocols such as ONDC which aims to make digital commerce accessible for SMEs and the skill and livelihood ecosystem DESH, setting up a digital university and intensified focus on financial intrusion.

- **Digital Transformation of Services:** Based on APIs, rapid digitisation exercises are taking place in public service delivery systems. From filing of Income Tax returns to single window clearances for projects, the government has changed the way business and citizens interact with it. More than 4,000 e-government services across the country witness 385 million e-transactions every day. The Gatishakti initiative is an example of enabling efficiency and cost optimization in government processes enabled by planning and infrastructure projects and logistics. The Gem for digital public procurement and the e-bill system are other examples of platforms enabling transparent business to government transactions. The scalability and inclusivity of the platforms have the power to touch every citizen. The government has used Adhere as the primary mechanism to target the right beneficiary in the PDS programme.
- **Metropolitan Scale Deployments:** The Smart City Mission of GoI is one of the several planned or ongoing large-scale deployments of the IoT, to enable better management of cities and systems. It is a Centrally Sponsored Scheme as a part of Urban Rejuvenation focuses on promoting the cities that provide core institutional, physical, social and economic infrastructure; provide decent quality of life to city dwellers; sustainable environment and smart solutions. The Core infrastructure features of Smart City Mission would include robust IT connectivity and digitalization; good governance, especially e-governance and citizen participation along with basic civic amenities.

The smart solutions under the mission refer to use of technology in such a way that it leads Smart outcomes e.g. E-Governance and citizen services including public information and grievance-redressal, Electronic Service Delivery, Citizen Engagement, Video crime monitoring, smart water and electricity metering, intelligent traffic management, integrated multi-modal public transport, etc. Vijayawada, a city in Andhra Pradesh has started deploying technologies for Smart Wi-Fi, Smart Safety & Security, Smart

Lighting, Smart Parking, Smart Transports, Smart Bus Stops, Smart Kiosks, Remote Expert for Government Services (REGS), and Smart Education.

The auto industry is also adopting digital ecosystems. The automotive manufacturers have either formed an alliance with an original equipment manufacturer or built contractual relationships with hundreds of suppliers to obtain the necessary parts from a large number of partners covering industries in different countries to manufacture cars that are autonomous, and connected to the company's digital platform.

Chapter 5

MANAGE SERVICES

5.1. Introduction

As the world economy matured, it has become dominated by service-focused businesses. The service sector is generally grouped into three categories: 1. Public Services, 2. Consumer Services, and 3. Business Services. The services are delivered either in general, thereby catering to any sector, or as more industry-specific models for technical service. Essentially, a service delivery company provides to a customer a service they can't create or don't want to create on their own. These services could be anything from a task to a technology or information.

Broadly defined, service delivery is a business framework that supplies services from a provider to a client. A service delivery system is a set of interlinked functions that deliver services to customers or clients. The services are in terms of inputs, processes, outputs, and outcomes. It also includes the constant interaction between the two parties during the duration of the time in which the provider supplies the service and the customer purchases it. Sometimes service delivery may involve a third-party or outsourced supplier besides the provider and the client.

Service delivery processes typically aim to provide clients with increased value by setting standards, policies, principles and constraints to guide all aspects of their business and customer interactions. Typically, services are delivered by the vendors through three models: 1. Contracting, 2. Outsourcing, and 3. Manage Services. The focus of this handbook is on the latter, i.e., Manage Services.

5.2. Manage Services: An Overview

Manage services is the practice of outsourcing the responsibility for maintaining, and anticipating need for, a range of processes and functions, ostensibly for the purpose of improved operations and reduced budgetary expenditures through the reduction of directly-employed staff. It is an alternative to the break/fix or on-demand outsourcing model where the service provider performs on-demand services and bills the customer only for the work done. Manage services clients look beyond traditional outsourcing criteria or hiring short term contractual staff so as to get the longer-term benefits they expect from a solutions partner.

Manage Services are preferred over contracting or outsourced models because of a number of reasons, for example:

- Pay only for the actual use of the service
- Increased performance
- Optimised value-added use of internal resources
- Continuous Service Improvement (CSI) and efficiency gains over time built in
- Reduced risk due to business volatility directly driving service demand
- Suppliers have flexibility with staffing engagements and with utilisation and management of resources.
- Supplier assumes the risk of transition and future operations based on an agreed, committed scope and tenure.

5.2.1. Types of Services Delivered

There are different types of services being delivered that cover a range of products cutting across industries and businesses.

5.2.1.1. Information Technology Service Management (ITSM): IT Service Management is today one of the most common services delivery being consumed across the world. ITSM is the process of designing, delivering, managing, and improving the IT services an organisation provides to its end users. Being offered by a lot of provider organisations, ITSM is focused on aligning IT processes and services with business objectives to help an organisation grow.

ITSM service providers focus on supplying customers with technological and communication resources such as cable, internet, mobile phone service, streaming services and other related hardware, software, systems or infrastructures. ITSM companies may use tools like help desks, service catalogues, configuration management, databases and performance logs to provide service delivery and track its usefulness.

5.2.1.2. Local Services: States, cities and municipalities offer multiple types of service delivery for residents and business owners within their districts. These typically include healthcare, education, regulation of administrative proceedings, garbage collection or other related amenities. With local service delivery, the provider is generally a government organisation, and the client is its citizens or business owners.

5.2.1.3. Health Services: Health service providers use service delivery to ensure that patients receive the medical treatment and supplies they need and deserve. In a health services situation, the patients are the customers and the medical professionals, health institutions and insurance companies are the providers.

5.2.1.4. Legal Services: Legal service providers help businesses by giving legal advice and representing them in court proceedings in addition to conducting many services like understanding the terminology and processes of certain situations under local, state and federal laws. In this type, customers or clients are those seeking legal advice or assistance and the providers are attorneys, law firms, or other organisations.

5.2.1.5. Real Estate Services: Real estate services help people in finding a property to buy, finding purchasers for a property, coordinating inspections and appraisals, and working with legal service providers to create contracts.

In this type, the customers are those buying or selling property and the providers are agents or organisations facilitating the processes.

5.2.1.6. Consulting Services: Consulting service delivery is provided by consulting firms that offer a solution that an organisation doesn't have the knowledge or volume of staff to generate internally. Consulting firms can specialise in almost any area of business like HR, finance, marketing, IT, operations, safety etc.

5.3. Manage Services Management Model

Manage Services requires well coordinated Service Governance and Service Management functions in addition to the other functions in operation of a business model.

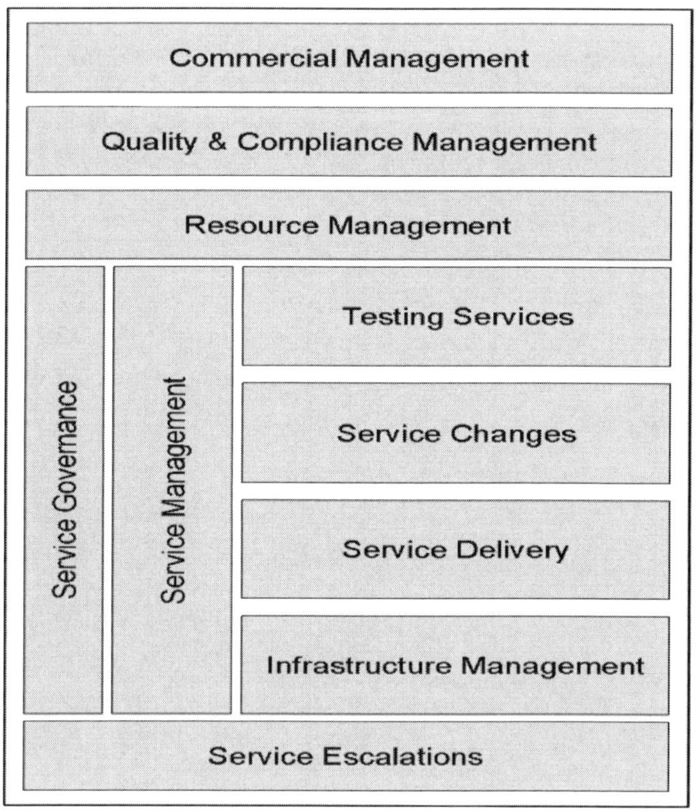

Figure 5.1: Manage Services Management Model: A Schematic Overview

5.3.1. SLA and MSA: In order to manage and monitor delivery of the contracted services and to ensure adherence to the desired levels of performance, the vendor and the customer organisations enter into different types of agreements. In the IT sector, the two common agreements are Service Level Agreement (SLA) and Master Service Agreement (MSA).

An SLA documents the agreed-upon level of service between a vendor and a client giving numerical metrics to determine success or failure of the agreement, along with clear repercussions for failing to meet the service level standards. These metrics enlist factors like response time, customer satisfaction, and replies to resolve etc. They help set a standard for measuring customer satisfaction level and team productivity.

There are three types of SLAs:

1. Customer-based SLA with individual customer groups covering all the services that they use.
2. Service-based SLA is a wider agreement between the service provider and all the customers using the services.
3. Multilevel SLA covers for a more variable level consisting of corporate-level, customer-level and service-level.

An MSA is a typical contract between two parties that lists out the terms that govern all of their future transactions or future agreements. On the other hand, a Service Level Agreement (SLA) is an agreement specifically between the service provider and a client / a service user.

Simply put, an MSA must state every important and minute detail to convey business expectations and provide financial guarantees to both parties. It should also be clear and understandable to guide project managers. The MSA document contains provision of services containing overall goals and objectives for future projects, client's expectations, services provided, clauses, fees, processes, progress reporting, guarantees of independence for the vendor and the client.

It also contains provisions for Communication and notices to stay in touch during the agreement period, representatives of each side, preferred methods, and tools for communications, locations chosen for real-life meetings, as well as the process of receiving official notifications. It establishes the process for delivering the MSA and its revisions and also procedure of approval or rejection of the deliverables.

5.4 Manage Services in Information Technology Service Management (ITSM)

Today, IT is a vital part of any business, linked by technology to a company's success. No longer is IT just a set of computer hardware operated by some specialists sitting in a corner office in the depths of the building who people call when their desktops refuse to obey them. Also long gone are the times when, if an organisation needed software they would call a software provider, who would deliver a bunch of CDs and licence keys that would be loaded in the systems and used.

Way back in the 1990s itself, the concept of remote support of IT infrastructure started taking shape when application software providers (ASPs) emerged, who focused on supplying and remote monitoring and management of application software. With time, the scope of services has expanded to include providing servers, networks, infrastructure, security, ongoing regular maintenance and development support, active system administration etc and has matured to the concept of managed service providers (MSPs) delivering them.

With the advent of the cloud and continually evolving business models, things have evolved even more now. Now, with the cloud services available as IaaS (Infrastructure as a Service), PaaS (Platform as a Service), SaaS (Software as a Service), and even FaaS (Function as a Service), service delivery systems have taken centre stage in terms of decision making relating to IT as well as overall business models.

This has set a trend of transition of the IT service delivery industry from SaaS, which offers a low-cost alternative to traditional, in-house solutions to Manage Services, which offer far more comprehensive solutions over and above SaaS by helping a company with maintenance, upgrades, and integration of software to create better workflows.

5.4.1. Information Technology Infrastructure Library (ITIL) services

With the proliferation of IT in every aspect of business across all types of industries as well as in day-to-day life of individuals, ITSM has gained a position of prominence in the strategies that companies adopt to evolve and remain competitive. To manage IT services, organisations must control performance and oversee problem resolution. ISTM has developed its own set of standard delivery practices to use in corporate business around the world. The Information Technology Infrastructure Library (ITIL) is a set of detailed practices for IT activities such as IT service management and IT asset management that focus on aligning IT services with the needs of business.

Information Technology Infrastructure Library (ITIL) services are a set of best-practice publications for IT service management that gives guidance on the provision of quality IT services and the processes, functions and other capabilities needed to support them. It also describes processes, procedures, tasks, and checklists which are not specific to any singular organisation or technology.

5.5 Manage Services Delivery Procedures in ITSM[1]

5.5.1. Incident Management: An incident management process is a set of procedures and actions taken to respond to and resolve critical incidents: how incidents are detected and communicated, who is responsible, what tools are used, and what steps are taken to resolve the incident. It includes functional and technical changes to maintain operational integrity of the applications.

In a business organisation, the IT service desk is responsible for addressing performance issues, restoring the service in case of an outage and making improvements where needed. They should also create and update procedures to stop incidents from happening again. The primary drivers in determining support work are the work types defined within the individual contracts.

Purpose: The goal is to restore normal service operation as quickly as possible and minimise the adverse effect on business operations, thus ensuring that the best possible levels of service quality and availability are maintained. The procedure starts when the user identifies a problem related to an application in a production environment, including emergency fixes. The procedure ends when the problem is closed or the problem has been resolved to the user's satisfaction.

Scope: Incident Management provides fixes for identified problems, which may or may not be critical situations and or escalation problems. It also provides an emergency fix for an identified problem, which will cause a negative impact to business function and / or processing. It handles activities to maintain operational control of systems, exclusive of security updates. It identifies activities related to Master Data change. It contains all user consultative activities, including 'How to' attend the incident.

---

[1]Checklists & Schematics for all Manage Service Delivery Procedures are given in Appendix I-X.

It assumes that the Client Support Agreement is in place and the support levels and criteria are available to the support team. The procedure does not include the development or coordination of any change requests.

Process Flow:

Steps in Incident Management

1. Record, Classify, and Route Incidents
2. Accept the incident & maintain SLA
3. Investigate and Diagnose Incident
4. Test in QA
5. Approval to move to PDR
6. Resolve Incident
7. Close Incident Ticket

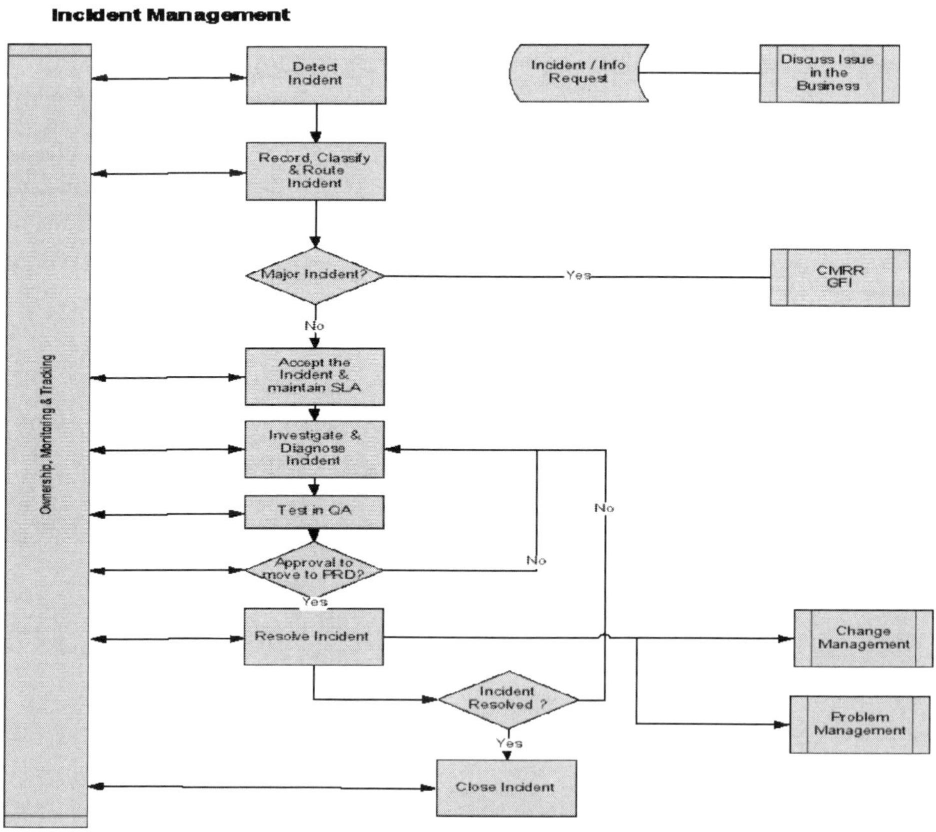

Figure 5.2: Incident Management: A Schematic Overview

5.5.2. Problem Management: Problem management aims to fix issues permanently and deliver a more performance-based service. The IT team's objective is to deal with the problems that include functional and technical changes to maintain operational integrity of the applications.

Purpose: The goal is to resolve the root cause of incidents and to minimise the adverse impact of incidents and problems on business that are caused by errors within the IT infrastructure, and to prevent recurrence of incidents related to these errors and eliminate Work-Around. The procedure starts when the Support Organisation identifies a problem related to an application in a production environment, including emergency fixes. The procedure ends when the problem is closed or the problem has been resolved to the user's satisfaction.

Scope: Problem Management provides fixes for identified problems, which are not critical situations and or escalation problems. It also provides an emergency fix for an identified problem, which will cause a negative impact to business function and / or processing. It handles activities to maintain operational control of systems, exclusive of security updates. It identifies activities related to Master Data change. It contains all user consultative activities, including 'How to' Support.

Process Flow: When a problem occurs, the Client business user / end user logs a call with Level 1 support team. Level 1 support team in turn analyzes the case and either resolves or forwards it to the proper Level 2 resolver group for resolution. A problem ticket may be related to one or many incidents and should be created under the following circumstances:

- A high impact/urgent incident is recorded
- Repeat incidents are observed
- A workaround is unsustainable
- Workaround or temporary fix is not available
- Monitoring events indicate likelihood of a future incident.

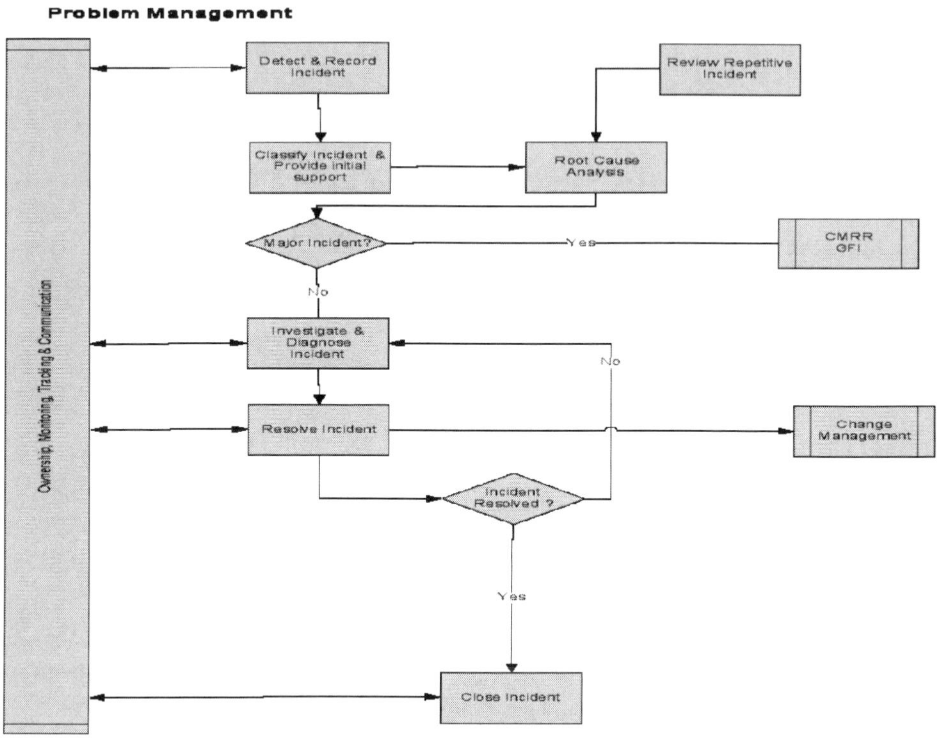

Figure 5.3: Problem Management: A Schematic Overview

5.5.3. Release Management: Release Management is the process responsible for planning, scheduling, and controlling, in addition to testing and deploying Releases. Release Management ensures that IS&T delivers new and enhanced IT services required by the business, while protecting the integrity of existing services. Release management can be treated separately or can be grouped with Change management.

Purpose: The purpose is to ensure that consistent and integral release packages are deployed in line with agreed policy and with plans agreed with the customers and stakeholders, and that this takes place under full and effective control. Any associated business and business process changes, including training and skills transfer, must be managed to take place in a timescale that is aligned with the release timetable.

The objective is to ensure that there are clear consistent plans that everyone understands and follows, that releases are managed efficiently and effectively through to deployment and use and that the new service and supporting systems are capable of being operated successfully and deliver the agreed service requirements (Utility and Warranty).

Scope: The scope of Release and Deployment Management includes the processes, systems and functions required to package, build, test and deploy a release into production in accordance with the Service Design Package (SDP). This includes handover to the Service Operation lifecycle stage.

Effective Release and Deployment Management adds value by ensuring that customers and users can use the new or changed service in a way that supports the business and by delivering change faster and at optimum cost and minimal risk. Well-planned and well-implemented release and deployment can make a significant difference to an organisation's service costs by minimising troubleshooting and rework.

Process Flow:

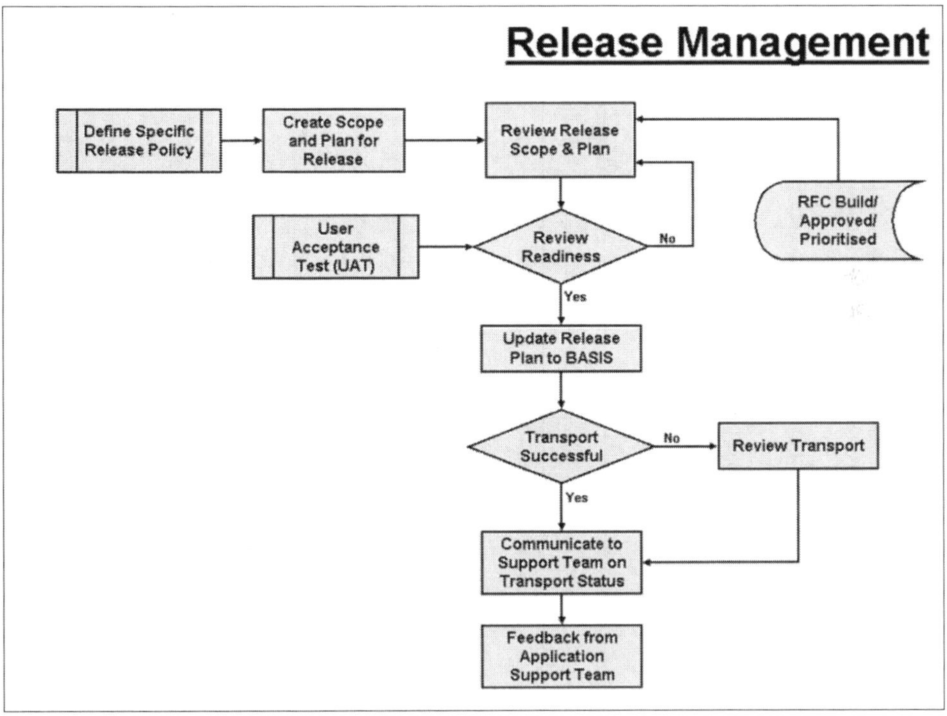

Figure 5.4: Release Management: A Schematic Overview

5.5.4. Service Level Management: Service Level Management is the process responsible for maintaining and improving IT service quality. It is achieved through a constant cycle of identifying, agreeing, monitoring and reporting on IT service achievements, and initiation of actions to eradicate poor service in line with the business or cost justification.

In this regard the Service Level Agreements (SLAs) serve as the guiding documents and therefore their drafting, negotiations, finalisation, authorization and signing need to be taken up with utmost care from the beginning itself. Severity levels of the services are predefined in the SLAs along with time standards of their resolution.

Purpose: This procedure is used to:

- Collect the metrics from the projects and to analyse them.
- Consolidate and analyse organisational metrics.
- Develop and publish the organisational quality objectives.
- Monitor and verify process effectiveness.
- Initiate process improvements to address the measurement related problem areas.

Severity Level Definitions: In the Service Level Agreements the clients in agreement with the vendor generally define a standard set of severity levels as outlined here:

- **Severity level 1 – Critical:** A problem has a severe business impact and must be responded to immediately, e.g. Critical Interfaces (such as payroll) delayed during month-end.
- **Severity level 2 – High:** A problem has a major business impact affecting 1 or more people, e.g. System performance unexpectedly significantly slower than usual for multiple users.
- **Severity level 3 – Medium:** A problem has a minor business impact that introduces business risk and cost, e.g. New user requests
- **Severity level 4 – Low:** A problem is an inconvenience or is minor with no business risk, e.g. New Minor Enhancements

5.5.5. Security Management: Security Management records include the complete history of Security Requests via the service management system, where these records include all approvals and attachments relevant to a security request and will provide evidence of the procedures carried out in providing access.

Purpose: The primary goal of Security Management is to ensure that appropriate access is provided to the business and support organisations. It reduces the risk of business exposure and service disruption by adhering to CLIENT's global rule set for Segregation of Duties, sensitive transaction access, password management and user currency.

Scope: Security Management consists of a number of processes:

- **"User Creation / Change"** - assignment of existing roles to users.
- **"Inactive User Lockout / Deletion"** - removal of inactive users.
- **"Role Creation / Change"** - development of roles.
- **"Open Configuration"** - temporary unlocking of the system for changes.
- **"Access Security Review"** - regular checkpoint of security activity and status.

Process Flow: Security Management activities can be grouped under two headings based on their interrelation as follows:

5.5.1.1. Production Access

- **User Creation / Change**: Business and IT users can be assigned existing roles on request as determined by the security design for each application.
- This process is triggered by a Security Request being raised for a user for new or changed access when a Security Request record is created in the service management system.
- The Security Request in alignment with the Security Management process of Enterprises, and appropriately approved and authorised for access are delivered as per the approved request in line with local security standards and policies.
- The security request record is updated with the user confirmation and then closed.
- For certain applications the Security team has a list of sensitive transactions.
- **Inactive User Lockout / Deletion**: If a user is inactive for a period their user id is locked, and after a further period if there is no request to unlock it then the user id is deleted. The periods are agreed with the

Business for each application, taking account of business life cycles and frequency of access.

- **Role Creation / Change:** Business organisation changes and application enhancements may require modifications to existing role definitions or new roles, being updates to the security design for each application. Role changes are handled by the Change Management process as small enhancements.

5.5.1.2. Production Change

- **Firecall**: In the Manage Services framework support users are assigned roles on production systems which are restricted to identified support tasks. During critical periods, authorizations may be missing which prevents them from performing a critical task. In order to allow them to complete the task a Firecall role can be assigned temporarily.

This process is triggered by a Security Request being raised by a support user for the Firecall role:

- The Firecall role is delivered as per the approved request, with an automated expiry time set, in line with local application security standards for handling user details and access security strategies. Details related to assigning the emergency role and revoking it are noted in the ticket.
- The user is contacted to confirm the role is available and access meets requirements.
- After the expiry period the role is removed from the user. When the ticket is due for time out and business has not confirmed if successful, it needs to be escalated to Client business contact.
- The security request record is updated with a summary report of the users' activity during the period they had the Firecall role and the users' activity (trace log) is stored as the Fire-fighter log report which is sent to the Application Manager for review.
- **Open Configuration:** Application production systems are locked down at system level to prevent any code changes. During critical periods when addressing emergency or out of package changes, this may prevent support staff from performing a critical task. During scheduled release implementations, this lock down would also

prevent deployment. In order to allow the support staff to complete their tasks the system is unlocked temporarily. This unlock is defined, requested and formally approved, and then closely monitored to closure when the system is locked down again.

5.5.6. Root Cause Analysis (RCA) Management: In case of a severe deviation from expected results an analysis will be performed to find the root cause of the issue and document it for future reference.

Purpose: Analyse and identify the situation (root cause) of incidents in order to determine:

- Corrective (or preventive) actions to resolve the incidents and prevent their recurrence.
- Identify opportunities for improving the quality of both the work product deliverable and the process with which it was created.

Scope: RCA is conducted proactively and reactively as recommended by the Delivery Excellence Team. Proactive RCA is triggered when a number of instances of the same type of incident or a pattern of similar incidents are detected in terms of increase in the number of incidents over time or there is a significant positive or negative trend in the outcome of any activity.

Reactive RCA are initiated when a priority 1 (one) incident has taken place or any incident/issue has been escalated to level 4 as per escalation matrix.

Process Flow:

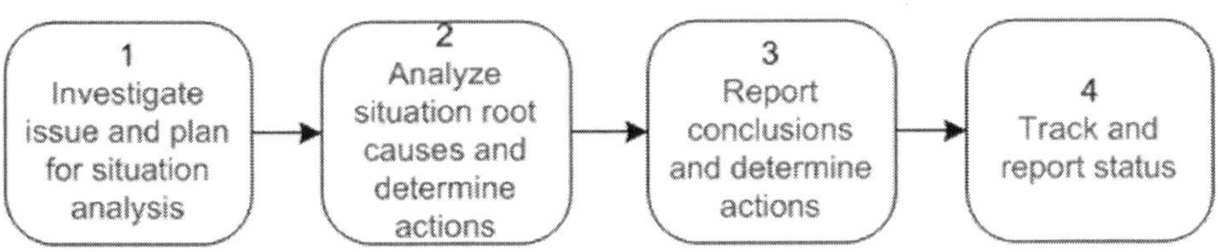

Figure 5.5: RCA Management: A Schematic Overview

5.5.7. Change Management: Management of change is a critical factor in a project's success. When an IT service is not answering business expectations, they must be modified or suppressed. The process of Change Management defines how these modifications will impact service deployment and facilitate the IT team to make adjustments before executing them. The IT controls if the adjustments have the effect that were anticipated.

All activities related to enhancements/ changes to both software and non software functions affects Change Management, which can be categorised as:

- Architectural Change and Exposure
- Business Process Change and Exposure
- Organisational Process Change and Exposure

Purpose: The goal of Change Management is to ensure that standardised methods and procedures are followed for efficient handling of any type of change, in order to minimise the impact of change-related incidents and to improve on day-to-day operations. All the changes that arise during the course of a contracted engagement that affect the contract's Terms and Conditions should be controlled.

The changes have to be managed by ensuring that they are identified and various parameters (such as cost, effort, content or schedule) are agreed, recorded and tracked.

It should be ensured that each request for change is properly assessed, approved or rejected by appropriate stakeholders and approved changes are implemented with updation of affected deliverables. Documents and plans must be revised as required and affected groups should be made aware of the status of all the changes.

Scope: Change Management includes queries related to functional enrichment. It may be a small adhoc one-time extract required to support activities such as audit, lawsuit, and other decision support requests. It may be a functional enrichment that may involve varying engineering characteristics and business change or service requests such as consulting or training. It may be a large functional enrichment. The Change Management scope also includes changes implemented as a result of break fix incidents.

Process Flow

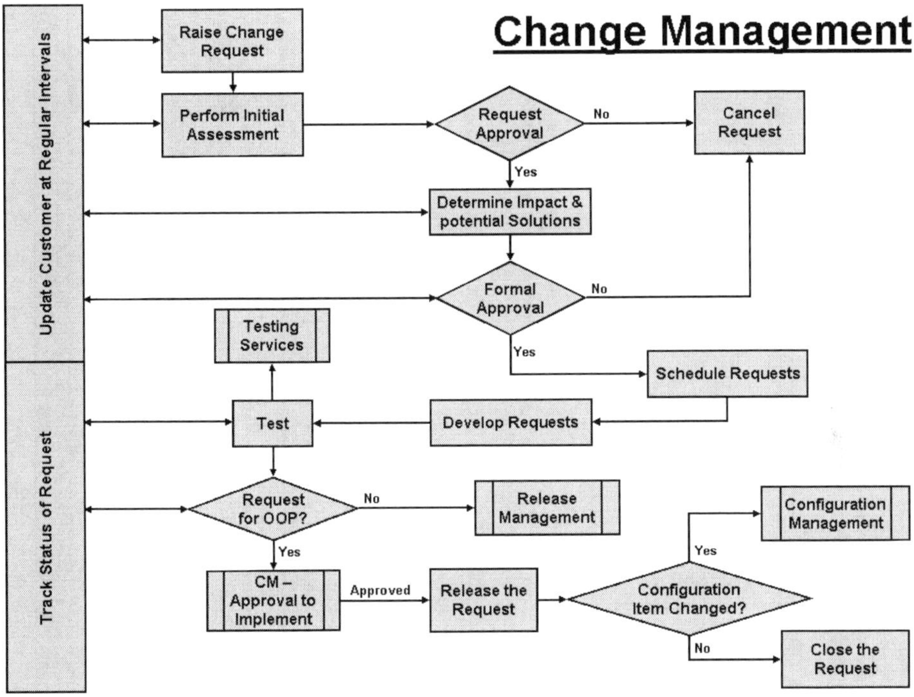

Figure 5.6: Change Management: A Schematic Overview

5.5.8. Risk Management: The process adopted for identifying and managing the project risk is called Risk Management. It is used to reduce the impact of risk within a project by identifying, analysing, reporting and managing risks on a continuous basis. It should be initiated at project level when the project has commenced and it should be repeated throughout the duration of the project or contract with the organisation.

5.5.9. Enhancement Request Management: Enhancements requests from the client regarding Changes and Exposures in Architecture, Business Processes, and Organisational Processes need to be handled following standardised methods and procedures. The objective should be efficient implementation of the Enhancement-related incidents in order to minimise their impact on the project.

Just like Change Management, Enhancement Request Management ensures that all requests are assessed in terms of various parameters (such as cost, effort, content or schedule) and they are agreed, approved/rejected, recorded and tracked by appropriate stakeholders. Simultaneously, the affected groups are aware of the status of the changes and the documents, plans and deliverables are revised / updated as required. Any Enhancement that arises during the course of a contracted engagement and affects the contract's Terms and Conditions should be controlled.

5.5.10. Testing Services: Testing is a set of activities conducted through scripts with the motive of finding errors in software. It deals with tests for the entire application. It helps to enhance the quality of the applications while reducing costs, maximising ROI, and saving development time. Application testing can be done in various categories like GUI, functionality, database (backend), load test, etc. For Application Testing, the testing life cycles involve various phases which include requirement analysis, test planning, test analysis, test design, test execution & bug reporting, etc.

Purpose The major objectives of Software testing are as follows:

- Finding defects which may get created by the programmer while developing the software.
- Gaining confidence in and providing information about the level of quality.
- To prevent production defects.
- To make sure that the end result meets the business and user requirements.
- To ensure that it satisfies the BRS (Business Requirement Specification) and SRS (System Requirement Specifications).
- To gain the confidence of the customers by providing them a quality product.

Scope: Development and quality assurance teams are under strict deadlines to send out deliverables and complete other tasks within a sprint. The teams need to effectively use agile testing methodologies to keep up with the requirements of Quality Assurance. It must be realised that a major amount of available time goes toward creating features and there is little space available for QA processes. Thus it is important to have a testing scope strategy in place that defines 'What features are to be tested', 'When to implement the change', and 'Clear acceptance of the procedure'.

Process Flow: Software testing helps in finalising the software application or product against business and user requirements. Once the delivery is made to the end users or the customers they should be able to operate it without any complaints. In order to make this happen the tester should know how the customers are going to use this product and accordingly they should write down the test scenario.

Good testing coverage means that various areas like functionality of the application, its compatibility with the OS, hardware and different types of browsers, its performance, and its load taking capacity are tested so that the system is reliable and should not crash or have blocking issues. The software application should be deployed easily to the machine and without any resistance with all functions performing well and as per the specifications and it is easy to install, learn and use.

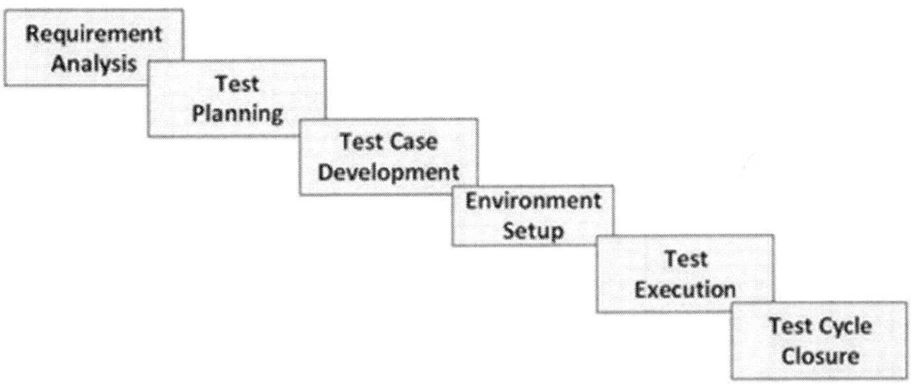

Figure 5.6: Testing Services: A Schematic Overview

5.5.11. Transition Management: Transition is the process of moving work to a Delivery Centre from another organisation providing support to the client applications. Transition Management has to ensure successful migration activities so as to meet financial objectives and attain transfer of knowledge with minimal or no impact to client satisfaction and SLAs.

The objective should be to reduce and manage risks, manage staff morale, ensure security and controls while continuing business operations as usual while migration activities are in-progress.

Scope: Transitions for the project involve Knowledge Transfer (KT), Primary support, Integration Testing with the project team, Bubble support till secondary support, and achieving Steady state. The transition processes also include Due Diligence, Pre-Planning, and Application Specific Migration Plan. It is important to have Primary Support and Secondary Support teams in place at appropriate times so as to ensure timely and effective implementation of the project.

During the Primary Support, the supplier team takes responsibility and controls the ticket flow and is expected to undertake all ticket resolution (under normal circumstances). During Secondary Support, the incumbent team is responsible to manage the tickets with the supplier team providing support to them.

Transition Management Checklist: The client is required to appoint quality managers for each transition from project to support and a suggested checklist for each transition should include;

- Quality requirements and associated reviews for each transition gate
- Risk and Issue management in control
- Organisation and roles effectiveness
- Approval processes for critical documentation
- Any sampling requirements for other documentation
- Process readiness tests requirements
- Project sign-off / handover quality assessment (through UAT – User Acceptance Testing, and OAT – Operational Acceptance Testing)
- SLA –Service Level Agreement, and OLA- Operational Level Agreement understanding and readiness
- Data controls approvals
- Compliance approvals and process readiness
- Governance processes and engagement

Chapter 6

DATA SCIENCE AND INTELLIGENCE

6.1. Introduction

Data science is the field of applying scientific principles and advanced analytic techniques to extract valuable information from data for decision-making, strategic planning, and other fields in business or industry. It encompasses preparing data including cleansing it, aggregating it, and then manipulating it to perform advanced data analysis. As an umbrella term, it incorporates various disciplines like data engineering, data preparation, data mining, predictive analytics, machine learning and data visualization, as well as software programming along with statistics and mathematics.

Companies, today, are sitting on a treasure trove of data. As modern technology has enabled the creation and storage of increasing amounts of information, data volumes have exploded. But this data is often just sitting in databases and data lakes, mostly untouched. The wealth of data being collected and stored by these technologies can bring transformative benefits to organizations and societies around the world—but only if we can interpret it. It is the bedrock of innovation, but its value does not come by itself, but from the information that the data science professionals can glean from it, and then provide to the right persons, in the right format, and at the right time to be acted upon. Data science reveals trends and produces insights that businesses can use to make better decisions and create more innovative products and services. Perhaps most importantly, it enables machine learning (ML) models to learn from the vast amounts of data being fed to them, rather than mainly relying upon business analysts to see what they can discover from the data.

In today's information driven business world, data science plays an important role in virtually all aspects of business operations and strategies. In the field of marketing, it provides information about customers with regard to their requirements, preferences, helps companies create stronger marketing campaigns and targeted advertising to increase product sales. From an operational standpoint, data science initiatives can optimize management of supply chains, product inventories, distribution networks and customer service. On a more fundamental level, they point the way to increased efficiency and reduced costs. Data science also enables companies to create business plans and strategies that are based on informed analysis of customer behaviour, market trends, future projections, and competition. Without it, businesses may make flawed decisions and miss opportunities. It is becoming increasingly more critical to businesses as the insights that data science generates help organizations increase operational efficiency, identify new business opportunities and improve marketing and sales programs, among other benefits. Ultimately, they can lead to competitive advantages over business rivals. It furthermore aids in managing financial risks, detecting fraudulent transactions and preventing equipment breakdowns in manufacturing plants and other industrial settings. It also helps block cyber attacks and other security threats in IT systems. Beyond regular business operations, in healthcare, data science uses include diagnosis of medical conditions, image analysis, treatment planning and medical research. Academic institutions use data science to monitor student performance and improve their marketing to prospective students. Sports teams analyze player performance and plan game strategies via data science. Government agencies and public policy organizations are also big users.

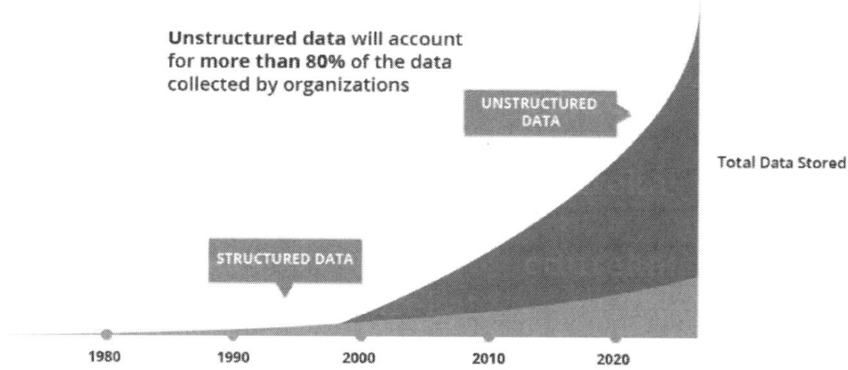

Figure 6.1. The Exponential Growth of Data Uses & Stored: A Visual Representation

Data science combines multiple fields including statistics, scientific methods, artificial intelligence (AI), and data analysis to extract value from data. Those who practice data science are called data scientists, and they combine a range of skills to analyze data collected from the web, smart phones, customers, sensors, and other sources to derive actionable insights. The practice of data science encompasses preparing data for analysis, including cleansing, aggregating, and manipulating the data to perform advanced data analysis. Analytic applications and data scientists can then review the results to uncover patterns and enable business leaders to draw informed insights.

6.2. Evolution of Data Science

During the 1960s data analysis was considered to be intrinsically an empirical science and till late 1990s, it kept on looking for a place of recognition as '*the science of data and data processes*' distinct from the two established fields - Statistics, and Computer Science. However, with the growing need for designing data, collection of data, and analysis on data for supporting the decision-making process, '*the science of dealing with data*' – Data Science has continued to grow in prominence, fuelled partly by increased use of AI and machine learning in organizations.

Traditionally, the data that we had was mostly structured and small in size, which could be analyzed by using simple statistical tools. However, today most of the data is unstructured or semi-structured, maybe upto 80 % of it. Moreover, this data is generated from different sources like financial logs, text files, multimedia forms, sensors, and instruments across vast geographical and sectoral expanses of the business world. Simple Business Intelligence tools are not capable of processing this huge volume and variety of data. This is why we need more complex and advanced analytical tools and algorithms for processing, analyzing and drawing meaningful insights out of it.

With the advanced tools and techniques of data science, today businesses are able to understand the precise requirements of their customers from their past browsing and purchase history, age, social strata and income. Although all this data was available earlier too, now the data scientists can train models more effectively and help businesses recommend the product to the customers with more precision bringing more business to the organization.

For example, today, cars are being equipped with the intelligence to drive people home in which self-driving cars collect live data from sensors, including radars, cameras, and lasers to create a map of its surroundings. Based on this data, it makes decisions like when to speed up, when to speed down, when to overtake, where to take a turn – making use of advanced machine learning algorithms. In the field of weather forecasting today, the data from ships, aircraft, radars, satellites is being collected and analyzed to build models that are not only helping forecast the weather but also help in predicting the occurrence of any natural calamities and help in taking appropriate measures beforehand so as to save many precious lives.

Most of the technology vendors of today like Google and Amazon were early users of data science and big data analytics for internal applications like other internet and e-commerce companies like Facebook, eBay, Yahoo etc.

6.3. Data Analysis, Business Intelligence, and Data Science

Data analytics is devoted to realizing actionable insights that can be applied immediately based on existing queries. While data science focuses on finding meaningful correlations between large datasets, data analytics is designed to uncover the specifics of extracted insights. In other words, data analytics is a branch of Data Science that focuses on more specific answers to the questions that data science brings forth. The two are trending fields that are used to mine large datasets. Data analytics software is a more focused version of this and can even be considered part of the larger process.

Data analysts are often responsible for designing and maintaining data systems and databases, using statistical tools to interpret data sets, and preparing reports that effectively communicate trends, patterns, and predictions based on relevant findings. Analytic applications and data scientists can then review the results to uncover patterns and enable business leaders to draw informed insights. It's primarily done by skilled data scientists, although lower-level data analysts may also be involved. In addition, many organizations now rely partly on citizen data scientists, a group that can include business intelligence (BI) professionals, business analysts, data-savvy business users, data engineers and other workers who don't have a formal data science background. In practice, data science is primarily being used to make decisions and predictions making use of causal analytics, decision science, machine learning, and Artificial Intelligence. The different use cases of causal analytics include the following:

- **Predictive Causal Analytics**: If a model is required that can predict the possibilities of a particular event in the future, predictive causal analytics is to be applied. In practice, the organisations providing money on credit are using such models to predict the probability of customers making future credit payments on time based on the payment history of the customers.
- **Prescriptive Analytics**: If a model is required to have the intelligence of taking its own decisions and the ability to modify it with dynamic parameters, then prescriptive analytics is to be applied. It is an emerging field and it not only predicts but suggests a range of prescribed actions and associated outcomes. Google's self-driving car is the present day best example of this combination of causal analytics and decision making process in which the data gathered by a large number of vehicles is used to train the cars to take decisions like when to turn, which path to take, when to slow down or speed up, and when to stop.
- **Predictions through Supervised Machine Learning**: If a large inventory of data is already available and a model is built to determine the future trend and program the machine learning process, then it is possible to train the machines to predict and identify fraudulent actions of users based on historical records of transactions.

- **Pattern discovery through Machine Learning:** If enough parameters are not available on which predictions can be made, then it is possible to dig out hidden patterns within the dataset to be able to make meaningful predictions. Techniques like Clustering used by telecom companies to finalize tower locations to ensure that all the users receive optimum signal strength use this methodology of unsupervised machine learning.

All the above techniques are used both in Data Analysis as well as in Data Science, yet there is more emphasis on descriptive analytics and prediction in Data Analysis while Data Science is more about Predictive Causal Analytics and Machine Learning. It is to be noted that data science is often confused with Business Intelligence. Business Intelligence (BI) basically analyzes the previous data to find hindsight and insight to describe business trends. Here BI enables organisations to take data from external and internal sources, prepare it, run queries on it and create dashboards to answer questions like quarterly revenue analysis or business problems. BI can evaluate the impact of certain events in the near future.

In contrast Data Science is a more forward-looking approach. It answers the open-ended questions as to "what" and "how" events occur in an exploratory way with the focus on analyzing the past or current data and predicting the future outcomes with the aim of making informed decisions.

As such, the two have quite contrasting features in terms of the data sources, the approach, the focus, and the tools used. BI uses highly structured data sources with focus on past and present taking Statistics and Visualization approach, whereas Data Science uses both structured as well as unstructured data sources with focus on the present and future using the Statistics, Machine Learning, NLP (Natural Language Processing), Graph Analysis etc.

6.4. Data Science in the Industry

Since the advent of the 4th Industrial Revolution multitudes of emerging technologies have transpired around the power of digital world. Technologies such as digital twins, Industrial Internet of Things (IIoT), and cyber-physical systems have come into the scene as core elements, providing the necessary ingredients for a paradigm shift in manufacturing. Data science is becoming an invaluable discipline in industry in order to transform information into knowledge. There is a growing need to pre-process all the collected IoT data in place, and move only the resulting insights, alarms and alerts, or trends to the enterprise. To understand how to build a smart plant in the industry 4.0 world, it's necessary to understand the typical data workflow in this space. The spread of data science across various sectors is growing at a pace that is creating disruptions in their business models overnight.

- **Entertainment:** Entertainment industry is one of the most widely impacted industries by proliferation of digital transformation. Data science enables the companies to track and analyze what users watch, and they are able to determine what to stream, develop new shows, and produce films and other services. Based on the viewing history of a user, personalized recommendations are made using data-driven algorithms.
- **Financial Services:** Financial institutions, banks, credit card and insurance companies use data science to mine and analyze data to manage financial risks on loans and credit lines, to detect fraudulent transactions, and to evaluate customer portfolios to identify up-selling opportunities.
- **Healthcare:** Hospitals, healthcare providers, biotech companies use data science tools and machine learning models to automate diagnostic analysis of radiological and pathological reports. Data science also helps in providing historical medical history of the patient and helps doctors in diagnosing illnesses and planning treatments. Telemedicine and robotics aided surgery has revolutionised the medical industry and patient experience.
- **Manufacturing:** Optimization of supply chain management and distribution, condition monitoring for detecting potential equipment failures in plants and predictive maintenance to avoid breakdowns, logistics optimization, quality control, customer feedback and quick response to the market demand are some of the areas where data science is helping manufacturing industry.
- **Retail:** The industry that has the closest link with the customers is retail and thus retailers are using data science to analyze customer behavior and buying patterns to drive personalized product recommendations and targeted advertising, marketing and promotions. They are also able to manage optimum product inventories and keep their supply chains lean to maximize their profits as well as to give customers an experience of delight.

- **Transportation:** Logistics services providers, transporters, freight carriers, and delivery companies are optimizing delivery routes and schedules, modes of transport for shipments, consignment warehousing and clustering using data science. Tracking of the consignment on a real-time basis not only ensures efficiency of the services but also gives the customer a sense of control.
- **Travel and Hospitality:** Airlines use data science in planning flights to optimize routes, scheduling crew, and managing passenger loads as well as to implement variable pricing for flights. Hospitality industry, in a similar way, uses large volumes of data to manage their properties, products, and pricing.

Every industry requires different set of tools, technologies, and data processing systems. The retail sector is very customer oriented and opportunities lie behind the buyer preferences and needs. The natural language processing and media analytics are tools widely used to make attractive suggestions to the final consumer. For example, fintech requires specific algorithms for fraud detection, aggregation, and anomaly detection in commercial transactions in real-time, and for insurance policies dependent upon medical and health risk indicators. In the production and manufacturing plants at least three very different types of data are being produced at different rates, with different volumes, for different purposes, each with its own sensitivity regarding when the data needs to be accessed for processing and decision making.

It is to be noted that even though industries, customers, and end products vary dramatically, for Data Management & Storage it's all about data volumes, data flows, data protection, and ultimately the analysis of that data at the locations where the decisions are made. Industrial plants of different sizes and complexity and their various Industrial processes might also be connected in different ways to the enterprise to help condition monitoring, inventory optimization, centralized quality assurance.

- **Condition Monitoring:** Equipment uptime and machine availability as well as the quality of products conforming to specifications are directly dependent upon health of the machine and its maintenance. Robotics is being used to a greater degree in modernized plants, to gain accuracy and efficiency and to reduce overall operating costs. These systems generate tremendous amounts of data. The information coming from such systems is typically referred to as "time series data." Per second or sub second, vibration, temperature, pressure, RPM, strain, etc. are monitored as indicators of how the system is functioning. This data is aggregated in a local data historian that is optimized for such data. Through equipment condition monitoring, enterprises are moving away from time-based maintenance of the equipment to condition-based maintenance. This increases uptime, overall throughput, and Profitability.

- **Inventory Optimization:** Inventories are monitored constantly in most plants to keep track of the balance between too much inventory and insufficient inventory. Too much can take up precious space, while insufficient levels can cause unplanned downtime due to lack of raw input materials. Supply-chain management is essential in modern plants. Data from this cell typically uses RFID tagging of both input and output materials and products. Different data repositories and algorithms are used to monitor and optimize these processes, as well as operator health and safety.
- **Centralised Quality Assurance:** Many industry regulatory bodies are demanding quality inspections of manufactured products. These inspections might include X-rays and various forms of image scanning to identify invisible defects. It could also include using 4K resolution cameras with sophisticated algorithms, instead of people, to conduct visual inspections. Image data might not be conducted at the same rate as the time series data from condition monitoring, but the volumes of each data sample are vastly greater. Image data does not compress effectively, and because it's tied to the quality of the sold product, it's likely that it is required to be persisted for a longer period of time.

There are some uses of data science that are common across different industries, viz. cyber security, customer service, business process management including human resource management. Recruitment, talent acquisition, performance management, effectiveness of job postings, skill inventory, etc are taking advantage of the data science knowledge in hiring, retention, and rewarding process.

6.5. Data Science Processes

Data Science is a systematic process to analyze, visualize, and model large amounts of data by using tools to find unseen patterns, extract data, and convert information to actionable insights that can be meaningful to the process of decision making. It also helps in turning a problem into a solution by treating the business problem as a project and adopting a systematic step by step approach towards it. The six broad steps of the data science process include the following.

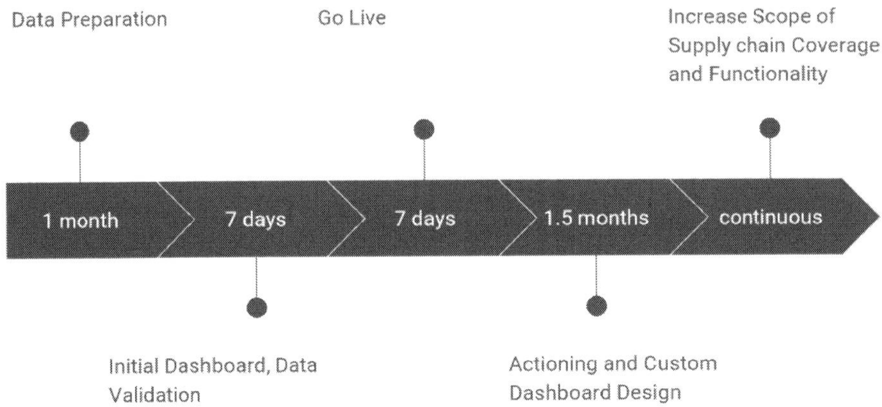

Figure 6.2: A Reference Timeline of Data Science & Analytics Process in Organizations

1. **Problem Framing:** Data related problems are more often than none expressed in quite ambiguous terms. It becomes a challenge to know what exactly the problem is. Asking the right questions is the first and most effective way of getting the right inputs in this regard. Business questions in terms of who, what, why, when, where, and how relating to the product, people, place etc will result in those inputs giving insight into actionable outputs. As an outcome of this step, the data scientist must have as much information about the problem at hand as possible.
2. **Collecting the Raw Data for the Problem:** The process of data collection involves thinking and finding ways to collect and get the data related to the problem in the required format. It may be obtained from internal databases or purchased from external sources specialising in this field. The requisite data need to be collated and verified for being relevant to the business problem.

3. **Processing the Data for Analysis:** The data so collected can be messy if it had not been appropriately maintained, leading to errors that easily corrupt the analysis. Hence it has to be processed before analyzing in order to clean it and to eliminate possibilities of erroneous results. Common errors like missing values, corrupted values, invalid entries, time zone differences, null vs. zero, date range errors, etc need to be attended to. Further, aggregation of the data and validation across data-sets and files need to be done and in case of anomalies deletion or replacement of the anomalous data has to be done.
4. **Exploring the Data:** Exploratory Data Analysis (EDA) is the step where domain knowledge and business intelligence come together to identify hidden patterns and insights. Looking beyond the obvious to find patterns in the data requires thorough analysis and interpretation in proper context.
5. **Performing In-Depth Analysis:** The clean data is then subjected to the data science tools to crunch the data successfully and discover insights by using mathematical, statistical, and technological knowledge. Development of predictive models to compare averages with the underperformers or deviations may bring out several factors in the analysis. This analysis includes both the quantitative and qualitative data and the outcomes have to be translated into actionable recommendations.
6. **Communicating the Results of the Analysis:** Proper communication leads to action and data science is no exception. The insights and findings from the foregoing steps have to be conveyed to the stakeholders so as to make them understand the importance of the problem and the analysis. It should help them solve the problem and meet the organisational objectives.

Figure 6.3: An Overview of Data Science Processes in Practice

6.6. Components of Data Science

- **Data Strategy:** The most important component of data science is developing a data strategy that determines what data is collected and why. It requires the data scientists to make a connection between the business goals and the data going to be gathered. Not all data are equally important. Getting rid of "garbage" data that doesn't serve the business goals as well as formatting the collected data correctly is a tough task but quite valuable for the final outcomes. It involves identifying data that is mission-critical to the business goals and separating it from the nice-to-have data that won't contribute substantially in meeting the goals. Time and energy has to be invested in collecting and sorting the former one, while the latter has to be let go if it requires a lot of additional time and effort.
- **Data Engineering:** Appropriate technologies and systems to access, organize, and use the data have to be brought together to create appropriate software solutions. It involves establishing a data system that creates data endpoints and data pipelines connecting them so that data flows from or to the product and through the ecosystem to various stakeholders. Data engineering is, in effect, the plumbing that lets the data scientists make use of the data and it requires in-depth understanding of a wide range of data technologies and frameworks,

as well as how to combine them in algorithms to create solutions that enable business processes.

- **Data Analysis and Mathematical Models:** This component takes data and using mathematics, statistics, algorithm, and other scientific methods creates a model to mimic how the business system works. It can be called the heart of the data science ecosystem that describes, extracts insights or makes predictions about a service, product, person, business or technology. In the new era of more advanced computing power, data scientists are able to use many existing mathematical and statistical concepts that previously could not be utilized because of computational power limitations.
- **Visualization and Operationalisation:** It is important to convey the meaning of the data or analysis to the person whose job it is to interpret the output and take action. Data Visualisation comes into play here. It goes beyond just doing data analysis and presenting it correctly and many times involves going back into the raw data and understanding what needs to be visualized based on the needs and goals of both the user and the operations. It needs to take care of the needs and capabilities of the persons consuming the data, the context of use including physical location, devices being used, physical environment, and situational context. Data Operationalisation is what is done with the data that is presented to the stakeholders. Someone or some machine has to make a decision and take actions in terms of a real-time response, a long-term response, or carrying out a specific task. Data visualisation and operationalisation is the final component that justifies the very process of data science and analysis, because it is the resultant actions that make the impact on business outcomes.

6.7. Data Science in Practice

While it is great to have a theoretical foundation and academic skill-set about data science, how do you apply it to the business environment of a company is the real task. The data scientist has to think about how to communicate it to management, leadership and the business context at large. Adopting a strategy of thinking backwards would be effective here.

- Communicate data insights in a simple story to empower the decision-makers to act on.

- Collaborate with business stakeholders to identify their business needs and convey the expected results.
- Use Data Scientist skills on Big Data platforms and analytics tools to gain business insights.
- Identify/create appropriate algorithms to solve business problems.
- Craft experiments to corroborate the assumptions and make available scenario models as and when necessary.
- Support data collection, integration, and retention requirements based on the collected data.

Data Science Tools: Data science involves quite a complex set of processes for building, evaluating, deploying, and monitoring machine learning models. Data scientists use many types of tools to accomplish these tasks. With data science proliferating every aspect of industry, business, and life as a whole, there has been an increase in the number of data science tools.

To determine which data science tool is right for a project, it's important to find answers to the questions like, what kind of languages are the data scientists using, what kind of working methods do they prefer, what kind of data sources are they using? Some users prefer to have a data-source-agnostic service that uses open source libraries, while some others prefer the speed of in-database, machine learning algorithms. In order to have some understanding of the tools it is better to categorize them according to their processes.

Figure 6.4: Data Scientist Skills: A Pictorial Representation

6.7.1. Data Collection Tools: Although data can be collected through various methods, which include online surveys, interviews, and forms, the information gathered has to be transformed into a readable form for the data analyst to work on. Example tools for this purpose include Semantria, Trackur, Open Text, Opinion Crawl, NLTK, and TensorFlow.

6.7.2. Data Storage Tools: These tools are used to store a huge amount of data – which is typically stored in shared computers – and interact with it. These tools provide a platform to unite servers so that data can be assessed easily. Example tools include Apache Hadoop, Apache Cassandra, MongoDB, CouchDB, Apache Ignite, and Oracle NoSQL Database.

6.7.3. Data Extraction Tools: Data extraction tools are also known as web scraping tools. They are automated and extract information and data automatically from websites. Some commonly used options include OctoParse, Content Grabber, Mozenda, Pentaho, and Import.io.

6.7.4. Data Cleaning / Refining Tools: Integrated with databases, data cleaning tools are time-saving and reduce the time consumption by searching, sorting, and filtering data to be used by the data analysts. The refined data becomes easy to use and is relevant. The more commonly used tools include Data Cleaner, OpenRefine, MapReduce, Rapidminer, and Talend.

6.7.5. Data Analysis Tools: Data analysis tools not only analyze the data but also perform certain operations on the data. These tools inspect the data and study data modelling to draw useful information out of the data, which is conclusive and helps in decision-making for a certain problem or query. The most common tools used by data scientists to analyse data include SAS, R, Apache Spark, Python, BigML, Scikit-learn, and Excel.

6.7.6. Data Visualization Tools: Data visualization tools are used to present data in a graphical representation for clear insight. Many visualization tools are a combination of previous functions we discussed and can also support data extraction and analysis along with visualization. The industry makes use of tools including Python, Tableau, Orange, Google Fusion Table, DataWrapper, Qlik, Gephi, Matplotlib, ggplot2, and D3.js.

It is to be noted that many tools like Excel, Jupyter, and Weka can perform more than one or maybe all the functions of the data science project implementation.

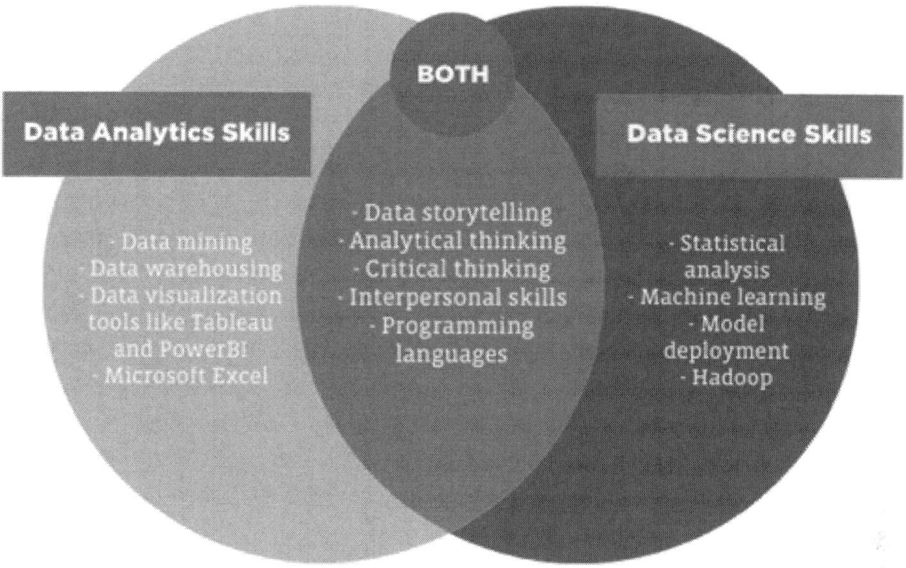

Figure 6.5: Data Analytics & Data Science: A Practice Pictorial

6.8. Challenges in Data Science Project Implementation

Although companies have already embarked upon ambitious data science projects and have made huge investments in data science teams, many of them are not able to realize the full value of their data. There has been a race to hire talent and create data science programs, but due to lack of technical discipline and with different people using different tools and processes that don't work well together, the companies that have experienced inefficient team performance are not able to get return on their investments. The major challenges in implementation of a data science project include:

1. **Access to data inventory:** Generally, access to data is granted by an IT administrator, the data scientists often have to wait for long to get access to the data and the resources they need to analyze it.
2. **Compatibility issues:** The data science team might use a different tool to analyze the data which may possibly be incompatible with the language in which the application was written. Due to this it can take weeks or even months to deploy the data science models into useful applications.

3. **Limitations in deploying machine learning:** Many times, the machine learning models that developers receive are not ready for being deployed in applications due to inflexible access points or incompatible data formats. In such cases models can't be deployed in all scenarios and scalability gets a beating.
4. **Need for excessive support and coordination:** As there is proliferation of open source tools, the central IT team can get overburdened by an ever-growing list of tools to support. The data scientist teams in different functions like marketing, finance, operations, etc might be using different tools. They might also have different workflows, and that would require excessive efforts from the IT team to continually rebuild and update environments as well as to coordinate between teams.
5. **Data Science being alien to Business managers:** The business decision-making processes and systems are not always integrated with data workflows, and that makes it difficult for business managers to collaborate knowledgeably with data scientists. They find it difficult to understand why it takes so long to go from conception to delivery of the projects and they perceive it as too slow.

6.9. Strategic Business Applications of Data Science and Analytics: The Case of the Utility Industry

6.9.1. About: Many electricity and gas distribution companies are now turning towards digital meters and also equipping them with IoT based software. This is helping them come over the limitations of the traditional counter rotation-based meters, in which many times digits are displayed partially due to the rotation at the time of reading, sometimes the meter sets itself to zero due to crossing the highest number, and sometimes they are rigged by unscrupulous users.

6.9.2. The Challenge: However, the existing system of taking pictures of the meters and then reading the images through OCR cannot be replaced overnight. Hence a project of improving the existing system was taken with the following main objectives:

- Enhancing the image as received.
- Detecting the area of Interest (Meter Number, Meter Reading).
- Identifying the numbers accurately (Even the floating up/down digits).

6.9.3. The Solution: Sub-Routine Work-flow Design

- All the consumers and representatives of the organization were provided with a cross-platform mobile application through which they can manage meter readings.
- A picture of the meter is taken and the subroutine developed enhances the image using computer vision and image processing techniques.
- If the enhanced image quality doesn't conform to the recommended threshold - image is not of the meter or the picture quality of the image is not fit for enhancement - then it is not uploaded to the distribution company's database. The consumer is requested to take another image or raise a complaint to be followed up by the organization.
- The enhanced images are then processed for extracting the meter number and the meter reading.

6.9.4. The Functioning:

- **Deep Learning Approach for Digit Detection and Recognition**: The process of getting the values from the images of the meter is two-fold. First, there is a need to detect the areas where the text is and to extract the coordinates of the bounding box. This cropped area is then passed through a text recognition algorithm to give the final output.
- **Detecting Area of Interest:** Deep learning based detectors will identify the region or the area of meter ID and the number counter area from the gas meter images. This means that intuitively, our

region of interest is the dark animated meter number area and the number counter.

- **Digit Extraction for Convolutional Recurrent Neural Network (CRNN):** The pre-processed image is fed into the Artificial Neural Network (ANN) in which the first layer is comprised of a Convolutional Neural Network (CNN) which divides the image into feature columns, i.e. convolutional feature is mapped and then fed into a bi-directional Long Short-Term Memory (LSTM) sequence as a feature sequence. This recurrent neural network is responsible for outputting a sequence, intended for finding relations between characters.

Finally, the output sequence which now consists of characters which may or may not have significance is passed onto the Transcription Layer, in which these characters are unified using a probabilistic method to extract information from the sequence.

6.9.5. Project Requirements: To reach the accuracy level of around ~ 90 - 95%, there would be a requirement of around 10,000 varied images. A typical Machine Learning model would give 60-70% accuracy with 1000 – 3000 images, 75 – 85 % accuracy with 3000 – 7000 images, and 85 – 90 % accuracy with 7000 – 9000 images. The project would be evolutionary in nature which means the images become available.

6.9.6. Project Roadmap Timeline:

1. Detailed Project plan and data cleansing - 1 Week
2. Data split and image processing - 1 Week
3. Training identified models - 2 Week
4. POC Validation (Go or No Go) - 1 Week
5. Develop, Analyse, and Fine Tune - 4 Weeks
6. Validation and Testing Model - 1 Week
7. Integration and Operationalize System - 1 Week
8. Live experiment for safe launch - 1Week
9. Monitor and Maintain - 13th Week onwards

6.9.7. Manpower requirement: Data Scientist, Image Processing and Machine Learning Engineer, Python Developers, Project Manager. The ML Engineer was deployed for a certain period even after successful commissioning of the project for the purpose of validating and enhancing the model.

6.10. Cases of Data Science & Analytics Use in the Indian Context

6.10.1. Synapsica for Radiology Reporting: India has over 10,000 radiologists and over a billion people, which means there is one radiologist for 1 Laky people. About 85% of the radiology market is fragmented with a huge shortage of radiologists creating margin pressures for diagnostics centres and hospitals. The scanning of patients is done by the equipment operated by trained technicians, yet the reporting gets delayed for want of availability of radiologists. As such, there is a huge potential to use AI to bring speed, standardisation, and objectivity into radiology reporting.

Taking cognizance of the situation, the startup Synapsica has built radiology workflow solutions using AI, Computer vision, NLP, and distributed computing to build new algorithms to address the problem. The solution involves reporting condition of spine, chest, and other body parts based on the scans of the body parts and their comparison with expected conditions. Its algorithm can automatically report degenerative (age related) pathologies.

6.10.2. Retigence's StockWise for Hypermarket Inventory Optimization: The key pain area for big retailers, especially in the hypermarket segment is the wafer thin margins. 60% of their business comes from food and grocery, where the inventory comes with an expiry date, high shrinkage and high pilferage. In the Indian retail scenario, where customer buying decisions are MRP determined, the retailer has limited scope to play around with the margins. Hence inventory management is key to profitability. Manual forecasting of demand at the stock keeping unit (SKU) level for more than 300,000 SKUs per store was a difficult task. For example, SPAR Hypermarkets placed orders once every fortnight by manually arriving at the order quantity. They were struggling to use the volumes of data effectively. In retail, speed of action is of utmost importance. The shelves need to be stocked adequately at all times. Considering the huge number of SKU's they deal with, it is not easy to forecast demand manually. Retigence's StockWise, powered by HANA, helped them maintain stocks in real time. Their biggest challenge was accurate inventory planning and ensuring availability of the right quantity of stock at the right time to be able to cater to their customer needs. StockWise provided them details to the granular level and that simplified the task of inventory management and ordering on a day to day basis. The innovative solution providing actionable insights helped the leading hypermarket register increase in operating margins with this SAAS based solution for inventory optimisation.

6.10.3. Retigence Technology & Rostering of Nurses at Manipal Hospitals: At all hospitals, nurses administer medications, monitor patients, maintain records, manage intravenous lines, and work with doctors to heal patients. They also provide advice and support to patients and their attendants, including training them how to administer medication outside a hospital setting. Thus their availability in proper numbers in every shift is critical for patient care. Thus, rostering nurses to work shifts is one of the most important tasks at Manipal Group corporate and teaching hospitals.

However, rostering at the group's hospitals was a time-consuming exercise. Senior nurses in each ward would have to spend up to 45 minutes per day manually amending paper-based rosters to accommodate requested changes to duty shifts for personal or other circumstances. The organization began receiving complaints from patients, doctors, and other hospital staff that occasionally too few nurses were present in certain shifts. At the macro level, the number of nurses was sufficient to man all the shifts, but at micro level there would be imbalance in shift-wise allocations.

In response, Retigence Technologies built an application using computing resources available through Compute Engine, a Google Cloud product. The organization deployed the application to a smaller hospital and secured user support before rolling out the application to its Bangalore flagship. The initial resistance from senior nurses to automation and consequent loss of their control was overcome by presenting to them the transparency offered by the solution.

At one end the project resulted in saving 30 man-hours per day, and brought out the buffer of about 100 nurses as redundant, while at the other end it eliminated the stress in rostering manually and meeting the demands for change of duty. The night shifts were also distributed equitably and team composition of nurses in each ward, each shift improved. It has facilitated better leave management and training of the nurses.

6.11. Cases of Data Science & Analytics Use Globally

6.11.1. AcademiSinica & Context-Aware Music Recommendation using Factorization Machines: As people are switching from limited private music collections to public music streaming services containing millions of tracks, the music industry, today, is facing an elementary change in the way people consume music. Hence, there is a need for efficient Music Information Retrieval practices to analyse the tons of data generated. In a project at AcademiSinica, a novel data set, #nowplaying-RS containing 11.6 million listening events was taken from Twitter, and audio features of the respective tracks were taken from Spotify. The dataset was split into training and test sets based on different scenarios (warm users, cold-start users etc.), and using state-of-the-art Machine Learning algorithm - Factorization Machines context aware music recommendations were made. Different user contexts and track content features were used and the hashtags were analysed to make sentiment based track recommendations.

6.11.2. NUS Singapore & Unsupervised Named Entity Recognition for Electronic Health Records using Bidirectional LSTM-CNN: Electronic Health Records (EHRs) are an important part of the knowledge concerning individual health histories. Extracting valuable knowledge from these records is a challenging task because they are often composed of highly codified notes diverse in language, acronyms and jargon. In a project at the National University of Singapore a transfer learning, in an unsupervised setting, approach was proposed for the medical concept extraction task from patient reports. It used a CNN to extract character-level features by converting discrete features into continuous vector representations. Entity labels for unsupervised dataset were generated using an LSTM model trained in a supervised setting. The extracted features along with the generated labels are used to train a hybrid Bidirectional LSTM-CNN model, to perform Named Entity Recognition in an unsupervised setting.

6.11.3. SERI & Estimating Uncertainty of Neural Network for Detection of Diabetic Retinopathy: Diabetic Retinopathy (DR) is a leading cause of vision-loss globally. Of an estimated 500 million people with diabetes mellitus worldwide, approximately one third have signs of DR and of these, and a further one third of these cases is vision-threatening. The Singapore Eye Lesion Analyzer (SELENA) project in collaboration with the Singapore Eye Research Institute (SERI) involves examining retinal fundus photographs for eye conditions like diabetic retinopathy; to deploy it as the first nationally-adopted automated screening solution. The uncertainty of neural networks for automated screening of DR has been estimated using the PyTorch framework. It also generates visual explanations of the deep learning system to convey the pixels in the image that influences its decision using the Integrated Gradient method. The complete workflow to input data, train models, finding uncertainty and visualization of the output, have been designed and structured such that it can be used by end-users like clinicians.

Chapter 7

CYBER AND INFORMATION SECURITY

7.1. Introduction

In the highly digitised world of today, businesses, governments, and individuals store a whole lot of data on computers, smart devices, networks, and the cloud. A data or information breach can be devastating in a variety of ways for the users and can have even catastrophic impact on them. A data breach is a security incident where sensitive information is copied, transmitted, viewed, stolen or accessed by an unauthorised individual. It can involve business, financial, and personal information like trade secrets, intellectual property, credit card or bank account details, protected health information, personally identifiable information etc. Data breaches can also occur when data leaks and cloud leaks are discovered and exploited by cybercriminals.

The data-driven approach to business today is leading towards a trend of ever-expanding volumes of data from many sources, including customers, financial transactions, marketing campaigns, the cloud, mobile apps, emails, text messages, social media, Internet of Things (IoT) devices, and more. In the past, organisations were concerned about the capacity storage constraints on hard drives and other storage mediums. Today, storage space has become much more available and less expensive in the cloud, so the quantity of data an organisation can manage is nearly limitless. This data is prone to breach throughout its life cycle i.e. from creation to deletion and it can be a challenging task to maintain integrity of data and information all through.

7.2. Cybersecurity & Cybersecurity Risk

Cybersecurity is the practice of protecting critical systems and sensitive information from digital attacks. It is the practice of application of technologies, processes and controls to protect systems, networks, programs, devices and data from cyber attacks. It aims to reduce the risk of cyber attacks and protect against unauthorised exploitation of systems, networks and technologies. Also known as information technology (IT) security, cyber-security measures are designed to combat threats against networked systems and applications, whether those threats may originate from inside or outside of an organisation. It encompasses within itself, Information Security, which is concerned with protecting the confidentiality, integrity, and availability of information.

On the other hand, the probability of exposure or loss resulting from a cyber attack or data breach and the potential loss or harm related to operations, functioning, infrastructure, use of technology, image or reputation of an organisation defines the Cybersecurity Risk of the organisation. In 2020 itself, the average cost of a data breach was USD 3.86 million globally, and USD 8.64 million in the United States. These costs include the expenses of discovering and responding to the breach, the cost of downtime and lost revenue, and the long-term reputational damage to a business and its brand.

The challenges of cybersecurity breaches are immense, and are ever-present risks in businesses of all sizes. Any breach opens a Pandora box of problems for an organisation. Cybercriminals target customers' personally identifiable information (PII) — names, addresses, national identification numbers (e.g., Social Security number in the US, fiscal codes in Italy, Aadhaar Number in India), and credit card information — and then sell these records in underground digital marketplaces. Compromised PII often leads to a loss of customer trust, the imposition of regulatory fines, and even legal action.

In response, a growing number of new and existing regulations are placing a higher penalty on noncompliance with data privacy regulations. In India, one of the primary legislations dealing with Cybersecurity, data protection, and cybercrimes is the Information Technology Act 2000 (the IT Act), read with the rules and regulations framed there under. The IT Act not only provides legal recognition and protection for transactions carried out through electronic data interchange and other means of electronic communication, but it also contains provisions that are aimed at safeguarding electronic data, information or records, and preventing unauthorised or unlawful use of a computer system. Some of the cybercrimes that are specifically envisaged and punishable under the IT Act are hacking, denial-of-service attacks, phishing, malware attacks, identity fraud and electronic theft.

While the role of regulations in managing cybersecurity risk is critical, one cannot lose sight of the internal functioning of firms and their technology systems. Security system complexity, created by disparate technologies and a lack of in-house expertise, can amplify these risks. But organisations with a comprehensive cybersecurity strategy, governed by best practices using advanced analytics, artificial intelligence (AI) and machine learning, can fight cyber-threats more effectively and reduce the lifecycle and impact of breaches when they occur.

7.3. Security Issues in the Data Life Cycle

Every data in a system goes through six stages during its life-cycle: creation, storage, use, sharing, archiving, and destruction.

- **Data Creation:** Every moment, organisations, during their operations, are creating massive amounts of structured and unstructured data in multiple formats. It includes both qualitative and quantitative data as alphanumeric, documents, spreadsheets, PDFs, emails, texts, images, and more. Data acquisition and capture occurs at the beginning of the cycle when an enterprise organisation obtains new, vetted information, including creating data internally, purchasing third-party data, and collecting data as it streams from apps. Data discovery and classification procedure keeps all the data organised, so that it's both usable for business purposes as well as protected from security breaches.
- **Data Storage:** The data that gets created needs to be stored as active data so as to speed up data retrieval, prevent data loss, meet data retention requirements, and reduce IT expenses. The process generally includes replication, mirroring, security, compression,

redundancy management, storage capacity provisioning, and memory management. Data storage must be compliant with contracts and regulatory laws. It would mean storing data on servers or drives in such a way that it can't be accidentally altered. Commonly the stored data is specified in terms of its sensitivity, such as private, sensitive, restricted, or public. Also, the stored data is accessible only to assigned personnel so that the organisation's intellectual property and its customer relationships are protected. Data storage has to manage data recovery plans also, so that in case of occurrence of a failure, the organisation should be in a position to continue accessing the data. It may involve having a temporary backup plan on a hierarchical storage management system.

- **Data Use:** Similar to any asset, data has value only when it is usable and is used. Proper data usage requires ensuring that the records meet certain validations before being accessible to users. When a data set or a file is created, copied, edited, transmitted, retrieved, extracted from an archive, or otherwise modified, it should be instantly searched, classified, made available, and reported. The process also defines who can use the data and for what purposes. Optimum data security and role-based security controls need to be applied to all sensitive data via tagging based on internal security policies and compliance rules.
- **Data Sharing:** Data is constantly being shared among employees, users, customers, partners, and other stakeholders through different devices and platforms. A published data is available to people even outside of an organisation's system, and the more the people who share data, the higher is the risk that the data is not compliant with governance and legal or policy regulations. Also, as the data moves between a variety of public and private storage locations, applications, and operating environments, it is important that it should be discoverable no matter how many times and where it's moved, copied, and shared.
- **Data Archiving:** Archived data is that stored data which is not active yet is needed to be accessed from time to time. Such data can eventually be stored within an organisation's storage systems and on drives that are not on the network, but accessible for ad hoc reporting and analytics. During archiving, data undergoes an archival process that ensures redundancy and accurate classification according to all

pertinent internal and external guidelines. Depending on what the data is, it is decided when, where, and for how long data needs to be archived. The guiding factors for such decisions may be internal company policies as well as legal regulations. Once archived, it's important for the data to be both available and protected according to industry compliance rules relating to personal, research, or medical data etc.

- **Data Destruction:** In the final stage of the life cycle, significant amounts of data are needed to be purged from the records and destroyed to reduce the storage burden and improve overall data security. Data classification and local as well as international laws mandate the disposal method. Before destroying any data, it is critical to confirm that the activity is in conformity to the policies in place that require retention of the data for a specific period of time.

7.4. Cyber Security: An Evolutionary Perspective

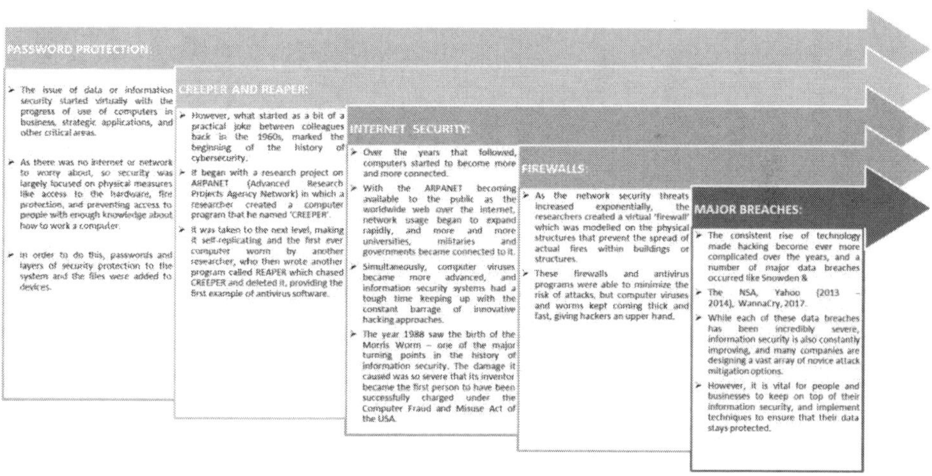

Figure 7.1: Cyber Security through ages

7.5. Contemporary Cyber Security Threats

Although cybersecurity professionals work hard to close security gaps, attackers are always looking for new ways to escape IT notice, evade defence measures, and exploit emerging weaknesses. The latest cybersecurity threats are putting a new spin on "known" threats, taking advantage of work-from-home environments, remote access tools, and new cloud services. The threats countered by cyber-security are three-fold:

- **Cyber-crime**: When single actors or groups target systems for financial gain or to cause disruption, it falls under the category of cybercrime.
- **Cyber-attack**: When politically motivated groups or political entities breach the security of others for information gathering to their own advantage.
- **Cyber-terrorism:** When unscrupulous actors or agencies try to take control of strategic systems and undermine electronic systems with an intention to cause panic or fear.

Some common and evolving methods used to threaten cyber-security are listed below for general appreciation.

- **Malware**: The term "malware" derives its name from 'malicious software'. One of the most common cyber threats, malware is a software that a cybercriminal or hacker has created to get unauthorised access to a computer so as to disrupt or cause damage to it. Often spread via an unsolicited email attachment or legitimate-looking download, malware attacks are increasingly becoming "fileless" and designed to get around familiar detection methods, such as antivirus tools, that scan for malicious file attachments.

There are a number of different types of malware, like worms, viruses, Trojans, spyware, Adware, Botnets etc. While worms and viruses are self-replicating programs that attach themselves to files and spread throughout a computer system, infecting files with malicious code, Trojans are a type of malware that is disguised as legitimate software and the users are tricked into uploading them onto their computer where they cause damage or collect data. Spyware and Adware are programs that secretly record what a user does, so that cybercriminals can make use to their advantage.

Ransomware is a malware that locks down a user's files, data or system, with the threat of erasing, destroying or making private or sensitive data public unless a ransom is paid. Some Ransomware attacks have targeted state and local governments, which are easier to breach than business organisations and are under pressure to pay ransoms in order to restore applications and web sites on which citizens rely.

Botnets are networks of malware infected computers which cybercriminals use to perform tasks online without the legitimate user's permission.

- **Phishing**: When cybercriminals target victims with emails that appear to be from a legitimate source asking for sensitive information, it is called Phishing. It is a form of social engineering where people lie outright about their identity and dupe people into handing over sensitive information like credit card data, login details, and other personal information. A surge has been noted in pandemic-related phishing that is directly linked to the growth of remote work.
- **Identity Theft:** Identity Theft involves the stealing of personal information of the victims from social media websites such as Facebook, Instagram, etc. and using that info to build a picture of the victims. If sufficient sensitive information is gathered it could allow the cybercriminal to pretend as the person in some way and cause immeasurable damage to the public image, cause financial loss, and breach security of the victim.
- **Password Attacks:** Hackers attempt to crack the passwords of the user with the help of a hacking tool and they may gain access to the victim's account credentials. They may also attack a computer login screen to gain access to a victim's computer and reach the data stored in it.
- **Insider Threats:** Many times, current or former employees, business partners, contractors, or anyone who has had access to systems or networks in the past abuse their access permissions. These are called Insider Threats and they can be invisible to traditional security solutions like firewalls and intrusion detection systems, which focus mainly on external threats.
- **Man-in-the-Middle Attacks:** A man-in-the-middle attack is an eavesdropping type of cyber threat, where a cybercriminal intercepts communication between two parties and relays messages in order to steal data. It can happen on an unsecure Wi-Fi network, an attacker

can intercept data being passed between a user's device and the network.

- **Distributed Denial-of-Service (DDoS) Attacks:** A DDoS attack attempts to crash a server, website or network by overloading it with traffic, usually from multiple coordinated systems so as to prevent a computer system from fulfilling legitimate requests. DDoS attacks overwhelm enterprise networks via the simple network management protocol (SNMP), used for modems, printers, switches, routers, and servers rendering the system unusable, and the organisation is not able to carry out its vital functions.
- **Advanced Persistent Threats (APTs):** When an intruder or a group of intruders infiltrate a system and remain undetected for an extended period, it causes APT. Such intruders leave networks and systems intact so that they can keep spying on business activity and steal sensitive data while avoiding the activation of defensive countermeasures. The recent Solar Winds breach of United States government systems is an example of an APT.
- **SQL Injection:** In the vulnerable data-driven applications, cybercriminals are able to insert malicious code into a database via a malicious SQL (structured language query) statement. An SQL injection gives the attacker access to the sensitive information contained in the database and it is used to take control of and steal data from the database.

7.6. Impact of Cyber Crimes

Given the nature of cybercrimes and the difficulties in detecting them, it is difficult to ascertain the direct and indirect costs of these security breaches. So many factors contribute to the cost of cybercrimes and each of these factors can be attributed to a lack of robust cybersecurity practices. A lack of focus on cybersecurity can damage a business in a range of ways including economic, reputational, and regulatory.

- **Economic Costs** include the theft of intellectual property, corporate information, disruption in trading, and the cost of repairing damaged systems.
- **Reputational Costs** include the loss of consumer trust, loss of current and future customers to competitors, and poor media coverage.

- **Regulatory Costs** include General Data Protection Regulations (GDPR) and other data breach laws which would mean that the organisation could suffer from regulatory fines or sanctions as a result of the cybercrimes.

With increasing cyber-crimes, consumers are expecting increasingly sophisticated cybersecurity measures as time goes on and the reputational damage of even a small data breach or other security may be quite large.

7.7. Deploying Cybersecurity

Individuals and organisations can't remain complacent when it comes to their privacy and security. With cyber attackers becoming more innovative and users having more than one device, it can be a challenge to protect people and businesses from cyber threats. In order to combat the cyber threats, a structured approach to cybersecurity is necessary. Some of the following types of cybersecurity initiatives are being put in place by the concerned agencies to protect the information, the systems, and the individuals' privacy.

- **Network Security:** Network security includes the deployment of software and hardware technologies to protect the usability, integrity, and safety of a network, associated components, and data shared over the network or VPN. In a secured network, potential threats get blocked from entering or spreading on that network as if by a wall standing between the organisation's network and the malicious activity.

Network security includes Firewall that acts as a barrier between the trusted internal network and external network, Email Security that prevents any incoming attacks through emails which are the most common carriers of cyberthreats, Anti-virus and anti-malware software that scan for malware upon entry, monitor files for anomalies, and remove it to fix any damage, and Data Loss Prevention (DLP) that prevents users from sharing, uploading, or forwarding critical information in a risky manner.

- **Information Security:** Information security aims to protect the critical business and private information from unauthorised access, theft, destruction, disruption, and alteration. It is a crucial factor in cybersecurity as it is specifically designed for data security to protect the confidentiality, integrity, and availability (CIA) of data and hardware that handle, store and transmit that data ensuring that only authorised users, apps, or systems can access.

Information Security initiatives include Cloud Security that focuses mainly on the vulnerabilities coming from Internet services and shared environments, Cryptography that involves obscuring content to secure information so that only the user with the correct encryption key can access it, Incident Response that monitors and probes possibly malicious behaviour, and Vulnerability Management that scans the environment for any weak spots, such as unpatched software and other factors to monitor potential exposures.

- **Application Security:** Application security aims to protect software applications from vulnerabilities that occur due to the flaws during application design, development, installation, upgradations, or maintenance. A compromised application can provide access to the data it is designed to protect. Such a security system begins at the design stage itself, well before a program or a device is deployed.
- **Infrastructure Security:** In order to protect critical infrastructure, such as communication network, data centre, servers, IT centre, power generation and transmission, water supply, air conditioning and other systems from cyber attacks it is necessary to limit their vulnerabilities and to develop a contingency plan. IoT security also forms part of the infrastructural security requirements.
- **End-point Security:** End- point security or end-user protection is a crucial aspect of cyber security. Mostly, it is the end-user, an individual, who accidentally downloads malware or another form of cyber threat to their desktop, laptop or mobile device. The end-user security software scans computers for pieces of malicious code, quarantines this code, and then removes it from the machine. It confines the potentially malicious programs to a virtual bubble separate from a user's network.

7.8. Technologies for Cybersecurity: An Overview

Organisations are implementing some key technologies and adopting the best practices to have strong cybersecurity that reduces vulnerability of their systems to cyber attacks and protects their critical information systems, without intruding on the user or customer experience.

- **Identity and Access Management (IAM):** IAM defines the roles and access privileges for each user, as well as the conditions under which they are granted or denied these privileges. Identity and Access

Management methodologies include single sign-on that enables a user to log in to a network once without re-entering credentials during the same session; multifactor authentication that requires two or more access credentials; privileged user account that grants administrative privileges to certain users only; and user lifecycle management that manages each user's identity and access privileges from initial registration through retirement. IAM tools can also give the cybersecurity professionals of the organisation deeper visibility into suspicious activity on end-user devices, including endpoints where they may not have physical accessibility. This helps speed investigation and response times to isolate and contain the damage of a breach.

- **Comprehensive Data Security Platform:** A comprehensive data security platform protects sensitive information across multiple environments, including hybrid multi-cloud environments. The best data security platforms provide automated, real-time visibility into data vulnerabilities, as well as ongoing monitoring that alerts them to data vulnerabilities and risks before they become data breaches. They also simplify and facilitate compliance with government and industry data privacy regulations. Having regular hierarchical backups and mandatory encryption are also vital for keeping data safe.
- **Security Information and Event Management (SIEM):** SIEM aggregates and analyzes data from security events to automatically detect suspicious user activities and trigger a preventative or remedial response. These solutions include advanced detection methods such as user behaviour analytics and artificial intelligence (AI). SIEM can automatically prioritise cyber threat response in line with the organisation's risk management objectives. Many organisations are integrating their SIEM tools with security orchestration, automation and response (SOAR) platforms that further automate and accelerate an organisation's response to cybersecurity incidents, and resolve many incidents without human intervention.

7.9. Practices in Cybersecurity Management: An Overview

- **Plan**: All technology implementations in the organisations of today should begin with a plan that includes cybersecurity. A sound cybersecurity plan not only helps businesses identify and improve their current security protocols, it also positions them to manage future risks. Key stakeholders should identify the most critical information assets to protect, map how that information flows through the organisation (currently and with any proposed technology or process changes) and determine the level of risk if that information gets lost or is compromised.

Planning in this order sets the foundation for how the company will address risks to that information and can be used to assign risk management roles, develop secure procedures, and implement appropriate safeguards. To cover all of its bases, an organisation should develop a comprehensive plan with an eye not only on the types of cybersecurity, but also on the three components that play active roles in a cybersecurity posture - people, processes and technology.

- **People:** No matter what precautions are put into place, if people don't follow the rules, the risk remains unattended. Mostly, people don't bypass the security protocols intentionally– it is mostly a mistake. They are either not trained to handle the situation, or not educated about the significance of their actions. Common ways through which the human factor impacts cybersecurity risk are:
- **Suspicious URLs and Emails:** Staff should pay attention to URLS, delete emails that don't have content or look like they are coming from a spoofed address, and the importance of guarding personal information should be stressed.
- **Password Idleness:** Frequent changing of passwords and using strong combinations should be emphasised.
- **Personally Identifiable Information -**Personal browsing, like shopping and banking tasks, should be done from people's own devices. They also share too much information (PII) on social media like Facebook, Twitter, Instagram, etc.
- **Backups and Updates -** Many consumers and users go about their daily business without backing up their data regularly and updating their system antivirus, thus inviting many potential cybersecurity threats.
- **Physical Security of Devices -** People in offices leave their desk for meetings, gatherings and lunch breaks without locking their devices. An unattended device is prone to unscrupulous interference with the system causing security breach.

As such, conducting regular security awareness training and reinforcing the most basic cybersecurity principles with employees both inside and outside of the IT department can make a big difference in an organisation's security posture.

- **Processes:** The processes by which confidential data are protected are multi-faceted. Cybersecurity professionals are employing standardised procedures for detecting and identifying threats, protecting information and responding to incidents as well as recovering the system from them. Cybersecurity Frameworks have been developed by various agencies like the National Institute of Standards and Technology (NIST) of the U.S. for use by companies as a guide in creating their own best practices.
- **Technologies:** Cybersecurity initiatives in the present context have to focus on technological aspects in two broad areas. The first one is to prevent and combat cybersecurity attacks, like DNS filtering, malware protection, antivirus software, firewalls and email security solutions etc. The other one is to provide protection to the data that resides on computers, smart devices, routers, networks, and the cloud.

7.10. Cyber Risk Management Frameworks

A cyber risk management framework can help organisations effectively assess, mitigate, and monitor risks; and define security processes and procedures to address them. There are several cyber risk management frameworks, each of which provides standards organisations can use to identify and mitigate risks. These frameworks are used to assess and improve the security posture of the organisation.

- **ISO 27001:** The International Organisation for Standardisation (ISO) and the International Electrotechnical Commission (IEC) have jointly issued ISO/IEC 27000-series of standards for information security. The ISO/IEC 270001 cybersecurity framework offers a certifiable set of standards defined to systematically manage risks to information systems. Organisations can also use the ISO 31000 standard, which provides guidelines for enterprise risk management.

- **NIST CSF:** The National Institute of Standards and Technology Cybersecurity Framework (NIST CSF) is a popular framework. It integrates industry standards and best practices to help organisations manage their cybersecurity risks. It defines a map of activities and outcomes related to the core functions of cybersecurity risk management—protect, detect, identify, respond, and recover. The Framework not only helps organisations respond to and recover from cybersecurity incidents, but also prompts them to analyse root causes and consider how they can make improvements. The CMF that was initially developed for critical infrastructure has also been recommended for use in organisations including industry regardless of size, degree of cybersecurity risk, or cybersecurity sophistication
- **DoD RMF:** NIST has also developed the Department of Defence (DoD) Risk Management Framework (RMF) that defines guidelines that the US federal agencies use when assessing and managing cybersecurity risks. RMF provides a comprehensive, flexible, repeatable, and measurable 7-step process that any organisation can use to manage information security and privacy risk for organisations and systems and links to a suite of NIST standards and guidelines to support implementation of risk management programs. These key steps are, 1. Prepare, 2. Categorise, 3. Select, 4. Implement, 5. Assess, 6. Authorise, and 7. Monitor.
- **FAIR Framework:** The Factor Analysis of Information Risk (FAIR) framework developed by The FAIR Institute is defined for the purpose of helping enterprises measure, understand, manage, and report on information risks from a business perspective. The goal is to guide enterprises through the process of making innovative well-informed decisions and sharing cybersecurity best practices.

7.10.1. Checklist for assessing Cyber Risk and Compliance to ISO27001 or NISTIR 8183:

- Are you using confidential information supplied by your customers?
- Is your computer system in constant or regular contact with those of your customers and/or suppliers?
- What information security controls are in place to protect all the data concerned?

- Do you provide a service requiring access to customers' personal details?
- Do you have control over the devices being brought to your site or of the information being downloaded by those with legitimate access?
- Are there policies and procedures in place to reduce the risk of a security breach?
- What controls do you have in place to prevent those sitting outside your premises from downloading your confidential data?
- What controls do you have around your premises, or indeed within the premises to prevent prying eyes from seeing something to your disadvantage?
- Do you have access control within your buildings to restrict access to places where the highly confidential activity takes place?

7.11. Critical Aspects of Cybersecurity Management

7.11.1. Security Maturity Assessment: Before attempting to implement a cybersecurity plan it is important to conduct a Security Maturity Assessment and design a Maturity Improvement Roadmap. This approach is based on analysing the enterprise's cyber security operational and technologies framework capabilities as they provide a lower level of granularity and rigorous assessment of cybersecurity functions.

7.11.2. Cyber Breach & Ransomware Prevention Readiness: It is important to assess the cyber breach and Ransomware prevention preparedness of the organisation because the costs attached to such breaches are far more than loss of operations. The average cost of a Data Breach in the Industrial space is USD 4.24 Million (Statista). Ransomware Readiness includes a multi-pronged approach. The assessment is to be done with regard to the following:

- People preparedness using Tabletop Exercises to gauge employee responsiveness to a Ransomware attack.
- Technology preparedness through Ransomware simulation to gauge technology responsiveness to a Ransomware attack. Technology implementation by auditing technology deployment to detect and prevent a Ransomware attack.

- Readiness with regard to the Incident Response Plan for Recovery.
- Forensics Investigation Capability of the enterprise.

7.11.3. Cybersecurity Ratings: Cybersecurity rating is a tool that an organisation can rely on to proactively reduce risk throughout the cyber attack surface. Ratings use expansive data-scanning technology to provide an outside-in view of the organisation's security posture, along with the third-party ecosystem.

These ratings are similar to a credit score and can range in value from 250 to 900, with a higher rating equalling better cybersecurity performance. Presenting risk in this format makes it easier for everyone to tell how well–or poorly–their organisation is protected.

7.12. Implementing Cybersecurity Systems

An organisation's efforts to digitise its business operations without a robust plan can lead to unbounded investment costs. This is especially true when considering the cybersecurity aspects of a digital environment where investments can become reactive if not thoughtfully prepared for in advance. An Enterprise-wide Disaster Recovery Policy should be implemented to keep the operations continuously available.

7.12.1. Return on Security Investment (ROSI) on Cybersecurity System Implementations: Once a plan is implemented, it enables the business to sensibly invest in advanced production technology capabilities and get Return on Security Investment (ROSI) benefits over time. Some of the benefits of integrating cybersecurity in operational planning are:

- Increased operational efficiency and agility
- Reduced downtime
- Improved ability to predict and adjust to facility and supply changes
- Improved security posture & maturity across the IT and OT environment
- Reduced cyber risks and liabilities
- Improved cyber risk compliances
- Enhanced cyber defence against potential breach

There is also the cost of non-adoption to consider when it comes to digitising business operations, such as failing to keep pace with competitors or struggling to meet current market expectations. A thorough investment plan considers the cost and benefit of implementing – or not – any changes, when those changes should occur, and how much money to set aside to prepare for those changes.

7.12.2. Challenges to Implementing Cybersecurity Systems: The top challenges for enterprises when it comes to implementing advanced production technology applications include capital investment, people awareness, equipment obsolescence, and privacy concerns.

- **Learning Curve Aspect of Cybersecurity Systems Management:** One of the biggest digitization challenges in businesses is the lack of relevant knowledge to implement advanced digital technologies in a safe and secure manner. But overcoming this learning curve may be as simple as reaching out to external consultants experienced in providing guidance and facilitating availability of resources to enterprises. Enlisting outside expertise for any kind of technology implementation can help the organisation leverage knowledge, skills, and abilities they wouldn't be able to access otherwise.

In this regard, external experts can provide immediate implementation guidance and training to help organisations take advantage of innovations such as AI / machine learning, Advanced data analytics, Augmented / virtual reality, Automation, Cloud computing, Digital Twins, Sensors /IoT, Wireless infrastructure, Zero-trust models

It is also necessary that the Board Level Awareness regarding cybersecurity issues is enhanced so that the required investments and projects get their approval. Outside experts can be helpful in this area by enlightening the Board members on Cybersecurity & the Internet, Cybersecurity Governance Essentials, Cybercrime: Regional & International Legislation, Cybersecurity Ethics, Threats, and Consequences for Organisations, etc.

- **Insider Threat (Employee/Third-Party Vendor Awareness):** Human errors represent one of the most common risks facing organisations, including safety, quality, and cybersecurity risks. Humans can configure machines incorrectly or insecurely, forward unprotected business sensitive information to outside parties, and cause vulnerabilities arising through e-Mail/SMS Phishing. Third-

Party Risks arising out of vulnerabilities in supply chain and Insider Threat caused by intentional malicious behaviour also fall under this category.

The awareness process requires engagement at all levels of the business. It should begin with the company's president or leader and then continue through key multi-departmental staff, including decision makers at every level of the organisation. This process should consider the experiences and expertise of all employees, including but not limited to administrative staff, engineering staff, IT managers and staff, operations managers, shop floor employees, third-party vendors, and other stakeholders.

- **Use of Outdated Systems:** Technology changes are occurring in the digital world at a much faster pace than traditional industrial equipment. They often have an expected lifespan of less than 10 years and planned obsolescence around 3-5 years. The older a technology infrastructure is, the more difficult it is to make it compatible with a digitised manufacturing environment. In a fully realised digitised environment, appropriate data can be shared between a variety of systems. However, if business platforms and technologies are over five years old, they may not be able to read, write, or share data as needed.

Leveraging a more modular approach to technology, such as, by using standard application programming interfaces (APIs), can reduce these concerns for future innovation implementation.

- **Privacy Concerns:** Digitization challenges often include privacy concerns, as digitised production capabilities can provide a window into every aspect of operations of the whole business. Privacy should be considered whenever information is collected that could be used to identify a person. This may include employee or customer contact information as well as the data collected by certain IoT sensors, cameras, or biometric authentication devices. It is important to note that while data from one device might not present a privacy concern, that data combined with data from other devices could.

The risk profile in the business space is changing in the digital age. Data privacy is a key risk for any company handling potentially sensitive data related to its customers, employees and business partners. The reasons for adoption of Privacy Protection are:

- Increased privacy regulations (GDPR) and rising consumer privacy requests

- Emerging technologies and the expanding Internet of Things
- Adoption of Big Data due to the emergence of Industry 4.0
- Digitalization and integration of physical assets
- Shortage of data privacy expertise

Taking cybersecurity seriously at the outset will give enterprises the opportunity to protect privacy as well, especially in the areas of Contingency and Disaster Recovery Planning, Operational Security, Personnel Security, and Physical Security.

NOTES

Chapter 8

AI & BUSINESS APPLICATIONS

8.1. Introduction

Artificial Intelligence (AI) is one of the most complex and astounding creations of humanity till date. In particular, on hearing the term AI, the first thing that usually comes to minds is that of robots. However, nothing could be further from the truth. From facial recognition to auto-correction of textual data, AI can be found all around us. The transformation brought about by AI in different industries has made business leaders and the mainstream public perceive that we are close to achieving the peak of AI research and maxing out on AI's potential. Its rapid growth and powerful capabilities have made people paranoid about the inevitability and proximity of an AI takeover. This however disregards the fact that the field remains largely unexplored and it is still hard to comprehensively gain a clear perspective on the potential impact of AI in the future.

Nonetheless, AI provides us countless utilities that mankind has become almost dependent on. Let's take a look at some of the examples of application of AI in day-to-day affairs and their impact on people's life.

- **Maps and Navigation Apps** have drastically improved travelling and instead of having to rely on printed maps or directions, we can now type in the destination on the computer and get the directions as well as other details like the optimal route, road barriers, and traffic congestions.

- **Facial Detection and Recognition** used for unlocking our phones or using virtual filters on our faces when taking pictures are also based on AI. Facial recognition is also used for surveillance and security by government facilities and at airports.
- **Text Editors or Autocorrect Apps** have AI algorithms to identify incorrect usage of language and suggest corrections in word processors, texting apps, and every other written medium. Linguists and computer scientists have been able to teach machines grammar, just like we were taught at school.
- **Search and Recommendation Algorithms** provide smart recommendations aligned with users' interests or recent searches based on their behavior and interests learnt by the systems over time following their online activity. The data stored and analyzed through Machine Learning and Deep Learning helps the system to predict what the user might want to shop online, see or listen to next.
- **Chatbots** are becoming increasingly a popular AI solution to the typically expensive, hard to manage, inefficient and time-consuming customer service department. The programmed algorithms enable machines to answer frequently asked questions, take and track orders, and direct calls.
- **Digital Assistants** are examples of AI applications that are able to conduct voice and image search, identify words, access users' contacts, and make calls. These assistants use NLP, ML, statistical analysis, and algorithmic execution to decide what the users are asking for and try to get it for them.
- **Social Media** applications are using AI to monitor content, suggest connections, and serve advertisements to targeted users, among many other tasks to ensure that users stay invested and plugged in. AI algorithms are able to spot and swiftly take down objectionable posts that violate terms and conditions.
- **E-Payments** have eliminated the enormous waste of time and drudgery of running to the bank for every transaction. Using intelligent algorithms, payment processes have been simplified to make deposits, transfer money, and even open accounts from anywhere, leveraging AI for security, identity management, and privacy controls.

- **Speech recognition:** Also known as automatic speech recognition (ASR), computer speech recognition, or speech-to-text is a capability which uses natural language processing (NLP) to process human speech into a written format. Many mobile devices incorporate speech recognition into their systems to conduct voice search and provide more accessibility around texting.

In its simplest form, AI is a field, which combines computer science and robust datasets to enable problem-solving. Machines are wired using a cross-disciplinary approach based on mathematics, computer science, linguistics, psychology, and more. It also encompasses sub-fields of Machine Learning, Deep Learning, and Natural Language Processing which are frequently mentioned in conjunction with AI. These disciplines are at the core of AI algorithms which seek to create expert systems which make predictions or classifications based on input data.

8.2. The Rise of Artificial Intelligence

The concept of AI is based on the principle that human Intelligence can be defined in a way that a machine can mimic it and execute tasks. AI leverages computers and machines to mimic the problem-solving and decision-making capabilities of the human mind. Surprising rapid strides are being made by researchers and developers in creating machines that mimic the human cognitive activities such as Learning, reasoning, and perception. There are people who believe that innovators may soon be able to develop systems that exceed the capacity of humans to learn or reason out any subject. But others remain skeptical because cognitive activity is laced with value judgments that are subject to human experience and there are limitations to the extent that these can be concretely defined.

Decades before the term AI was coined, the concept of AI was indicated in the question "Can machines think?" posed by Alan Turing, often referred to as the 'Father of Computer Science', in his seminal work, 'Computing Machinery and Intelligence' published in 1950. He also propounded the Turing Test which is a method of inquiry in AI for determining whether or not a computer is capable of thinking like a human being. It is a three-person game in which a computer uses written communication to try to fool a human interrogator into thinking that it's another person. Interestingly, despite major advances in AI, no computer has ever passed the Turing Test.

Fictional presence of machines that think and act like humans have been there in books and movies since quite long, but the real application of AI in machines was noticed by the world in the 1960s when computers were developed to be able to play chess with human beings. It was followed by autonomous moving robots, machines playing music, translating written text, responding to text, and Learning by updating their stored database. With the panic of the Y2K bug over the trend of advancements in the world of AI surged like a phoenix in the 21st century.

AI is continuously evolving to benefit many different industries and as technology advances, previous benchmarks that defined AI become outdated. Today, machines that compute using basic functions or recognize text through optical character recognition (OCR) are no longer considered to embody AI, since this function is now taken for granted as an inherent function of computers. Even face recognition or voice recognition is not considered something involving Intelligence.

A lot of hype still surrounds AI development, which is expected of any new emerging technology in the market. As a characteristic of any hype, product innovations like, self-driving cars and personal assistants, have been following a typical progression of innovation, from over enthusiasm through a period of disillusionment to an eventual understanding of the innovation's relevance and role in a market or domain.

Researchers have been delving into two approaches with overall four potential goals or definitions of AI, which differentiate computer systems on the basis of rationality in thinking vs. Acting. The Human approach looks at AI as systems that think like humans and systems that act like humans, whereas the Ideal approach looks at it as systems that think rationally and systems that act rationally.

8.3. Understanding Artificial Intelligence

AI systems work by combining analysis of large sets of data with intelligent, iterative processing algorithms to learn from patterns and features in the data. With every round of data processing, the AI system develops additional expertise by testing, measuring, and upgrading its own performance. As it is a machine, it doesn't need a break and can run through hundreds, thousands, or even millions of tasks extremely quickly, learning a great deal in very little time.

It is important to understand that AI isn't just a computer program or application, but an entire discipline, or a science that utilizes a whole series of techniques, processes, and a vast array of different technologies. As such, an AI system consists of many different components that can be considered sub-fields of the overarching science of AI. The most important technologies that make up AI are Machine Learning (ML), Deep Learning (DL), and Natural Language Processing (NLP).

- **Machine Learning (ML)**: It is the process by which machines learn how to respond based upon structured big data sets and ongoing feedback from humans and algorithms. It allows the machine to find patterns in data, uncover insights, and improve the results of whatever task the system has been set out to achieve.
- **Deep Learning (DL):** It is a specific type of ML that allows the AI system to learn and improve by processing data through representation. Deep Learning can work even with data that isn't structured. It uses artificial neural networks which mimic biological neural networks in the human brain to process information, find connections between the data, and come up with inferences, or results based on positive and negative reinforcement.
- **Neural Networks:** It is a process in which data sets are analysed over and over again to find associations and interpret meaning from undefined data. Neural Networks operate like networks of neurons in the human brain, allowing AI systems to take in large data sets, uncover patterns amongst the data, and answer questions about it.
- **Natural Language Processing (NLP):** NLP is a linguistic tool in computer science that helps AI-enabled computers to recognize, analyze, interpret, and understand human language, either written or spoken. It translates human language into computer inputs and is critical for any AI-driven system that interacts with humans in some way.
- **Cognitive Computing**: It uses computerized models to simulate the human thought process in complex situations where the answers may be ambiguous and uncertain. These computer models mimic the way a human brain works when performing a complex task, like analyzing text, speech, or images and also imitate the interactions between humans and machines. Although computers are getting

faster by the day and are able to outpace humans at processing and calculating, they have yet to master some tasks, such as understanding natural language and recognizing objects in an image. Cognitive computing is an attempt to make computers mimic the way a human brain works.

- **Computer Vision** – It is the field of AI that trains computers to capture and interpret information from image and video data. By applying ML models to images, computers can classify objects via pattern recognition and response. Computer vision is the base for one of the prolific uses of AI technologies that is the ability to review and interpret the content of visual data and perform actions like face recognition, enhancing photos, putting filters on pics, detecting lung lesions in medical images, reading captchas in security systems, etc.

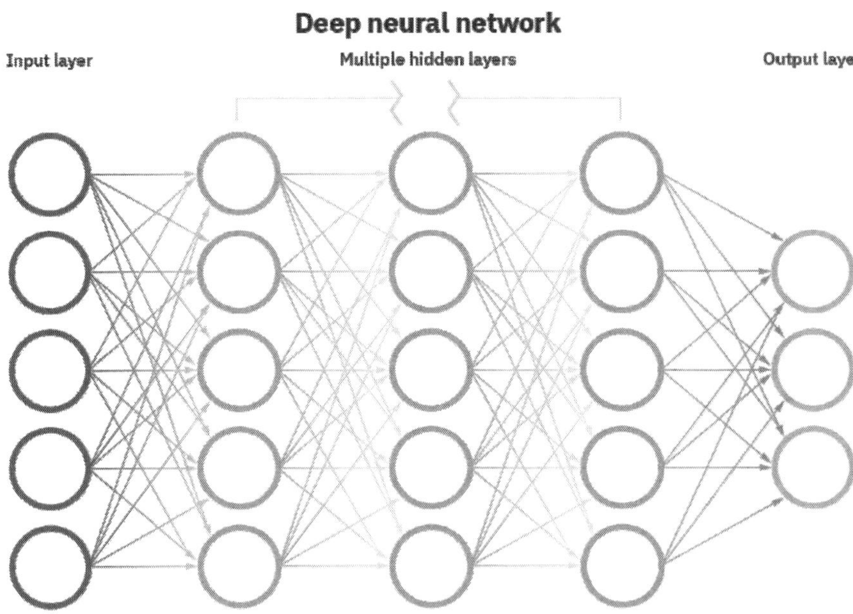

Figure 8.1: Deep Neural Network – a schematic representation

8.3.1. Clearing a Misconception: Deep Learning vs. Machine Learning

Many times Deep Learning and Machine Learning are used interchangeably, but there are nuances that differentiate the two. Although both of them are subfields of AI, Deep Learning is actually a specialised form of Machine Learning. At a fundamental level, Deep Learning comprises neural networks and the term 'Deep' in Deep Learning refers to a neural network that is composed of more than three layers through which the algorithm processes the data successively to come to a conclusion.

The fundamental difference between Deep Learning and Machine Learning is the way the two algorithms learn. Deep Learning automates much of the feature extraction part of the process and enables use of larger data sets, eliminating the manual human intervention to a large extent. On the other hand, classical, or "non-deep", Machine Learning is more dependent on human intervention to learn. They usually require more structured data and it is the human experts who determine the hierarchy of features to understand the differences between data inputs. As such, "Deep" Machine Learning doesn't necessarily require a labelled dataset. It can use unstructured data in its raw form (e.g. text, images), and can automatically determine the hierarchy of features which distinguish different categories of data from one another.

Although Deep Learning can be understood as 'Scalable Machine Learning', the difference between the two can be categorised under a few factors that separate them.

- **Data Dependencies:** The most important difference between Deep Learning & Machine Learning is their performance as the scale of data increases. When the data is small, Deep Learning algorithms don't perform that well, because Deep Learning algorithms need a large amount of data to understand it perfectly. On the other hand, traditional Machine Learning algorithms with their pre-formulated rules work well with even small data.
- **Hardware Dependencies:** Deep Learning algorithms require high-end machines for processing, while the traditional Machine Learning algorithms can work on low-end machines. The graphics processing units (GPUs) used by Deep Learning algorithms do a large amount of matrix multiplication operations requiring high-end hardware to process.

- **Feature Engineering:** In ML, most of the applied features like pixel values, shape, textures, position and orientation need to be identified by an expert and then hand-coded as per the domain and data type. The performance of the machine, then, depends on how accurately the features are identified and extracted. However, in DL, algorithms try to learn high-level features from data and this takes it steps ahead of traditional ML. It reduces the task of developing a new feature extractor for every problem.
- **Problem Solving Approach:** In solving problems using traditional Machine Learning algorithms, the problem is generally first broken down into different parts, solved part by part and then combined to get the result. In Deep Learning the problem is taken up to be solved end-to-end.
- **Execution time:** A Deep Learning algorithm takes a long time to train, maybe even weeks and months, because the number of parameters in it is very large. Machine Learning comparatively takes much less time to train, ranging from a few seconds to a few hours. However, during testing, Deep Learning algorithms take much less time to run compared to Machine Learning algorithms in which test time increases on increasing the size of data.
- **Interpretability:** As a factor for comparison of Machine Learning and Deep Learning, interpretability plays a major role in making a choice between the two. Although the results of Deep Learning are quite near to human performance, it does not reveal why it has given that result. As the layers of neurons and their nodes utilized in the process are too large it becomes difficult to distinguish the models through which the data has travelled and thus interpretation of the results is nearly impossible. On the contrary, Machine Learning algorithms like decision trees give crisp rules as to why it chose what it chose, so it is particularly easy to interpret the reasoning behind it. Due to this factor only Deep Learning is still lagging behind in its use in industry.

8.4. Types of Artificial Intelligence (AI)

Since AI purports to make machines emulate human-like functioning, the degree to which an AI system can replicate human capabilities is used as the criterion for determining the types of AI. Broadly, there are two ways in which AI is generally classified.

One is based on classifying AI and AI-enabled machines based on their likeness to the human mind, and their ability to 'think' and perhaps even 'react' like humans. On this basis there can be four types of systems: reactive machines, limited memory machines, theory of mind AI, and self-aware AI.

The other system of classification used mostly in tech parlance is based on the technology used namely, Artificial Narrow Intelligence (ANI), Artificial General Intelligence (AGI), and Artificial Super Intelligence (ASI).

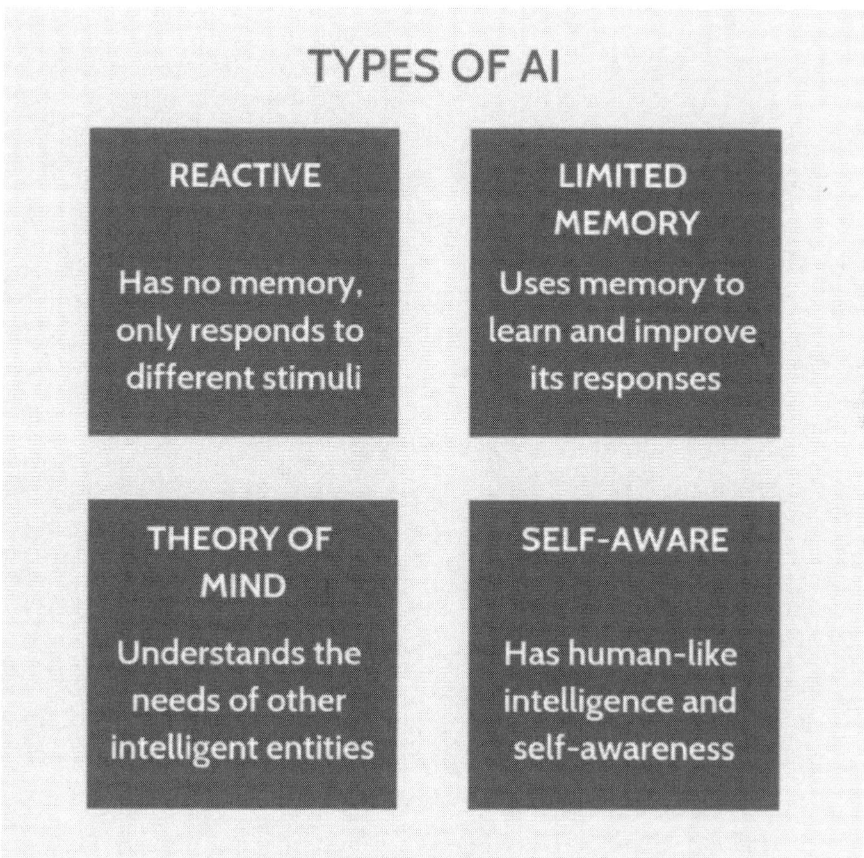

Figure 8.2: Types of Artificial Intelligence (AI)

- **Reactive Machines:** The oldest form of AI systems that have quite limited capability, but they emulate the human mind's ability to respond to different kinds of stimuli. They do not have memory-based functionality and thus cannot use previously gained experiences to moderate their present actions, i.e., these machines do not 'learn', they only respond automatically to a limited set or combination of inputs. A popular example of a reactive AI machine is IBM's Deep Blue, a machine that beat chess Grandmaster Garry Kasparov in 1997.
- **Limited Memory Machines:** These machines have capability of Learning from historical data to make decisions and they are not just reactive to the present stimuli. Almost all present-day AI applications, from Chatbots and virtual assistants to self-driving vehicles are all driven by limited memory AI, in which they are trained by large volumes of training data stored in their memory as a reference model for solving problems. By using these references the machine understands the contents of the problem presented to it by using Deep Learning and based on its "Learning experience" it labels new images with increasing accuracy.
- **Theory of Mind AI:** The next level of AI systems that researchers are currently engaged in innovating is integrating the Theory of Mind into machines. It aims at understanding human needs, emotions, beliefs, and thought processes so as to perceive humans as individuals whose minds are shaped by multiple factors. This level of AI will require collaboration of computer engineering with many branches of science, humanities, and psychology.
- **Self-Aware AI:** It is a stage of AI development that currently exists only hypothetically. This type of AI conceptualises a system that will not only be able to understand and evoke emotions in those it interacts with, but also have emotions, needs, beliefs, and desires of its own. It will be so akin to the human brain that it will have self-awareness. The doomsayers profess that such an entity may directly or indirectly spell the end for humanity, as it would be able to outsmart the intellect of any human being due to its power of interconnectivity and plot a catastrophe.
- **Artificial Narrow Intelligence (ANI): It** refers to the AI systems that can perform only a specific task autonomously using human-like capabilities and nothing more than what they are programmed to do.

They have a very limited or narrow range of competencies falling under the range of reactive and limited memory AI. Even the most complicated and capable AI of today that uses Machine Learning and Deep Learning to teach itself falls under this category.

- **Artificial General Intelligence (AGI):** It is a stage when systems will be able to independently build multiple competencies, form connections and do generalizations across domains. This will enable them to learn, perceive, understand, and function completely like a human being making the machines as capable as human beings exhibiting multi-functional capabilities.
- **Artificial Super-Intelligence (ASI):** It is a hypothetical stage of development of AI, when the system will be able to surpass the general human Intelligence and will be able to perform better in every field because of its overwhelmingly greater memory, faster data processing, and decision-making capabilities. It is a state called 'the technological singularity' in which the machine would enter a "runaway reaction" of self-improvement cycles resulting in Intelligence explosion with more and more intelligent generations coming out more and more rapidly with each cycle. While it is hard to picture the state of the world when more advanced types of AI come into being, yet it is clear that there is a long way to go in the field of AI both in terms of development of systems and in the field of ensuring safety of supremacy of men over machines.

8.5. Artificial Intelligence and Cloud

Nowadays, almost every technology comes with cloud backup services and the use of cloud computing services is continuously on increase. Also, AI has already started to dominate the tech-world and can be seen in different work domains.

In this regard, cloud computing offers enormous on-demand computer system resources, especially data storage and computing power, without direct active management and capital investment by the user. AI uses huge data and computing power to analyse, process, learn and take decisions for future action. An amalgamation of the two allows users not just to store and process data, but also to analyse it and draw conclusions from it. AI working with cloud computing has the power to revolutionize the Digital Transformation solutions. Without cloud computing, the current Machine Learning (ML) hype would not have been possible.

The integration of Machine Learning in the cloud is known as the Intelligent Cloud. Their combination is being used in IoT cloud, Business Intelligence, Chatbots, Cognitive cloud, AI-as-a-service platforms, Cloud AI platforms for improved decision making, minimizing costs and obtaining better output, analytics, data mining, and seamless data access.

Though the usage of AI and cloud together is in primary stage, companies are still investing enormously in cloud computing AI services. Over the years companies like Microsoft, IBM, Google, and Amazon have invested enormously in AI, especially in the cloud software solutions. This is because when both of these are merged, the quality and benefits of each are enhanced tremendously especially when it comes to their usage in the booming business world. This combination can be looked at as one of the most remarkable innovations in the future.

AI services and advanced analytics help generate more value from the cloud. Although 90% of today's businesses have adopted cloud, only one third are achieving the anticipated ROI. The most advanced companies understand that while cloud sets you up with next-level computing power and access to new kinds of data in the right quantity and quality, AI is the bridge to convert that data into business value. It's no surprise the entire Senior Management is now involved in the AI agenda

8.6. Artificial Intelligence in Action

Application of AI can be seen all around covering every aspect of business, industry, economy, and society.

- **Retail**: AI systems are being consulted by large retail outlets to design more effective store layouts, handle stock management, and provide shopping suggestions to the customers. Recommendations like 'You May Also Like' are a common feature today of most of the online shopping platforms.
- **Marketing:** AI applications are helping marketers deliver highly targeted and personalized ads with the help of activity monitoring, behavior analysis, pattern recognition, etc. It also helps with retargeting audiences at the right time to ensure better results and reduced feelings of distrust and annoyance.
- **E-Commerce:** AI technologies are finding major use in recommendation engines through which businesses can engage

better with their customers. They use browsing history, preference, and interests of the customers and it helps in improving relationships with customers and their loyalty towards the brand. Virtual shopping assistants and Chatbots help improve the user experience while shopping online by having real-time conversations that sound quite human and personal. Furthermore, credit card frauds and fake reviews are two of the most significant issues that E-Commerce companies deal with. AI can help reduce the possibility of credit card frauds and also identify and handle fake reviews.

- **Manufacturing**: AI solutions are helping forecast load and demand for factories, improving efficiency of production, quality control of products, assembly line optimisation, predicting possible equipment failure, spare-parts and inventory management etc. They are facilitating managers in making better decisions about ordering materials, completion timetables, project management, and other logistics issues.
- **Robotics:** The field where AI applications are used most commonly is robotics. Robots powered by AI use real-time updates to sense obstacles in the path and re-plan the journey instantly, respond to stimuli from human beings, perform tasks with real-time moderations in the operation sequence matching with the feedback from the foregoing actions. Such robots are already in use in carrying goods in hospitals, factories, and warehouses; cleaning offices and large equipment; inventory management, etc.
- **Automobiles:** The much talked about self-driving vehicles that use AI along with the vehicle's camera, radar, cloud services, GPS, and control signals to operate the vehicle. AI has been improving the in-vehicle experience by supporting additional systems like emergency braking, blind-spot monitoring, and driver-assist steering.
- **Finance:** AI tools are being leveraged to detect and prevent fraudulent financial transactions, provide more accurate assessments than traditional credit scores can, and automate all sorts of data-related tasks that were handled manually. AI can also detect changes in transaction patterns and other potential red flags that can signify fraud, which humans can easily miss, and thus saving businesses and individuals from significant loss. Aside from fraud detection and task automation, AI can also better predict and assess loan risks. Whether it's personal finance, corporate finance, or consumer finance, the

highly evolved technology that is offered through AI can help to significantly improve a wide range of financial services.

- **Healthcare:** Applications have been developed with AI technology that has been trained to provide personalized medication care, including giving reminders about when patients need to take their medicine, suggestions for specific exercises they should perform to improve their recovery from injuries, informing emergency services in case of unforeseen change in health parameters of patients, and so on.

There is a tremendous amount of data that is and has been generated and logged in different medical centers. Unravelling the data that has been captured as an initiative of Big Data implementation has farfetched benefits not only for the patients, but to the medical science field who will have better insights, access to different kinds of medicines, and the treatments that have to be administered to the patients. The sharing of this data across Government agencies will help in nurturing healthier societies.

- **Life Sciences**: AI capabilities are being extensively applied to combine the historical data and medical Intelligence for the discovery of new drugs by reviewing complex data sets used in testing new medicines, thereby helping life science organizations get effective medicines to market faster. They are used to build sophisticated machines that can help analyze chronic conditions with lab and other medical data to ensure early diagnosis, help in quicker detection of diseases and even identify cancer cells.
- **Education:** Even in the education sector, which relies heavily on human interactions, AI has made strong inroads and helped increase productivity of faculty and helped them concentrate more on students than office or administration work. The Creation of smart content through digitization of content like video lectures, conferences, and text book guides using AI and integrating different interfaces like animations and graphics has revolutionized the education industry. Without even the direct involvement of the lecturer or the teacher, a student can access extra Learning material or assistance through Voice Assistants and get answers to common questions easily. Similarly, the delivery of customized Learning content to students with different requirements has been made possible by AI helping in creating a rich Learning experience. Hyper-personalization techniques can be used to monitor students'

performance data and specific lesson plans, reminders, study guides, flash notes, frequency of revision, etc. can be easily generated.

- **Human Resource Management:** Today companies are already using intelligent software to ease the hiring process, more so in blind hiring. Using Machine Learning software, recruiters can examine applications based on specific parameters, and scan candidates' profiles and resumes to get an understanding of the talent pool they must choose from.
- **Lifestyle Practices:** AI already has a lot of influence on an individual's lifestyle. Facial Recognition is used in devices like phones, laptops, and PCs that use facial recognition techniques to detect and identify in order to provide secure access. The email that we use in our day-to-day lives has AI that filters out spam emails sending them to spam or trash folders, letting us see the filtered content only. Various platforms like e-commerce, entertainment websites, social media, video sharing platforms, etc., all use the recommendation system to get user data and provide customized recommendations to users to increase engagement.
- **VR & Gaming:** The sector where AI applications have found prominence is the gaming sector. It is being used to create smart, human-like NPCs (Non-playing Characters) to interact with the players. It is helping designers predict human behavior with which game design and testing is improving day by day. AI is used extensively in gaming to keep the player engaged throughout the game following the player by location, activity and behaviours.
- **Agriculture:** AI is being used to identify defects and nutrient deficiencies in the soil using computer vision, robotics, and Machine Learning, It can also analyze where weeds are growing and AI enabled equipment can help in harvesting crops at a higher volume and faster pace than human labourers.
- **Social Media:** Instagram, Facebook, Twitter, or you name any social media depends heavily on AI and considering the likes and the accounts the users follow they determine what posts are shown to them. They also use AI to understand conversations and to translate posts from different languages automatically. Fraud detection, removing propaganda, and hateful content et al are done with the help of AI only.

- **Smart Homes:** The revolution of IIoT and IoT is bringing intelligent devices to homes and integrating the abstract or granular data. Essential services can be monitored by the users of these homes as well by the authorities that manage and provide them. This includes fire detection, temperature monitoring, security systems, social network support, power demand and supply management, etc.

The list of industries that are having real-world applications of AI systems today is increasing by the day. Security Services widely use facial recognition in high security-related areas in several industries for safety, security and surveillance. Customer service companies are using online virtual agents which are replacing human agents along the customer journey and answer frequently asked questions (FAQs) around topics, like shipping, or provide personalized advice, cross-selling products or suggesting sizes for users, changing the way we think about customer engagement across websites and social media platforms. Automated stock trading applications are designed to optimize stock portfolios. AI-driven high-frequency trading platforms are making thousands or even millions of trades per day without human intervention.

8.7. Technological Requirements of AI

AI, as a concept, is not new, but its widespread application and utility have skyrocketed in recent years thanks to considerable improvements in technology. The explosive growth of AI's scale and value is closely related to recent technological improvements in certain areas.

- **Larger and Accessible Data Sets**: AI thrives on data, and has grown in importance alongside the rapid increase of data, along with better access to data. Without the technology to gather, store, process, and manage huge amounts of data that components like IoT generated from connected devices, AI would have far fewer potential applications.
- **Graphical Processing Units**: GPUs are one of the key enablers of AI's rising value, as they are critical to providing AI systems with the power to perform millions of calculations needed for interactive processing. GPUs provide the computing power needed for AI to rapidly process and interpret big data. They also form the basis for computer vision that is one of the most visible aspects of AI.

- **Intelligent Data Processing**: New and more advanced algorithms allow AI systems to analyze data faster and at multiple levels simultaneously, helping those systems analyze datasets far faster so they can understand better and more quickly the complex systems and predict rare events.
- **Application Programming Interfaces**: APIs allow AI functions to be added to traditional computer programs and software applications, essentially making those systems and programs smarter by enhancing their ability to identify and understand patterns in data.

8.8. Roles and Jobs description in Artificial Intelligence

One area that makes application of AI a complex activity in an industry is the need for a large variety of expertise required for AI implementation. An overview of the roles and the job requirements in the field of AI are listed below.

- **Chief Data Officer:** The person who brings in the data unification, and the data – driven culture inside the organization is the most important catalyst for implementation of AI.
- **Big Data Architects:** These are the experts who decide with all the above teams on how to architect the big fast data solution to derive a meaningful common business insight. They would also decide on the engineering solution, tools and technologies that would be adopted for implementing unified modern data architecture.
- **Integration Architects:** They play a complementary and highly supportive role in building the framework where the data flow would be outbound from a source system to a persistence layer.
- **Data Engineers:** Specialized expertise is required to work with the Big Data Architects, and Data Scientists to create the pipelines, the APIs, interfaces that would expose the data freely in a structured format, so that the data is consumed for bringing those benefits.
- **Data Scientists:** These professionals along with the team of Data Analysts and Big Data Architects bring meaning to the identified data through statistical algorithms.
- **Data Analysts:** They are the "data discoverers" who identify the data and its worth by considering the insights provided.

8.9. Challenges in Artificial Intelligence (AI) Implementation

Implementation of AI poses a variety of challenges in terms of requirement of resources like data storage, processing capabilities, investment, network capabilities, technical expertise as well as user's confidence, acceptance of outcomes, and threat to human Intelligence. Privacy concerns and the ability to manage large AI projects surface as the main challenges within AI. The latter is driven in large part by the lack of AI talent within teams.

- **Lack of Transparency:** Some AI models can be referred to as "black-box" models because it can be unclear why or how a model is arriving at a given result. The ability to understand and interpret these results is important for us to create impartial decision-making systems as it allows us to identify and adjust for bias effectively.
- **Capacity to Handle Large Data Sets:** AI solutions and Deep Learning algorithms rely on large datasets for model training. The accuracy of the DL models and their ability to evaluate new data depends on the depth of the neural networks and the amount and quality of the training data. The rate at which DL datasets grow can be astounding. Individuals as well as organizations are incessantly generating data records in humongous amounts in the form of documents, images, videos, social messages, search queries, news and so on. It is estimated that there is a piling up of at least 2.5 quintillion bytes of data per day.

This 'Big Data' is touching every business and life on earth now. It holds the potential to increase the business efficiency, augment the customer experience and reduce the cost. The data storage and processing capacities require huge infrastructure and investment in hardware, network, computing power, and operations. As such, training datasets for DL models must be managed across multiple physical locations throughout their lifecycle, from ingestion to transformation, exploration, training, inference, and archiving. The DL model deployment consists of three stages through which the data travels: edge (data ingest), core (training clusters, data lake), and cloud (data archival). Benefits from a holistic architecture with data management that extends across these three environments enrich the DL process.

- **Data Democratization:** Researches reveal that 90% of the data in enterprises is never analyzed and used for creating useful business insights. The major reason for this is that this data resides in

Enterprise Data Warehouses which are siloed in nature. Many organizations that have this data don't have the right resources to analyze it and churn insights from it. Availability of this data is only to a certain set of people and mostly inaccessible to the larger audience, thereby limiting the possibilities of using AI for improved decision making.

The business world has been looking towards making data available for the right people at the right time so that it is consumed, analyzed and applied in the organization. This has brought in a new concept of Data Democratization that is called Open Data. Organizations that are ready to embark on the journey of Data Democratization need the support of the people, technology and processes guided by the right strategies and implementation plans.

- **Privacy Concerns:** The challenge of security and privacy is the core of Data Democratization and thus a major concern in AI implementation. Safeguards can help overcome many concerns around privacy, such as designing AI systems that prioritize consumers' privacy and rights as well as disclose the data being collected and how it will be accessed, used and stored. The CDO office and the IT teams need to work in tandem with the internal and external legal departments to understand the impact of sharing data that could be in the privacy zone. The policies, frameworks, and guidelines should be built along these lines so that appropriate tools and technologies are used to encrypt shared data which is sensitive in nature.
- **Lack of Data-Driven Work Culture:** In the world of data, there are organizations in each field that collect data extensively, analyze it, derive insights from it and use it for the potential gains including financial growth as well as increased efficiency and better decision making that would lead to the overall growth of the organization. Sharing of data at various stages would give power to users to view the data closely and also from different angles thus bringing greater benefits. Inculcating a 'Data–driven Culture' requires sharing the data owned or accessed by multiple functions in the organization. It is a cultural change at the organizational level, and impacts the existing business processes. It involves decentralization of data systems, creation of appropriate policies, procedures, and security systems.

- **Limitations on Data Processing Technology:** With concepts like Big Data and Open Data becoming a core for implementation of AI, the requirement of managing the data processing load and ensuring the AIC triad (Availability, Integrity, and Confidentiality) poses a nearly insurmountable challenge. In this area, Enterprise Data Lake is the core and future of the modern data warehouse architecture, which is complemented by the components of metadata management, master data management, data governance, and security across the layers.

The data lake is the layer that will be exposed to different users, groups of users inside the organization, outside the organization through a service layer. Data lake layer is supported by metadata management below, and above with a unified data architecture or view that cuts across domains, subject areas persistence thus exposing the concept of data federation or virtualization without knowing the fact of what lies underneath to share the type of data.

The unified data model will be consumed by enterprise service bus or API. The data consumed by different users will tap the potentiality of the API hub, and is the connecting path to the external world. The entire reference view is tied with the layer of security and the practice of DataOps to ensure that all data that gets in is processed, used, and shared.

8.10. Artificial Intelligence in the Indian Context

For India, AI presents the potential to address some of the biggest challenges that are currently faced: availability, affordability, and access to quality healthcare, education, agronomics, mobility solutions etc. Government's focus on digitalization and impressive strides under Digital India has enabled generation of large quantum of digital data. Its support to three basic aspects: computing power, data storage, and volume of digitized data, have led to AI-based applications taking center stage in presenting a radical new approach to solving business and governance use cases.

AI has the potential to raise India's annual growth rate by 1.3 percentage points as per the studies by Accenture. Recognising the potential of AI to help achieve the goal of India becoming a USD5 trillion economy, NITI Aayog was tasked to establish the National Program on AI, with the aim to guide the research and development of new and emerging technologies. Given the nascent stage of India's AI ecosystem, a dedicated cloud based computing infrastructure is needed to facilitate and speed up AI research and solution development.

One of the key recommendations of the committee is to set up an AI-specific cloud infrastructure to facilitate research and solution development in using high performance and high throughput AI-specific supercomputing technologies, nicknamed AIRAWAT (**AI R**esearch, **A**nalytics and knowledge **A**ssimilation pla**T**form). AIRAWAT is envisioned to be a leading-edge AI computing technology platform, thus enabling the key players to bring an AI revolution in the country - students, researchers, startups, corporate and government organizations.

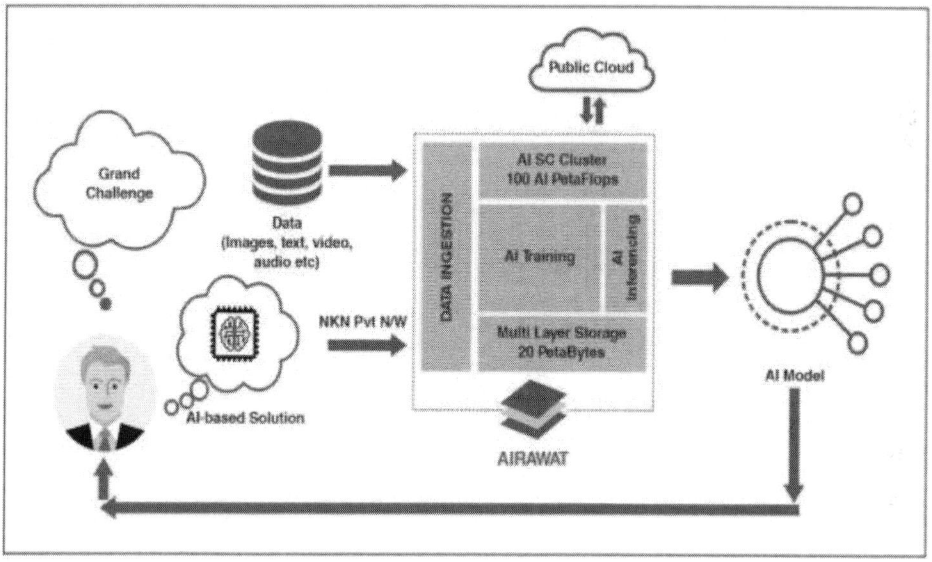

Figure 8.3: Proposed architecture of AIRAWAT.

8.11. Business Use Cases of AI

- **Accelerate Data Preparation and Improve Data Governance with AI:** Analysis using AI is only as good as the data that it uses, and as a result, many data scientists and analysts spend an exorbitant amount of time cleaning and organizing data to provide business value to their organizations. The raw data may not comply with the business taxonomy or there may not be a defined taxonomy for a new dataset and as a result, data may need to be classified in the given context or segmentation and clustering may be required. This can be a long, manual process for large datasets.

An approach for organizations is to use AI for data preparation. AI algorithms can assist in data classification tasks, reducing the cost and time to provide business insights. Labeled datasets can help categorize new data through supervised Learning algorithms, while unsupervised Learning can help businesses discover new clusters of data. Data management and classification has been identified as a key use case of AI. The results have been trusted analytical solutions that help reduce risk, detect fraud, assist commercial customers, and provide insights into consumers so organisations can better meet their needs.

- **Streamline Operational Efficiency with AI:** As a business expands in size, organisational complexity of IT function can also grow with new employees and processes. Over time, this can lead to operational inefficiencies, slowing IT response and eventually impacting businesses hindering their achievement of business goals. An approach for organizations can be to leverage log data from their information systems to understand performance of their processes, revealing bottlenecks and other areas of improvement. Specialized algorithms provide insight into the root causes of deviations from the process norm, which in turn arms managers with the information that they need to optimize them. The implementation is about bringing business efficiency by adopting a data democratization framework, stepping into the modern IT or data warehouse system where the above framework can be adopted yet again. The enterprise data hub consists of multiple operational data stores, a layer of data federation, and data virtualization. The data is consumed by IT teams and business users through collaborative tools hosted on cloud environments.
- **Forecasting Sales with AI:** Each year, business leaders are expected to set realistic goals for their organizations, setting the strategy for the upcoming year. Publicly traded companies also have the additional responsibility of sharing these future objectives during earning calls to maintain market confidence. However, in an ever-changing business landscape, it can be difficult to make commitments on sales goals with certainty, especially within large, complex organizations, where there are a variety of factors that can impact bottom-line sales numbers.

While sales forecasting isn't new to the business world, the factors that impact business sales have changed exponentially over the last decade, and they'll continue to do so. In firms, AI solutions allow data teams to adapt to changing circumstances, enabling them to make sales predictions with confidence.

- **Deep Learning for Identifying Important Motifs in DNA Sequences**: The analysis of gene structure is an important task in bioinformatics. The sequential nature of genomic data as well as the common syntactical structure between natural language and genetic code makes it suitable for NLP techniques to be applied to the genomics domain. The structure of the human genome was explored by training neural network architectures to distinguish between DNA sequences containing different types of genomic elements (intron, exons, splice junctions), as well as to predict the exact positions of splice junctions in DNA sequences. Subsequently, identification of important sequence motifs that code for exon location in the DNA sequences was done.

Deep Learning architectures like Convolutional Neural Networks and Long Short-Term Memory Networks were used, and DeepDeCode, an attention-based Deep Learning model was introduced to perform the tasks. Various intrinsic and extrinsic visualization techniques were used to infer biologically relevant information learnt by these models. These models successfully perform these tasks, while also attending to biologically plausible regions of the input while making the predictions. Given the results of the , it is expected that it can be extended to the discovery of splice sites that were not previously located through wet-lab methods as well as structural patterns of other subtle genomic elements.

8.12. Business Use Cases of Artificial Intelligence in the Indian Context

- **iSarthik (AI-Based Digital Learning Platform):** An AI-based digital Learning platform iSarthik, developed by Vitti, targets personalized tutoring using AI. It has some unique features which make it unique from the other Learning platforms. It just doesn't update the user in terms of knowledge but also it makes them job ready and helps them find job matching with their skill-sets. The digital learning platform helps reinforce learning and bring automation in analytics to enhance effectiveness. It brings consumer-preferred learning programs and uses AI to improve the completion rate. Furthermore, it provides AI-based digital tutors, making training accessible to a wide group of people, including differently-abled consumers.

- **AI in Industry: Steel Plant Deployment:** One of the key players in the field, Vitti AI has some key deployment in steel plants in process digitization, GPS monitoring of vehicles, temperature & vibration monitoring, and gas leakage alerts among others. The digitization process covers real time status updates on the production line and integrates with local ERP developed and customized as per plant requirements.

In terms of production process application, the AI-based system helps measure the actual heating temperature of all billet materials before hot forging, and can be used for steel-sheet width management during rolling, and for managing the roll chucking position of a slitter. It has the capability to track and control critical parameters of devices with moving parts like motors and fans, and can also assist with scrap management.

In terms of work process digitization, the AI-based system helps with assigning and monitoring worker tasks; it can monitor in real time workers' adherence to safety regulations (e.g., if they are wearing a safety wristband & helmet during working hours). Furthermore, the system helps with asset tracking in the production process and beyond it, and helps optimize resources to achieve production and business goals

- **Implementation of Remote Assist in Industry:** Remote Assist empowers vendors to collaborate more efficiently with the company by working together from different locations. Accessible via the AR Device, the field technicians can share their real-time view with the experts in remote locations to get the help they need and troubleshoot the problem faster. This is especially useful for new field technicians who may need assistance from their more experienced counterparts. The expert can virtually 'walk the site' with the technician, saving time and money by getting the job done right the first time.

Another benefit of Remote Assist is the ability to lower costs with remote inspections by combining video, screenshots, and annotations needed to ensure key safety protocols. It provides services like Group calls, thus enabling technicians to get inputs from multiple experts in one single session. In the context of extreme events like the pandemic, Remote Assist allows for social distancing, keeping your at-home experts safe yet virtually available for onsite needs and site visits.

- **Augmented Reality (AR)-based Training/Performance Support Tool:** Traditional training, testing and qualification methods of employees on the SOPs greatly inflate training time resulting in long training timelines, scheduling issues, and increased production cycle times, which impacts the productivity in any assembly line negatively. In contrast, the Augmented Reality (AR)-based training/performance support tool has been implemented at a Pharma Manufacturing Division with an objective to cut down training time and simultaneously accelerate the time to competency in operators to achieve desired business outcomes. The AR tool is designed to help new hires and less experienced operators working in high-speed pharmaceutical packaging lines to quickly up-skill on the standard operating procedure (SOP) of the splicing process of the machine.

The tool helps provide operators with the essential knowledge of the splicing process and enables real-time performance support to help execute the tasks of the splicing process at the job site. It reduces the time it takes a new operator with limited experience to do the reel change in the splicing by just 2 minutes (from current 12 minutes to 10 minutes). The tool also helps reduce the downtime of the equipment and can help in producing more packs per week to ensure more product reaches patients. Lastly, the tool can be used to train operators in better ways to ensure a faster supply of products to customers.

NOTES

Chapter 9

INDUSTRIAL ROBOTICS & INFORMATICS

9.1. Introduction

The relentless drive to operate more efficiently and sustainably has been pushing organisations to find innovative solutions to economic and environmental challenges. The increasing pressure from shrinking margins, global competition, and scrutiny of green certifications require more than just an incremental change in how industries work. However, continuing to drive operational efficiencies through traditional cost-cutting measures now provides only marginal gains.

Industry 4.0 is about the significant transformation taking place in the way goods are produced and delivered – moving toward industrial automation and the flexible factory. The industry needs an end-to-end transformation that improves performance at every stage of the value chain opening up huge opportunities in every aspect of business. To stay competitive, factories, warehouses, and industries as a whole have started leveraging digitalization, internet, and smart machines to become much more agile and efficient.

Industry 4.0 has been defined as a name for the current trend of automation and data exchange in manufacturing technologies, including cyber-physical systems, the Internet of Things (IoT), cloud computing, and cognitive computing with AI creating smart factories. It uses advanced robotics to increase productivity by taking over manual tasks and accomplishing them faster, which is known as the factory of the future. The flexible assembly line is one example where the assembling programme can accommodate variations in product specifications without requiring change in infrastructure. With real time data coming from the field, manufacturers, rather than becoming entirely computerised, are using advanced technologies to make man and machine reconcile and find ways to work together to improve the means and efficiency of production.

Industry 4.0 is characterised by smart machines, storage systems and production facilities that are capable of autonomously exchange information, trigger actions, and control each other without human intervention. It emphasises the transformation of factories into IoT-enabled smart facilities that utilise cognitive computing and interconnect via cloud servers.

In Industry 4.0, robotics is being used in many aspects of manufacturing to help increase productivity and efficiency while lowering production costs. Robots have been effectively being used in the healthcare industry, space technology industry, defence and security, as well as the hospitality industry for quite some time. Now, many robots in manufacturing collaborate with workers to perform repetitive, monotonous, or intricate tasks under the worker's guidance and control. The growth in the field of robotics has been quite stupendous in the recent past and it can be said that the robotics technology was one of the most significant drivers behind the start of the fourth industrial revolution, or Industry 4.0.

9.2. Industry 4.0 and Robotics 4.0: The Mutual Interdependence

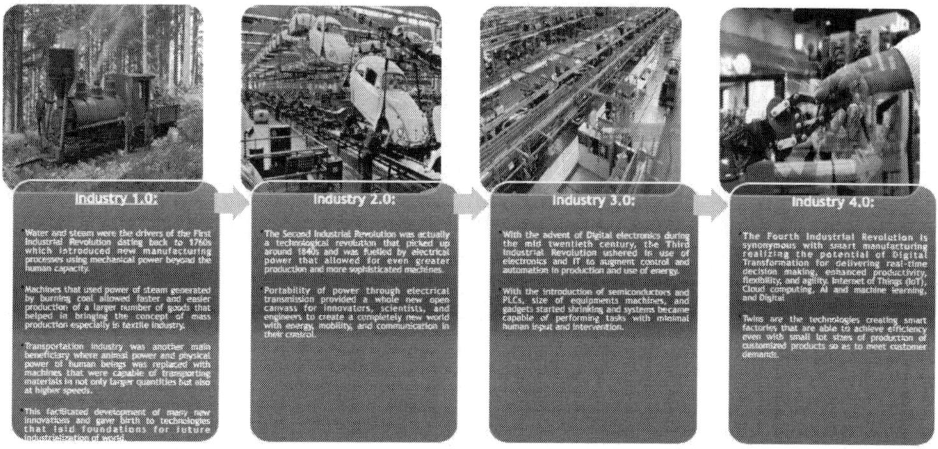

Figure 9.1: Industry 1.0 to 4.0: A Historical Timeline

The Digital Transformation of Industry 4.0 has made it possible to interconnect machines, processes and systems for maximum performance optimization. Given the efficiencies that are being achieved, the world is well past the point of going back, because now adopting the old way of doing things in industry would be like using typewriters in place of computers with word processing software. Industry is now moving towards a stage of people working alongside robots and smart machines. It would add a personal human touch to the pillars of automation and efficiency by allowing customers to customise the products at one end and return of human hands and minds into the industrial framework at the other.

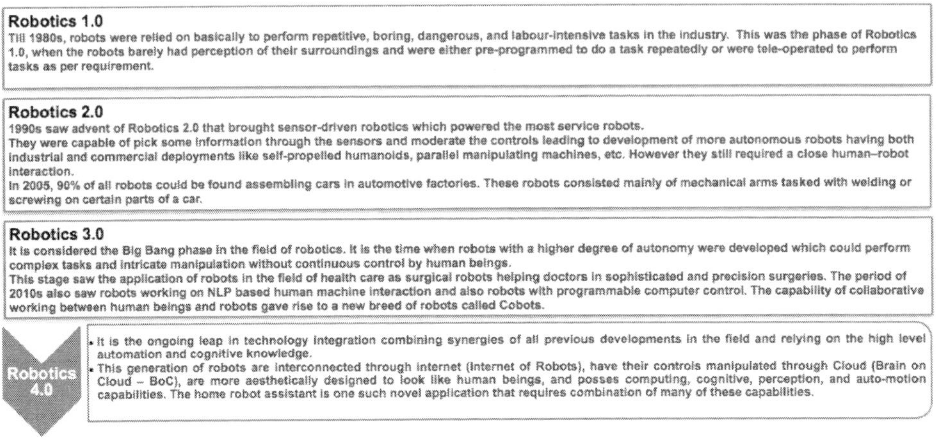

Figure 9.2: Robotics 1.0 to 4.0: A Historical Timeline

The robotics industry is expected to grow significantly over the coming years. Estimates suggest that the sector could be worth as much as $260 billion by 2030. Much of this growth will come from professional services robots that perform useful tasks for humans, such as cleaning, delivering, and transporting.

9.3. Robots: A Broad Categorisation

From 'RoboBee', a mere 0.2 millimetre-long robot that mimics a bee, to a 200 metre-long robotic shipping vessel *'Vindskip,'* robots are emerging in all shapes and sizes to efficiently carry out tasks for which they are designed. They all vary in design, functionality and degree of autonomy and carry out tasks that humans simply can't. They can be broadly categorised under five types:

- **Pre-Programmed Robots:** These are the simplest robots which operate in a controlled environment where they do simple, single function tasks, like a mechanical arm on an automotive assembly line that would weld a door on or insert a certain part into the engine, etc. Its job is to perform that task longer, faster and more efficiently than human beings.

- **Humanoid Robots:** These robots are designed to look like human beings and / or mimic their activities like running, jumping and carrying objects. Two of such humanoid robots are Sophia and Atlas.
- **Teleoperated Robots:** These semi-autonomous bots that are controlled by human beings from a safe distance through wireless networks. They usually work in extreme geographical conditions, dangerous circumstances, and difficult to approach locations etc. The submarines used to fix underwater pipe leaks during the oil spills, drones used to detect landmines in a battlefield, robotic bomb diffusers are some of their applications.
- **Autonomous Robots:** These robots are designed to carry out tasks in open environments and do not require human supervision. They work independently using sensors to perceive the world around them, and then take the optimal next step based on the data and mission using a computer for decision-making. They are widely used in Cleaning, Lawn Trimming, Hospitality, Drones, and the Medical field.
- **Augmenting Robots:** They are the newest form of robots that are making humans faster and stronger by either enhancing current human capabilities or replacing some lost capabilities of a human being. Robotic prosthetic limbs to help physically challenged persons, and exoskeletons used to lift hefty weights are examples of their application.

9.3.1. Industrial Robots and Non-industrial Robots: Application of robotics can be seen today in all aspects of life. However, there are certain characteristics that differentiate between them in their two major areas of operation.

- **Industrial Robotics:** Industrial Robots are usually not humanoid in shape, but are capable of reproducing human movements and behaviours with the strength, precision and speed of a machine. Their application is mainly in:
- Manufacturing – Automobiles, Electronics, maintenance, dangerous goods.
- Logistics – packaging, shipping, material handling, warehousing.
- Food Industry

- Agriculture
- Medical

The numerous benefits of the use of robotics in industry include not just improved productivity and safety of workers but also cost savings in the long run. This may be surprising, since smaller manufacturing businesses may assume that purchasing robotics is an expensive investment.

However, the first and probably the most obvious way that robots reduce manufacturing costs is that they do not require compensation. They can work 24/7 without interruption, if needed; they do not require lights all around reducing energy usage, and are precise in accomplishing repeatable tasks reducing the time spent correcting errors. They are able to produce high-quality products with little variation and greater consistency than their human counterparts. Once correctly programmed and trained to do a certain job, robotic workers do not need to take breaks, there are no shift changes, and can speed up production by decreasing part cycle times.

- **Non-industrial Robotics:** Also known as Service Robots, they are used outside industrial set-up like in areas such as education, travel, hospitality, healthcare, homes, offices, entertainment etc. They are more aesthetically designed to look like human beings and have capabilities for more efficient human interactions.

9.4. Robotics vs. Automation

In the industrial set-up, automation and robotics together have transformed the manufacturing space. Although these are two distinct technologies, the two terms are often used interchangeably.

Robotics is a field that combines engineering, computer science, and other applied sciences to design and build robots to perform tasks and work in place of human beings. Robots can be programmed and can be fully autonomous and automatic. However, not all robots rely on automation technology.

Automation is the process that uses software, machines, or other technology to carry out tasks without human intervention. It is applied to both virtual tasks and physical ones and can be used for simple functions, such as programmable thermostats to extremely complex processes in manufacturing.

- **Industrial automation** uses machines to control physical processes like CNC machines, automated inspection equipment, self-actuating equipments etc. Industrial automation faces limitations that the machines generally serve only one primary purpose. Creating machinery that can perform multiple purposes is what robotics and automation can do when they work together.
- **Software automation** uses a computer program to carry out repetitive tasks in a virtual environment like Chatbots that reply to texts or auto-fill forms or carry out scheduled computing operations.
- **Robotic Process Automation (RPA)** is a software technology that makes it easy to build, deploy, and manage software robots that emulate human actions interacting with digital systems and software. It allows the robot to interact with the user interface the same way a human worker would. Some RPA tools are enhanced with machine learning or AI to help them perform rule-based tasks more efficiently.

A well-implemented RPA can improve employee workflows and allow them to focus on high-value tasks. It can streamline various business tasks through help desk support with Chatbots, efficient meeting scheduling, or offering analytics on employee performance. The accrued benefits are in terms of the following:

- **Free up employee time,** by taking over tedious work so that people can focus their energy elsewhere.
- **Reduce costs,** by performing repetitive tasks continuously saving money on workforce.
- **Easy tracking,** by using much simpler analytics than required for human workers.
- **Improved governance**. due to strict adherence to protocols and flagging of activities that fall outside the scope.
- **Easily scalable**, by duplication and reprogramming for other purposes.
- **Better security**, as bots can't create security issues that human users possibly can.

Unfortunately, the process of automation in robotics is often disjointed because it is difficult to connect multiple systems without the right programming software. The main challenge is integrating the existing IT function and Robotic Process Automation.

RPA and AI can work together through intelligent bots, for example, the RPA tool "Automation Anywhere" allows bots to self-learn through the "IQ Bot". By integrating traditional RPA techniques with AI, the bot can perform tasks such as recognising unstructured data, learning from human feedback and many others.

It has been said that in Industry 4.0 '*the proliferation of robotic automation is inevitable.*' Robotic Automation is a key part of industries of the future that are adopting IIoT on a large scale. Some of the areas where it is being applied:

- Arc welding
- Spot welding
- Material Handling
- Manufacturing Line Automation
- Jigs & Fixtures –Development
- Welding SPM's
- Engineering Services
- IOT & Industry 4.0 Solutions

9.5. Role of Digital Twin in Industry 4.0

Industry 4.0 involves harnessing technology to automate industry and manufacturing. An important concept in Industry 4.0 is the digital twin, which lets the building of digital models of assets, processes, or products. While the concept of a Digital Twin has been around for more than two decades, it's only after the arrival of Internet of Things (IoT) that it has become cost-effective to implement. A digital twin is a dynamic, virtual representation of a corresponding physical product, process, or system. This technology has also been described by other terms like virtual prototyping, hybrid twin technology, virtual twin, and digital asset management.

The life of a digital twin starts with its creation by specialists, often experts in data science or applied mathematics, who research the underlying technology and critical factors of the physical object or system being mimicked. This information is used to develop a mathematical model that simulates the real-world original in a digital space. The twin could also be designed based on a prototype of its physical counterpart, in which case the twin can provide feedback to help refine the product. A twin could even serve as a prototype itself before any physical version is built.

After being tested in isolation, the digital twin is connected to the real-world counterpart so that the twin can receive input from sensors gathering data from the original. This allows the twin to simulate the physical object in real time offering insights into performance and potential problems of the physical entity.

In the age of Industry 4.0, digital twins help bridge the gap between the physical and digital worlds and serve as a powerful connection to the product for diagnostics and design changes. Companies are increasingly using digital twins to optimise their products in ways that were previously either unrealistic or impossible.

Companies use digital twin technology for many reasons including to improve ongoing operations, train employees, and to test new products or procedures before launching them to the real world where it becomes more expensive and complicated to fix any issues after production. Often AI and machine learning are used to analyse the model and operations represented by the digital twin of a remotely located real facility.

9.5.1. Benefits of Digital Twins

Digital twins offer a real-time look at what's happening with physical assets, and it can radically alleviate operational, quality, and maintenance burdens. In manufacturing engineering, changes to production are often tested on real systems, but this testing means that you must halt ongoing production. If errors occur, they must be eliminated before restarting production with the changed configuration. These downtimes are expensive and significantly decrease the flexibility of production.

Originally, the digital twin was conceived to virtualize expensive tests in the aerospace industry. Today, the automotive industry, among others, also uses digital twins to reduce development costs through virtual testing. The digital twin concept is mostly firmly established in the field of automation technology. The digital shadow of a product stores not only the current state, but also the history of production.

Digital twins are also useful in realising digital images of production processes and manufacturing equipment. Collecting and providing data makes it possible to identify optimization potential and to use predictive maintenance to avoid unplanned downtime. Some of their benefits include;

- Testing new systems prior to manufacture
- Improving efficiency and productivity

- Managing assets in real time
- Understanding data to provide better service

9.5.2. Data Management and Storage for Digital Twins

We have seen that Industry 4.0, the Fourth Industrial Revolution involves harnessing technology to automate industry and manufacturing using Digital Twin, which helps to build digital models of Industry assets, processes, or products. Virtual commissioning of production lines and manufacturing plants is also becoming more important. In this process, the team checks the software configurations and modifications on a plant's digital twins before the company applies them to the real plant. Digital Twins shadow work just like a Sandbox of the IT system. The whole process is extremely data intensive and an enormous amount of data gets generated that needs to be captured, stored, analysed, and used effectively.

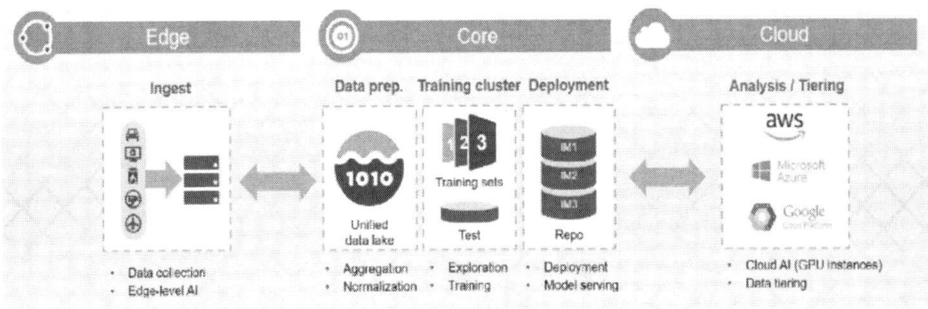

Figure 9.3: Digital Twins Data Management & Storage: A Pictorial Overview

The benefits of the cloud can be leveraged to use GPU instances for computation, and the team can use cloud for cold storage and for archives and backups. In many AI/DL applications, the data might span across the edge and/or the core and/or the cloud. As a result, the team must orchestrate data across these environments.

Depending on the scale of the AI/DL workflows and the criticality of an organisation's AI/DL strategy, the team should evaluate performance and TCO (Total Cost of Ownership) requirements before determining infrastructure deployment options (Cloud-only, On-premises-only, or Hybrid architectures).

9.5.3. Security Challenges with Digital Twins

Digital twins are generally based in the cloud, hence the associated security risks are somewhat lower than with other types of systems. However, the massive amount of data being collected and utilised is drawn from numerous endpoints, each of which represents a potential area of weakness. Every time a new connection is made and more data flows between devices and the cloud, the potential risk for compromise increases. When vulnerabilities are exploited, it forces companies to manage the security crisis on fire-fighting mode leading to the loss of time and profits. Thus businesses considering digital twin technology must assess and update their security protocols and ensure data encryption, controlled access privileges, clear definition of user roles, addressing known device vulnerabilities, and conduct regular security audits

9.6. Virtual Reality and Augmented Reality in Industry 4.0

In order to build exact virtual simulations of products, processes or production plants so as to see their operation in first person and in an immersive way, the industry today is using Virtual Reality technology. Virtual reality and its variations are being used for creating Digital Twins during the design phase, validation of prototypes, and training for operations as engineers can check and present the progress made in a more visual and interactive way through a virtual simulation.

The technology in this field has progressed manifold by incorporating added features for bringing the virtual twin as close to the real entity as possible.

- Virtual reality (VR) presents a complete immersive experience in which the physical world is shut out and the user is virtually transported into an imaginary environment where his senses perceive and believe what is being presented to them.
- Augmented reality (AR) places a layer of imaginary environment over a live view of the real entities by adding digital elements. It gives a new immersive experience that has the real world as the canvas and the imaginary world as the paint creating a completely new picture.
- **Mixed Reality (MR)** is a combination of both AR and VR in which the real-world and digital objects can interact and influence each other on real-time basis. Though nascent as yet, MR promises to be the technology that will impact the industry extensively.

- Extended Reality (XR) is an umbrella term that covers all of the three technologies helping in enhancing the senses, providing additional information, and creating simulated worlds for people to have immersive experience of the real and virtual worlds.

The application of virtual reality in Industry 4.0 has a different orientation due to the level of immersion it provides to the user. It enables training in complex or dangerous tasks before having to perform them in the real situation, avoiding any associated risk and obtaining cost savings for companies. In addition, due to the level of immersion it offers, virtual reality maximises the assimilation of knowledge, optimises the learning process and provides personalised and autonomous training for each user.

While the initial application of VR and AR was in the military and gaming industry, the technology has now reached the industry in a big way.

- **Design and Construction:** Probably the most common industrial application for AR today helps designers see what hypothetical products (or structures) would look like in real environments and make virtual modifications to existing products without actually touching them.
- **Maintenance and Repairs:** This technology helps technicians by guiding them through steps of repairing, upgrading, and maintaining products, industrial equipment, even entire buildings.
- **Training and Education:** HR departments and institutions are using AR technology to provide immersive experience during training employees, allowing them to comprehensively visualise products, processes, and concepts.
- **Healthcare & Surgery**: Surgery rooms, ICUs, and wards are the new destinations where AR technology has revolutionised the services by supporting critical steps of an operation, providing interactive nursing care, and continuous monitoring of a patient's vital parameters.
- **Retail & ecommerce:** Businesses are using AR to give retail shoppers a personalised dynamic experience of using the product before buying, viz. virtual makeup, virtual changing rooms, virtual product display like seeing how a piece of furniture will look and fit in a particular space.

- **Technology & Innovation**: Companies are able to improve responses to the breakdowns by having full visibility into the affected area and connected areas affected by the outage.
- **Marketing & Sales:** AR is being used by businesses to create memorable ways for customer interactions through new concepts in packaging, point-of-sale experience, billboards, and much more.
- **Navigation & Routing:** Enhanced navigation systems use augmented reality to superimpose a route over the live view of the road.

9.6.1. Example Business Cases of Augmented Reality (AR)-based Projects

- **Xerox** used AR to connect field engineers with experts instead of providing service manuals and telephone support. Rate of first-time fix of equipment increased by 67%, and the engineers' efficiency jumped by 20%. Meanwhile, the average time it took to resolve problems dropped by two hours, so staffing needs fell. Now Xerox is using AR to connect remote technical experts directly with customers. This has increased by 76% the rate at which technical problems are resolved by customers without any on-site help, cutting travel costs for Xerox and minimising downtime for customers. Perhaps not surprisingly, Xerox has seen its customer satisfaction rates rise to 95%.
- **Lee Company** (construction-management) saves more than $500 per technician per month in labour and travel costs. The company calculates a return of $20 on every dollar invested in AR.
- **KPN**, a European telecommunications service provider, field engineers conducting remote or on-site repairs use AR smart glasses to see a product's service-history data, diagnostics, and location-based information dashboards. These AR displays help them make better decisions about how to resolve issues, producing an 11% reduction in overall costs for service teams, a 17% decrease in work-error rates, and higher repair quality.

9.7. Future of Maintenance in Industry 4.0

Industry 4.0 is ushering in new and emerging technologies, redefined workspaces between people and machines, and as such, it is imperative that the maintenance activities keep pace. A concept of Maintenance 4.0 aligned with the global movement towards a fully digitally integrated world is emerging which is poised to revolutionise maintenance operations around the complex equipment. Maintenance 4.0 would mean application of machine learning, automated processes and robotics / drones to reliability and maintenance activities. Each stage of the repair process is depicted in an AR environment bringing in a scenario where unscheduled downtime is replaced by scheduled downtime. The key to this latest generation of maintenance management is that machine learning is used to detect when an asset is likely to fail, and plant maintenance experts receive an automated alert. Based on this alert, work orders are initiated, spare parts and tools requisition are raised, and other resource allocations with protocols are generated automatically. During the repairs, robotics, drones, and digital twins are used to replace or augment manual human efforts.

The arrival of Maintenance 4.0 on the horizon signals near real-time monitoring of assets in all the critical as well as semi-critical areas with alerts being triggered using real-time data and predictive analytics. The whole gamut of maintenance management and its integration with other departments like operations, materials management, finance, logistics etc is getting integrated with machine learning bringing improvement in the level of inherent expertise of the system with successive iterations of maintenance activity.

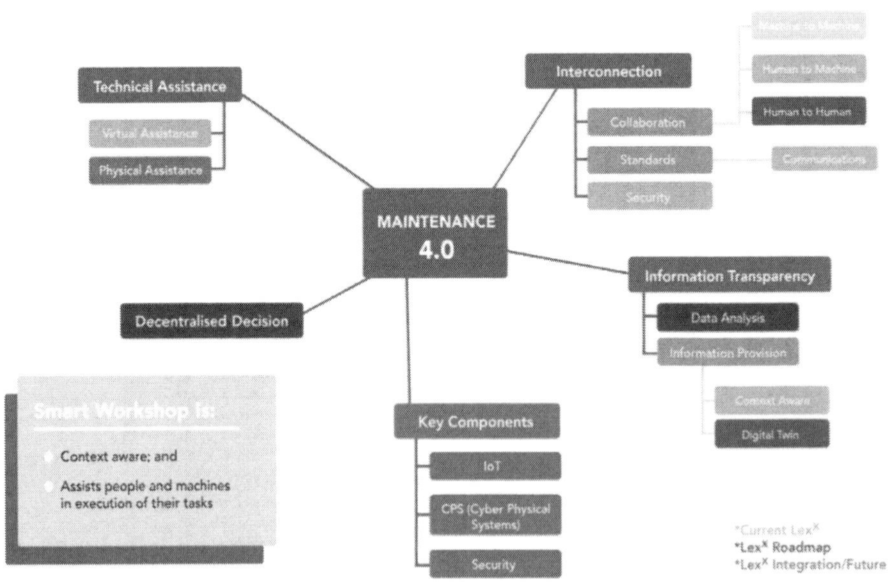

Figure 9.4: Maintenance 4.0: A Pictorial Overview

9.8. Use cases of Digital Transformation in Industry 4.0

9.8.1. Supply Chain Management

9.8.1.1. 'Stock*Wise*' is a SaaS product which is a real time analytics app that accurately predicts what, when, and how much stock in inventory should be reduced or replenished, in order to increase sales, maximise profit, minimise slow or dead stock and eliminate stock outs as well as optimise working capital needs. It uses the SAP-HANA Engine to tackle the scale, complexity and frequency of computation associated with supply chain volatility. It is hosted on Google Cloud Platform and APIs can integrate with other ERP's as well.

Following are the reported Business Benefits of this DT project:

- **Increased Sales:** Everyday demand predictions at each location/SKU results in higher availability and sales including eliminating stock-outs.
- **Higher Profits**: Higher sales result from optimum higher availability maximises profits.
- **Reduced Costs:** Determination of slow or dead stock thereby reducing inventory write off costs.
- **Optimised Working Capital**: By eliminating non-productive expenditure and resource stagnation through supply chain visibility on availability, stock-out, overstock etc drives reductions in investment in Inventory

9.8.1.2. SPAR, the online hypermarket, needed a comprehensive and robust solution which would increase availability of stock at store-SKU level, identify potential sales loss due to stock-outs, and improve working capital utilisation. Robotics has been implemented at SPAR, the online hypermarket, to increase availability of stock at store-SKU level, identify potential sales loss due to stock-outs, and improve working capital utilisation. It provided the customer with store level / SKU level suggestions for order placement on a daily basis, identification of excess inventory, and inter-store stock shuffling recommendations based on sales. Within six months of deploying the solution, the distributor was able to get an increase in its operating margins by increasing the sale, margins, and profitability without any increase in working capital.

9.8.1.3. 'DutyRota' is a SaaS based scheduling software that assigns the right number of staff according to process and compliance requirements, managing operational challenges of sudden absence and volatility of load, avoiding unnecessary overtime duty. Its application has led to cost saving, improving employee satisfaction and quality of service through equitable distributions of work.

At one of the hospitals of a large medical corporation, it has provided skill based auto-generated schedule saving cost, reduced demand for addressing personal requirements, and alleviating nursing stress on staff. At one end it has given saving in the time required for scheduling, it has given the flexibility of managing schedule anytime, from anywhere with a simple web-based mobile application enhancing productivity of staff. It's easy integration with Biometrics, HR, and HIS systems has ensured equitable distribution of workload, leaves, performance and other analytics on a dashboard for administrative decision making.

9.8.2. Environmental Management

Vitti, an innovation driven DT solutions provider has come out with a robot DUDI to provide a cognitive AI based robotic solution for better solid waste management in water bodies to reduce water pollution as pilot initiative. This project involves design and development of a small autonomous robotic device along with an AI based command & control cloud platform. The prototype is already under testing for conducting a comprehensive pilot to prove the efficacy of the Project.

To provide an overview, Dudi is a hermetically sealed Amphibious Robotic Implementation capable of working underwater for long periods, which is operated through an AI Platform Cloud infrastructure that makes it learn while in operation and improve future actions. Data security in Dudi is ensured through encryption. It has Computer Vision with 4K camera, LIDAR, and Forward-Looking Sonar (FLS) and is connected to devices over 4G/5G.

The robot is a GPS enabled location aware device and it can do systematic mapping of water bodies as well as create its own swim plan. Being an auto navigation robotic system it can do auto docking. It is built with solar charging, making it power independent with wireless charging for contingency. Furthermore, being a 3D-printing enabled bio-mimicked design makes it aesthetically attractive and kinetically efficient. The Dudi robot has been built in three variants – Placid water, Flowing water, and Coastal Sea areas water.

Sensor based water condition reporting is done in terms of micro-pollutants, chemical pollutants, oxygen solubility etc. Cloud based reporting, data collation, and water management analytics makes Dudi a useful implementation for agencies managing water bodies.

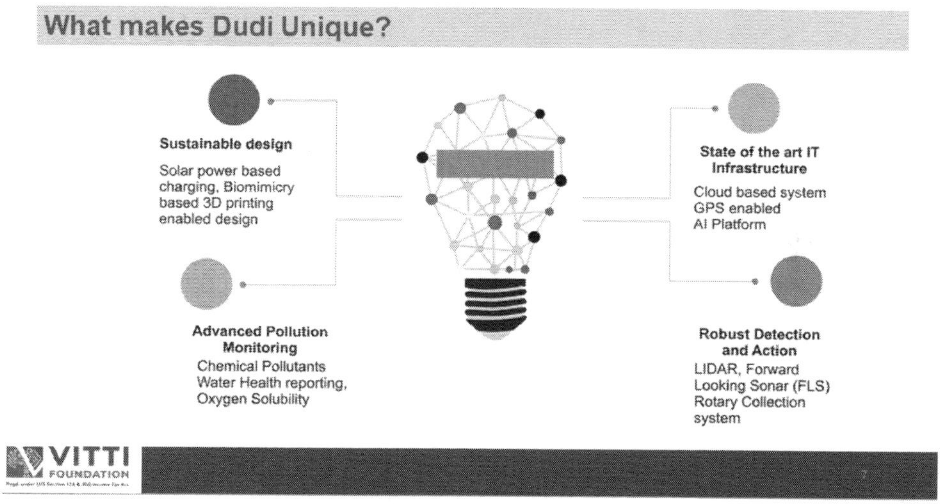

Figure 9.5: Dudi: An Overview

9.8.3. Maintenance Management

A global company in Power Generation has got a Proof of Value conducted for using AI based Maintenance Platform. The site comprises two 700MW coal-fired steam turbine generators fulfilling the energy needs of 1.18 million homes every year. The proposed maintenance management system would bring improvement of availability/up time of power generation using artificial intelligence and machine learning capability. The process includes ingestion of all organisational data, such as equipment manuals, maintenance logs, and work orders. It has realised improvement of up time & business continuity in terms of greater "on-tool" time, enhanced job satisfaction, and brought improvement in knowledge retention to develop a proper growth environment.

Another Proof of Value project has been completed for the AI, ML & NLP based Platform to reduce mean time of repair at a leading airlines company. The trials were conducted for Proof of Value (PoV) to solve the issue of traditional maintenance, repair and operations inefficiencies by enhancing data acceptability and instantaneous availability by applying Intelligent Assistant and Natural Language Processing. This would help engineers to troubleshoot in a conversational manner at the point of fault generation.

Chapter 10

SOFTWARE PROJECT MANAGEMENT

10.1. Introduction

Digital transformation projects are generally considered to be high stake exercises; they reflect the ambition and potential of organisations, as well the willingness and promise to deliver high quality outcomes. For individuals involved in such projects, the interest comes from the challenges and opportunities associated with DT exercises. Everyone loves to see a successful digital project launch that gets great feedback and has encouraging levels of adoption with satisfied clients, delighted customers, and happy project teams. And just like any other project, a software project is a temporary endeavour undertaken to create a unique product, service or result.

However, digital transformation exercises are not a onetime project, but are about continual change and evolvement. It does involve a onetime implementation, but the process is much longer: it requires careful consideration and preparation prior to the project start, as well as continuous follow-up engagements after the implementation of the starting architecture. The kind of research and scoping done, and the questions asked before taking up DT process can make all the difference to the success of the project. Similarly, the intensity of post-implementation follow-up would decide on the worthiness of the whole process.

However, unlike most of the technological projects, digital transformation exercises don't come with an owners' manual that "explains" or "shows" the procedure easily; this could be attributed as the reason as to why enterprises face unique (and significant!) challenges in the process of DT implementation. The challenges can come in different hues - from micro-challenges (e.g., taking too much time to implement change, not delivering satisfactory results, or spending too much to implement the initiative) to grander ones like (e.g., project dying on the vine before it gets implemented, desired changes impacting the business negatively, or key customers and employees defecting because of the changes).

However, well executed digital transformation cases prove that successful DT implementation exercises are achievable and are worth the effort. Often organisations believe that purchasing a software package is all that is necessary; however in reality, it is just the beginning. It is just half of the solution, and organisations need to be prepared to invest in this change, the time and commitment from their staff. A good Project Management Process is the key in this transformation journey.

10.2. Software Project Management: A Process Overview[2]

A software is an inherently intangible product because it is not present in a physical form to be seen, measured, and manipulated. Moreover, software development is a new stream in world business, and the experience in creating and consuming software products is still quite nascent. In the software industry, a unique factor is the underlying technology changes and advances that are so frequent and rapid that the experience of one project might not be applicable to another one. Such business and environmental constraints bring risk in software development, and as such, it is essential to manage software projects efficiently.

Also, due to the unique nature of the industry most software products are tailor made to fit client's requirements. Thus, a software project is a loosely defined task, which is a collection of several operations done in order to achieve some goals in terms of software development, delivery, and maintenance. It involves the complete procedure of software development - from requirement gathering to testing and maintenance, carried out according to the execution methodologies, in a specified period of time, to achieve the intended software product.

[2]Temporary means a defined start and end date.

For a software project, time, cost, and quality are the triple constraints that keep the process under control with very little degree of freedom as in a triangle. It is an essential part of a software organisation to deliver quality products, keeping the cost within budget constraints, and deliver the project as per schedule. There are several factors, both internal and external, which may impact this triple constraint triangle. Any one of three factors can severely impact the other two. Therefore, software project management is essential to incorporate user requirements along with budget and time constraints.

A typical job pattern of any IT initiative in a company can be split in two parts:

- Software Creation
- Software Project Management

The whole process of software development goes through a well defined life cycle called SDLC – Software Development Life Cycle. It is a structured sequence of stages in software engineering to develop the intended software product. These stages are steps to be followed to design and develop a software product efficiently.

10.2.1. SDLC – Software Development Life Cycle

A typical Product Life Cycle (PLC) starts with the conception of the product and goes until its withdrawal from the market or when it becomes obsolete. A product can require or spawn many projects over its life. For example, a project during the product conception phase could be "Determine customers need", while another project during product maturity phase could be "Do Competitor analysis".

However, the Software Development Life Cycle (SDLC) focuses broadly on requirement analysis, planning, design, and implementation of the software. The framework of SDLC, as such, involves the following steps:

- Communication
- Requirement Gathering
- Feasibility study
- System Analysis
- Software Design
- Coding

- Testing
- Integration
- Implementation
- Operation & Maintenance
- Post implementation Support and Disposition

10.3. Software Management Process: A Phase Overview

Project management of software development, enhancements, and rollout of IT projects allow companies to become competitive in their environments, optimising time and effort and keeping projects on track. It comprises a number of activities, which include planning of project, deciding scope of software product, estimation of cost in various terms, scheduling of tasks and events, and resource management. These activities can be grouped under four broad categories.

1. **Project Planning**
2. **Project Execution and Monitoring**
3. **Risk Management**
4. **Configuration Management**

10.3.1. Project Planning Phase

Development of the project management plan is the process of documenting the actions necessary to define, prepare, integrate and coordinate all the subsidiary plans. It also contains the performance measurement baseline. Examples of subsidiary plans include Cost Management Plans, Time Management, Human Resources, Quality Management and Risk Management. It defines how the project is to be executed, monitored &Controlled, and closed. It needs the acceptance of all the stakeholders so that the execution can take place and risks mitigated. In this phase we establish the total scope of effort, objectives and course of action to attain the objectives.

A software project in an existing industry or business entails blended ways of working where parallel online and offline working is involved as well as client's and vendor's personnel work together. In such a situation a project plan serves as the anchor point. Software project planning is the task, which is performed before the software project actually starts. Although it has the highest impact on the software project but involves such activities that seemingly have very little connection with software development. They include collecting requirements, scope management and project estimation.

10.3.1.1. Requirements Gathering: It is the process of defining and documenting shareholders' need to meet the project objectives. It is undertaken after the feasibility report is found to be positive towards undertaking the project. Analysts and engineers communicate with the client and end-users to know their ideas on what the software should provide and which features they want the software to include.

One of the important documents of this phase is SRS (Software Requirement Specification) that is created by the system analysts after the requirements are collected from various stakeholders. It defines how the intended software will interact with hardware, external interfaces, speed of operation, response time of system, portability of software across various platforms, maintainability, speed of recovery after crashing, security, quality, limitations etc.

In the SRS, the user requirements as expressed by them are recorded in natural language, and the technical requirements are in structural language as they are to be used within the software developing organisation. Pseudo code should be used to depict the design requirements with formats of forms and GUI screen prints while conditional and mathematical notations should be used for DFDs etc.

The process of communication with stakeholders for gathering requirements may include interviews, surveys, and document / report reviews. The interviews can be structured, non-structured, oral, written, and one-to-one or group as per the convenience of the stakeholders and the analysts. Organisations may conduct surveys among various stakeholders by querying about their expectations and requirements from the upcoming system. The existing reports, formats, SOPs (standard operating procedures), manuals, and publications are thoroughly examined to get the first hand idea about requirements.

10.3.1.2. Requirement Validation: After the requirement specifications are developed, it is important to validate the requirements because the users might ask for impractical solutions or the analysts might interpret the requirements incorrectly. There can be technical, legal, social, and organisational issues that might crop up due to such non-clarity. Thus it is important to check the requirements in the SRS against certain parameters.

- Are they practically implementable?
- Are they valid and as per functionality?
- Are there any ambiguities?
- Are they complete?
- Are they demonstrable?

For the process of validation, requirements are first arranged in order of importance, urgency and convenience and then negotiation & discussions are held with stakeholders. As the requirements come from various stakeholders, there are possibilities of ambiguity and conflicts, which are discussed for clarity and correctness. The unrealistic requirements are reasonably compromised and agreed upon. Finally the SRS gets modified as a mutually agreed document that contains all formal and informal, functional and non-functional requirements that become the foundation for the next phase of the project.

10.3.1.3. Scope Management: Scope Management includes the processes required to ensure that the project includes all the work required and only the work required to complete the project successfully, and should be defined and controlled what is to be included in the project. Defining the scope of the project that includes all the activities and processes needed to be done in order to make a deliverable software product is essential because it creates boundaries of the project by clearly enumerating what would be done in the project and what would not be done. It involves defining the scope, dividing the project into various smaller parts for ease of management, verifying the scope, and controlling the scope by incorporating any changes thereby.

- **Define Scope:** It is the process of developing a detailed description of the project and product.
- **Create Work Breakdown Structures (WBS):** It is the process of subdividing project deliverables and projects into smaller, more manageable components.
- **Verify Scope:** It is the process of formalising acceptance of the completed project deliverables.

- **Control Scope**: It is the process of monitoring the status of the project and product scope and managing changes to the scope baseline.

10.3.1.4. Project Estimation: Accurate estimation of various resources like time, money, labour, materials, risks etc is critical for managing and controlling the project efficiently and effectively. It may involve software size estimation in terms of coding requirements, effort estimation in terms of personnel and man-hour requirements, time estimation for the project, and cost estimation in terms of expenditure required for software, hardware, licences, manpower, travel, communication, training and support etc.

There are various techniques for Project Estimation like Decomposition Technique using line of code and function points, Empirical Estimation Techniques like Putnam Model (using time and effort required) and COCOMO - Constructive COst Model (based on type of software – organic, semi-detached, embedded).

10.3.1.5. Project Plan Document: When the above activities are completed a project plan is developed, discussed with the stakeholders and finalised. This document works as the base and guides the project deliverables and work required to complete them.

- Get stakeholder approval on scope
- Select project team
- Break down work into smaller manageable pieces (WBS)
- Develop Project schedule
- Determine project quality standards
- Determine project teams roles and responsibilities
- Complete Risk Identification, Analysis and Risk Response Planning
- Document project Management Plan

10.3.2. Project Execution and Monitoring

Project Execution & Monitoring is the phase during which the tasks described in project plans are executed according to their schedules and requires not only execution, but also monitoring in order to check whether everything is going according to the plan. During the process itself it is necessary to observe and report the status of various tasks, the probabilities of risk, and take measures to address the risks. The process of project execution starts with project scheduling and resource allocation and progresses under continuous monitoring and feedback through communication.

10.3.2.1. Project Scheduling: It refers to a roadmap of all activities to be done in specific order and within the time slot allotted to each activity. Project managers tend to define various tasks and project milestones, and arrange them keeping various factors in mind. They look for tasks that lie in a critical path in the schedule, which are necessary to be completed in a specific manner (because of task interdependence) and strictly within the time allocated.

Tasks that lie out of critical path and are less likely to impact the overall schedule of the project may be arranged as per convenience of the teams.

For scheduling a project, it is necessary to:

- Break down the project tasks into smaller, manageable jobs.
- Find out correlation between various tasks.
- Estimate time frame required for each task.
- Divide time into working teams and assign an adequate volume of labour for each task.
- Maintain the total time required for the project from start to finish under control.

10.3.2.2. Resource Management: Like any other project, software projects require resources specific to that project. Understandably these include human resource, developmental tools, hardware availability, and software libraries. In any organisation, resources are available only in limited quantities and mostly are as a pool of assets. Optimum allocation of each resource is necessary, because shortage of resources hampers the project and may cause it to lag behind the schedule, whereas extra resources increase the project cost.

As such, Resource Management includes defining the proper organisational structure of the project team and allocating responsibilities to each team member. Determining requirements of other resources at a particular stage and making arrangements for their availability becomes the first responsibility of the project team. Due to the nature of software projects, there is a necessity for dynamic management of resources so as to meet the requirements by allocating them when requests arise and de-allocating when they are no longer needed.

10.3.2.3. Project Monitoring: The intangibility of software projects makes it difficult to keep track of the progress and adherence to timelines unlike other projects where the work-done can be physically measured. Thus, it becomes imperative to have a check on the activities and on achievement of the milestones as per the schedule. Regular structured status reporting is a must for executing a software project.

- **Activity monitoring** involves the juxtaposition of actual activities carried out on a day vis-à-vis the schedule for the task. Completion of all the sub-tasks or activities within the task and their integration marks completion of the task.
- **Status reporting** involves generation of periodic reports on status of activities and tasks completed within a given time frame that need to be created where the status of each broken-down task can be marked as finished, pending, or work-in-progress etc.
- **Milestones achievement checklist** is created for the project in which major tasks are designated as milestones based on the various phases of SDLC. This milestone checklist is prepared periodically for monitoring status of the project and making mid-course corrections, if required.

10.3.2.4. Project Communication Process: Effective communication plays a vital role in the successful implementation of a software project. Communication is a two way process of transferring information from one entity to another. It bridges gaps in communication between the client and the company, among the team members, with stakeholders of the project, and vendors of hardware, network, etc.

The communication process needs to be well planned and mutually agreed. It should include identification of key stakeholders in the project, the mode of communication with them, and any additional communication facilities required. It should be ensured that the right information is shared with the right person at the right time. Typically, project management plans, project charter, status reports, emails, notes, and other conversations are the communication methods used. There has to be an inbuilt continuous feedback channel that ensures that everyone involved in the project is up to date with project progress and its status.

The Project Communication Process involves the need to...

- Identify Stakeholders
- Plan Communications
- Share Communications
- Manage Stakeholders Expectations
- Report Performance

An important aspect of software project communication is to have a well defined procedure for closure at every stage. At the end of each major event, milestone, or end of a phase of SDLC, closure should be formally announced to update every stakeholder so that there is minimum scope of ad-hoc requests for changes.

10.3.3. Risk Management

Software projects face risks that are typical to the IT industry and the risks become more pronounced in case of digital transformation projects. Risk is an uncertainty that can positively or negatively impact a project. There is a need to have a risk management process that takes care of all activities pertaining to identification, analysing and making provision for predictable and unpredictable risks in the project. These risks may include, but may not be limited to the following:

- Experienced people leaving the project.
- New hands coming in with different ideas and skills.
- Change in management of the software company or in the client organisation.
- Frequent changes in requirements or misinterpretation of requirements.
- Poor estimation of required time and resources.
- Technological changes, environmental changes, business competition.

In order to alleviate and minimise the risk impact, the software management team should follow the process of identification, categorization, management, and monitoring of all possible risks in an ongoing manner. Risk identification should look for early symptoms and categorisation should focus on the possible impact the risk would have therefore mark them as high, medium and low risks. Emphasis should be on avoiding the occurrence of risks and once they occur on mitigating them with least side-effects.

- Plan Risk Management
- Identify Risks
- Perform Qualitative and Quantitative Risk Analysis
- Categorise risk as per severity of impact
- Manage Risk Response
- Monitor and control Risks.

10.3.4. Configuration Management

Configuration management is a process of tracking and controlling the changes in software in terms of the requirements, design, functions and development. Once the SRS has been finalised there should be as little requirement of changes from the user as possible. There should be a policy to implement a change control system for formally collecting documented procedures, paperwork and authorised changes.

If such requests come up, they are to be addressed only with prior approval of appropriate level of management as they may cause cost and time overrun. The changes in the identified and defined configuration of the system should be controlled throughout their life cycle, by recording and reporting the status of items and change requests as well as verifying the completeness and correctness of the requests.

- **Baseline**: Every phase of SDLC is assumed to be over when all activities pertaining to it are finished, documented, and communicated. This becomes the baseline for configuration management for taking care of occurrence of any change (process, requirement, technological etc.).
- **Change Control**: Change control is the function of configuration management, and it ensures that all changes made to software systems are consistent, properly approved, and as per organisational

rules and regulations. Every request for change should go through the steps listed below.

- **Identification**: A change request received from either an internal or an external source is documented and is first examined in terms of its context, content, and relevance to the system, and only then it is formally identified as a change request.
- **Validation**: A standard process of checking the validity of change requests has to be established at the project planning stage itself. A change request goes through the validation and its handling procedure is confirmed.
- **Analysis**: Impact of the requested change in terms of schedule, cost, and required efforts is analysed. Special emphasis is put on any possible prospective changes in the system.
- **Control**: Depending upon the impact and prospective changes resulting from the requested change, it is decided if the change is worth incorporation or not. If the change is unavoidable and it is decided to go ahead, it is mandatory to take approval of the appropriate authorities before the change is incorporated into the system. In any case, if the change is not being incorporated, the request is refused formally.
- **Execution**: Whenever a change request is executed in any phase, it is imperative that appropriate actions are taken in subsequent phases to do a thorough revision and incorporate relevant changes, if necessary.
- **Close Request**: Once a change is implemented and is merged with the rest of the system, this newly incorporated change in the software is documented properly and the request is formally closed.

10.4. Software Project Quality Management

Quality is defined as conformance to requirements and fitness for use. When project requirements are met and the resulting product / service is usable then the quality has been met. Cost of quality includes all costs incurred over the life of the product by investing in preventing non-conformance to requirements and ensuring that the product conforms to requirements eliminating any rework.

Although "fitness of purpose" is a satisfactory interpretation of quality for many devices such as a car, a table fan, a grinding machine, etc. but for software products, "fitness of purpose" is not a wholly satisfactory definition of quality. For software products, the fitness of use is generally explained in terms of satisfaction of the requirements laid down in the SRS document.

In general, quality control refers to the process of monitoring and recording results of executing the quality activities to assess performance and recommend necessary changes and is performed throughout the project. Software Quality Management ensures that the required level of quality is maintained throughout the product development process. SQA aims to develop a culture within the team and quality is the responsibility of each and everyone in the organisation. Software Quality management should be independent of project management to ensure independence of cost and schedule adherences.

Some of the parameters that are inexplicitly desired in quality software even though they may not form part of the SRS are listed below.

- **Usability**: A quality software product has good usability i.e. various categories of users can easily invoke the functions of the product.
- **Correctness**: Various requirements as specified in the SRS document have been correctly implemented.
- **Portability**: The software should be portable i.e. can work on various operating system environments, in multiple machines, with other software products, etc.
- **Reusability**: The software should have reusability and modules of the product may be reused to develop new products.
- **Maintainability**: Maintainable software product allows for easy correction of bugs as and when they show up, addition of new tasks to the product, and modification of functionalities of the product, etc.

10.4.1. Activities of Software Quality Management

Software project quality control management can be segmented into four key components to be effective: quality planning, quality control, quality assurance, and quality improvement.

10.4.1.1. Quality Control Planning: The first step of quality management is planning. Organisation needs to take time to identify the goals and the baseline for quality standards. In this planning stage, the following should be considered:

- Stakeholders' expectations and priorities.
- Company's definition of successful software product.
- The legal standards or requirements that must be abided by.
- People to handle the quality management roles of supervision, testing, validation, approval etc.
- Frequency of review and evaluation for improvement.

10.4.1.2. Quality Control: It is the process of inspecting and testing the process as well as the product at different stages in line with what has been laid out in the planning stage to make sure that they are being achieved. Conforming to the standards that have been put in place and identifying any deviations or errors that need to be corrected should be done as soon as possible. The inspection data, once collected should be analysed and shared to make sure that all concerned have access to them.

10.4.1.3. Quality Assurance: Quality control involves inspecting the process and products while under development, quality assurance involves reviewing the delivery of products or services before delivery. It eliminated mistakes or defects reaching the customer. The feedback from Quality Assurance helps fine tune the processes to prevent errors in the future. To be effective, quality assurance should be conducted regularly through independent audits and it is preferable to have the audit done by a third-party which is not invested in the outcome, financially or emotionally.

10.4.1.4. Quality Improvement: Continual improvement is the key to successful quality management. The quality management process needs to gather all relevant data, re-evaluate both the processes and the product keeping compliance in mind, thoroughly review the findings, and come up with a way to improve the methods going forward. Quality control management is fruitless if the changes are not made when they are necessary.

10.5. Software Project Management: The Complexities

Software project management is not just different from any other type of project management, but it is much more complex. These complexities refer to the various difficulties in managing a software project because of the typical nature of the activities in software development and implementation. The complexities manifest themselves in different forms:

- **Time Management Complexity:** Estimation of the duration of the project is quite difficult because of the interdependence of multiplicity of activities and interlinkages amongst the functions, routines, and protocols.
- **Cost Management Complexity:** Total cost of the project is dependent upon the manpower requirement, skill-set requirements, possibilities of time over-run due to multiple stages of user interaction etc.
- **Quality Management Complexity**: Quality of the project must satisfy the customer, who is many a time a party to the ad-hoc change requests that might have been disagreed by the software development team.
- **Risk Management Complexity**: Risks in a software project relate to such areas that generally are not anticipated by managers from other area. They include licences, IPR, resource crunch, frequent changes in requirements, industrial disputes, etc. Serious efforts are required to identify these risks and make amendment plans to reduce impact of these risks.
- **Human Resources Management Complexity:** ICT is a very high manpower turnover area with quick mobility of skilled personnel. It causes difficulties in organising, managing, leading the project team, and delivering the project in time.
- **Communication Complexity:** Interconnectivity of the sub-systems makes it necessary that the members must interact with other members on regular basis, and there must be effective communication with the customer.
- **Procurement Management Complexity:** Software projects need many services from third parties like hardware vendors, network providers, and application tools providers to complete the task. Ensuring all such resources increases the complexity of the project.

- **Integration Management Complexity:** Coordinating integration of the sub-tasks, ensuring their mutual agreement, adherence to sequential schedules, managing slippages from some of the sub-teams, keeping the change management aligned to the project plan are complex activities, but they are necessary to ensure completion and delivery of the software project.

10.5.1. Factors which drive Software Project Complexity

- **Invisibility**: Softwares are inherently invisible, and until the software project development is complete, the software remains invisible. Anything that is invisible is difficult to manage and control. Software project managers and clients cannot see the progress of the project on a continuous basis. They can monitor the modules of the software that have been completed by the development team and the documents that have been prepared, which are a rough indicator of the progress achieved.
- **Changeability**: Software is not a physically visible structure being built, hence it is prone to requests for change. Most of these change requirements come from the customer during the software development phase and many of them result in redoing some work. Frequent changes to the requirements play a major role in making software project management complex.
- **Interaction Protocols**: These days, software of even moderate size has millions of parts functions interacting with each other in many ways like data coupling, serial and concurrent runs, state transitions, control dependency, file sharing, etc. The inherent complexity of these interactions among the basic parts making up the software creates many types of risks in software development.
- **Uniqueness**: Usually a software project is associated with many features or situations unique to the particular customer requirements. This makes every software product completely different from the other software products. Due to this software project turns out to be completely different from projects in other domains such as building and bridge construction, equipment and machine erection etc. where the projects are predictable to a large extent. Every software project brings unknown problems that are quite dissimilar to other software projects that managers would have encountered in the past.

- **Exactness of the Solution**: A software solution is expected to be exact according to the requirements and the design. A small error can create a huge problem in the software project acceptance. The parameters of function calls in the program have to be correct to the micro-level in line with the function definition. This requirement of exact conformity at micro–level as well as macro-level introduces additional challenges and increases complexity of software projects.
- **Intellect-intensive and Team-oriented Work**: Software development is an intellect-intensive work and project requires a team-oriented workforce, because a software cannot be developed without interaction between developers. There are requirements of synergy, collaboration, and compromises throughout the life cycle of the project and the need for interfacing with several team members creates complexity in managing the project.
- **Lack of Standardization in Estimation**: Project estimation sets the foundation of project planning. However, software project estimation is highly empirical and there are no set standards for predicting time, manpower, network, and software application tools requirements as everything depends on the size of the project. This makes the whole exercise of project estimation very subjective, ad-hoc, and complex.

10.6. Project Management Tools

Project management includes processes required to manage timely completion of the project and is concerned with developing a realistic project schedule and controlling changes to the schedule including contingencies management. The risk and uncertainty of delay in completion of the project rise multi-fold with the size of the project and even when the project is developed according to set methodologies there is a need for continuous monitoring.

The project schedule assigns to the activities a duration and sequence in a logical order. It also defines the start and end dates of the project and the project activities, but a software project has many requirements cropping up incessantly and they have potential to disrupt the whole development process. It is necessary to have project management tools like Gantt Chart, CPT-PERT etc to monitor the project progress and find any slippages from the schedule.

For monitoring the project against a schedule we need to define activities in the schedule by identifying specific actions to be performed to produce the project deliverables. Then sequencing of activities is done by identifying and documenting relationships (dependencies) among the project activities. Estimation of resources for activities is done to assess the types and quantities of materials, people, equipment or supplies required to perform each activity.

- **GANTT Chart:** A typical GANTT Chart displays the start and end dates of a project schedule with respect to time periods. It is a horizontal bar chart with bars representing activities and time scheduled for the project activities.

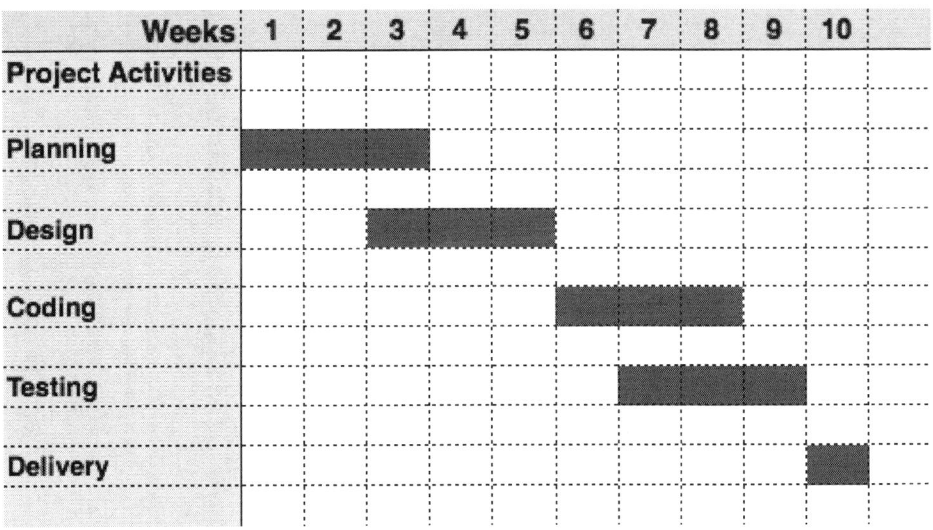

Figure 10.1: Example of GANTT Chart

- **PERT Chart:** PERT (Program Evaluation & Review Technique) chart is a tool that depicts project as a network diagram graphically representing main events of project that can be carried on parallel or sequentially. Events are shown as numbered nodes while activities are shown as connecting labelled arrows. The sequence of tasks in the project shows dependency of the later event on the previous one.

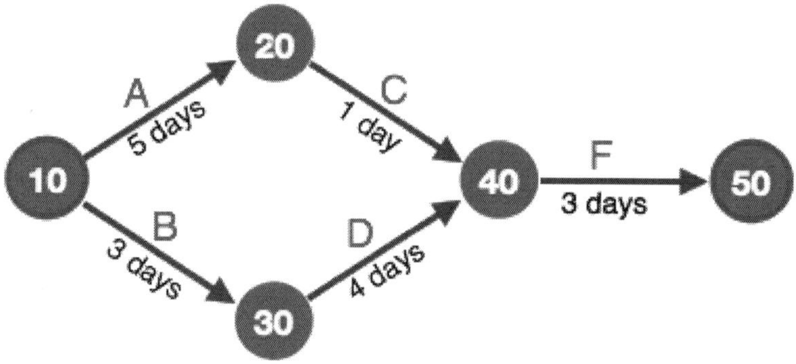

Figure 10.2: Example of PERT Chart

- **Critical Path Analysis (CPM):** Similar to the PERT diagram, in CPM each event is allotted a specific time frame and the dependency of the event dictates that the team can proceed to the next task only if the previous one is completed. This tool helps in recognizing interdependent tasks in the project and identifying the shortest path or critical path to complete the project successfully. The events are arranged according to their earliest possible start time.

Path between start and end node is a critical path which cannot be further reduced and all events are required to be executed in the same order. The path in which there is slack can be analysed to reallocate resources for completing the task more efficiently.

- **Resource Histogram**: Project time management of a software project is highly dependent on effective management of the human resources in terms of their quality, skills, numbers, and availability. Resource Histogram is a graphical tool that contains a bar or chart representing the number of resources required over time for a project event or phase.

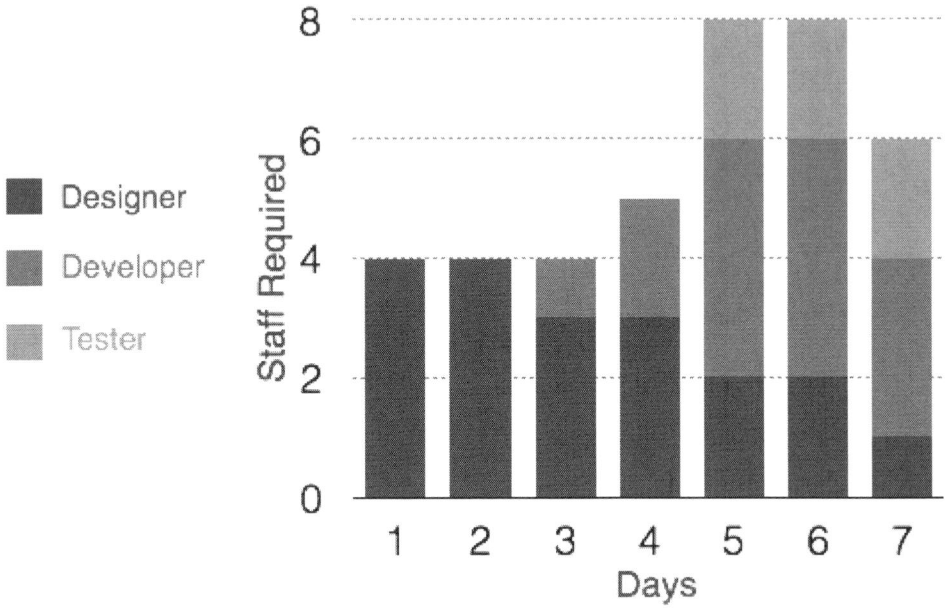

Figure 10.3: Example of Resource Histogram

10.7. Implementing a Digital Transformation Software Project

Managing a digital transformation project requires identifying project requirements, managing stakeholders, balancing project constraints (e.g. time, cost, quality, etc.). Digital transformation software projects are characterised by some unique features. They include:

- Every DT software project may have a unique and distinct goal.
- A DT project is not routine activity or part of day-to-day operations.
- Just like any project, DT projects also come with a start time and end time.
- It is expected that, similar to a technology project, the DT project should end when its goal is achieved.
- Similar to any project it needs adequate resources in terms of time, manpower, finance, material and knowledge-bank.

The process of implementation of a DT software project typically involves the following broad phases:

1. Initiating Phase
2. Execution Phase
3. Closing Phase

10.7.1. Initiating Phase

In the first phase, the objective is to define a new project. When the Project Charter is approved the project is officially authorised.

- **Project Charter:** The Project Charter formally authorises the existence of the project. It is a document that officially starts a project or a phase. It provides authority to the project manager to spend money and other corporate resources. The Charter defines the high-level project requirements and is issued by the Project Sponsor. It provides a reference source for the future and gives a direction and a sense of purpose to the management from start to end. It is broad enough not to require any changes during project execution.
- **Project Objective:** It is important to articulate the Project Objectives so that it works as the guiding document throughout the SDLC process for various process groups and sub processes to get the benefits.

10.7.2. Execution Phase:

The second phase involves the planning, execution, monitoring and control activities. The process group completes the work defined in the project management plan to satisfy project specifications.

- Manage stakeholder expectation
- Complete work packages
- Implement Quality Assurance
- Produce project reports
- Remove project bottlenecks
- Organise team building activities
- Organise training for team members
- Conduct project progress meetings
- Milestone approvals from clients

10.7.3. Closing Phase:

A project comes to an end when either its objectives are met or its objectives are not met due to various reasons. In the third phase, all the activities across all the project management process groups are formally announced to have been completed thereby marking completion of the project, or contractual obligations. At this stage it is necessary to cross check that the following have been achieved:

- Confirm all project requirements are met.
- Obtain formal sign off from customer
- Make payments to all parties and update cost record
- Complete contract closure
- Update lessons learnt database
- Measure customer satisfaction
- Handover project deliverables to Operations Team.

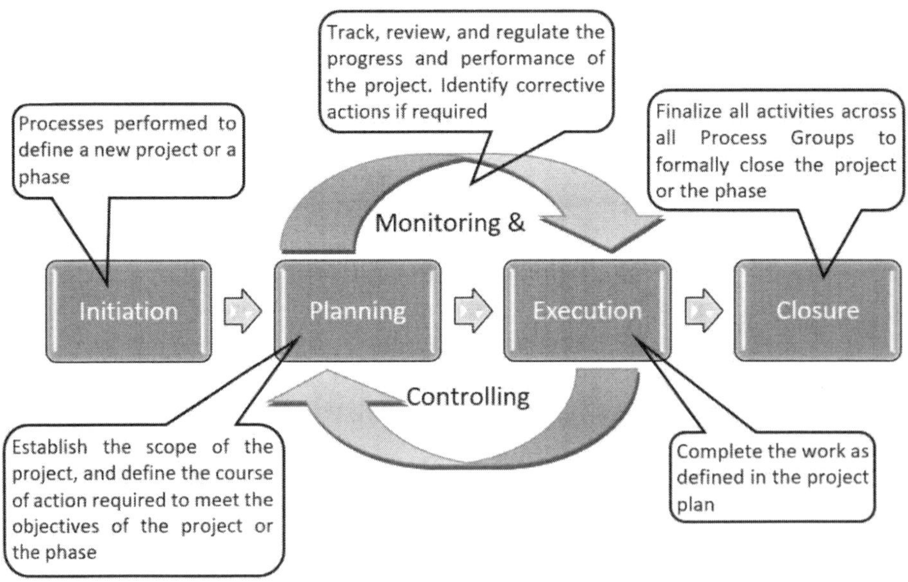

Figure 10.4: Flow Chart of DT Software Project Implementation

10.8. Project Management Office (PMO)

There is a need to have a Project Management Office (PMO) that has very critical roles to play in terms of providing policies, methodologies, tools and templates for managing projects within the organisation. It arranges for providing support and training to the concerned in the organisation as to how to manage projects and manages interdependencies between sub-projects, programs and portfolios.

While a program is a group of related projects managed in a coordinated way to obtain benefits and control not available from managing them individually, a portfolio refers to a collection of projects or programs and other work that are grouped together to facilitate effective management of that work to meet strategic business objectives.

The PMO has certain specific managerial responsibilities to shoulder throughout the currency of the project.

10.8.1. Stakeholder Management:

Stakeholders are people or organisations actively involved in the project or whose interests may be positively or negatively affected by the performance or completion of the project e.g. sponsors, customers, project managers, functional managers, unions, users, etc. The keys steps in stakeholder management include:

- Identification of Internal and External Stakeholders
- Determining stakeholder requirements
- Determining Stakeholders expectation
- Communication with Stakeholders.
- Obtaining concurrence of stakeholders on the processes.

10.8.2. Project Cost Management

Project cost management includes the processes involved in estimating budgeting and controlling costs so that projects can be completed within the approved budget. It contains details like how to go about planning the project cost and how to effectively manage and control the project to the cost baseline and manage cost variance. Determining the budget is an important step in project cost management. It is the process of aggregating the estimated costs of individual activities or work packages to establish an authorised cost baseline. Monitoring of the Budget Vs Actual expenditure and taking corrective steps for any variance deviation is a key part of the Monitoring and Control phase.

10.8.3. Project Human Resources Management

In a DT project the most important task of the PMO is to manage the human resources because of the complexities of high turn-over, specialisations, interpersonal relations among individuals, and requirements of team working. The project team is composed of the people with assigned roles and responsibilities of completing the project. HR management of a DT project includes the processes of organising, managing, and leading the project team.

The components of the HR management include developing Human Resource Plan, creating and developing the project team, managing the team effectively so as to deliver the project in time and without cost over-run.

10.8.4. Project Procurement Management

It is the process necessary to purchase or acquire products, services, or results needed from outside the project team. The PMO is required to Plan, Conduct, Administer, and Close procurement so as to provide the project team all the resources required by them towards completion of the project. Although it may not seem to be a major task in a software project because of lack of tangible assets, the procurement management for a software project is a complex task due to the intricacies of licences, regulations, modes of delivery, fast changing versions of products, and pace of change of technology.

10.9. Some Critical Concepts in Digital Transformation Software Projects

10.9.1. Digital Transformation - a Brownfield Project

Almost every Digital Transformation project today is a brown-field software development project, in which the development and deployment of a new software system is done in presence of an existing or legacy software systems. The new software architecture must consider and coexist with systems already in place so as to enhance existing functionality or capability. There are certain advantages of brown-field projects and some disadvantages.

The advantages of brown-field software development include availability of a reference place to start, a predetermined direction, and opportunity to bring improvements to existing technology solutions. It supports working with defined business processes and technology solutions and also allows possibilities of using existing codes with added new features.

Some of the disadvantages of brown-field projects include requirement of thorough knowledge of existing systems, services, and data on which the new system needs to be built, need to re-engineer a large portion of the existing complex environment, and precise understanding of the constraints of the existing IT so that the new project does not fail.

Dealing with legacy code not only slows down the development process and adds to overall development costs, but may even cause major roadblocks in the process.

10.9.2. Agile Methodology of Software Project Management

There is a shift in the way software projects are managed and modern day software development projects work on the Agile Methodology. Agile is technically more of a framework than a distinct model. Within Agile, there are sub-models in place such as Extreme Programming (XP), Rapid Application Development (RAD), Kanban and Scrum methodology. The main benefits of adopting Agile methodology is in selecting, managing and deploying shared resources. These benefits result in:

- Consistent communication
- Effective resource allocation
- Higher productivity
- Quality improvement,
- Production cost reduction,
- Error rate reduction,
- A higher level of customer service,
- Increased customer retention rate.
- Learning by Retrospection

10.10. Starting a Digital Transformation Project: A Checklist for Practitioners

Digital transformation projects are about change. Inevitably, they involve hard work both during the project and after the launch. They also require careful preparation prior to the project start; the kind of of research and scoping done and the questions asked can make all the difference to success.

10.10.1. Does the digital transformation project align with wider organisational goals?

When a digital transformation project is being planned, it's quite possible to get caught up in the minutiae and miss the bigger picture. Every digital transformation project must align with the wider goals of the organisation and its key strategic objectives. Every digital transformation project should be easily expressed as part of a wider digital strategy and being explicit about a project's wider value is key in aligning different stakeholders and project team members, framing expectations for digital implementation partners, scoping out details of the project, defining what success looks like and helping ensure everyone maintain focus.

10.10.2. Has thorough user research been carried out?

In order to ascertain the details and scope out the requirements of the DT project, a thorough understanding of the customers, the users, and other stakeholders is a must. A digital transformation project should never be based on assumptions and the decisions must be based on data and evidence.

10.10.3. Is the project just recreating the old process with new digital tools?

Many digital transformation projects face the typical pitfall of taking an old inefficient process and turning it into a new inefficient digital process. They miss out on eliminating unnecessary steps, driving innovation, creating unexpected outcomes and improving customer service. Digital transformation is about more fundamental change and instead of reproducing what organisation already does, it should focus on rethinking a process from the ground up, starting with the problem the organisation is trying to solve and the outcome they are trying to achieve.

10.10.4. Are the right skills and resources available and accessible?

While there is a lot of emphasis on assembling the right project team, it is important not to forget the wider team which plays the peripheral but still critical role in the digital transformation project implementation. Early conversations between the digital implementation partner and the organisation are a good idea here. However, in-house resources can also be a rich stream of experience to draw upon, especially in the area of user testing.

10.10.5. Have change management and communication activities been planned?

Digital transformation is as much about changing behaviours as it is about new technology. It is essential to include change management and related communications in project planning and give them necessary time and resources. How to involve the users and stakeholders from the beginning should be a matter of concern and carrying out user research and gathering ongoing feedback not only brings in critical data to fuel the project but is a change tactic in itself. Unfortunately, when budgets are tight, it's usually the change aspects that are left under-resourced. .

10.10.6. Have the risk and compliance teams been involved?

Most of the regulated industries such as financial services already have processes in place to make sure that any and every activity aligns with the organisation's legal and regulatory commitments, navigating GDPR concerns, and confirming legal, regulatory and security concerns. However, in the less regulated industries teams can forget to get the compliance team on board early and may miss on communicating with the trade unions or workers' councils. It should be endeavour of DT project implementers to involve the legal, risk and compliance teams in the project as early as possible and identify the risks and deal with any potential showstoppers upfront, as well as work on critical elements like Terms and Conditions.

10.10.7. Are there any technical and data dependencies?

The roadblocks in Digital Transformation projects don't come only from compliance areas, but also from technical and data areas. Data cleanliness, data duplicities, data incompleteness, and technical as well as data dependencies need to be identified that could delay the project or limit its success.

10.10.8. Has success been defined as to what it looks like?

The DT project management team should know where to end so as to align the requirements, garner efforts to drive adoption, and solicit any improvements that need to be made after launch. Success can be achieved only when it is defined what success looks like. The user research provides baseline data that can be used to compare before and after status of data, information, processes, productivity, and performance of the organisation.

10.10.9. Has provision been made for after launch resources by organisation?

After launch of the Digital Transformation projects, the systems, sites, and apps developed thereof can't sustain by themselves. They would require further iteration and evolution, continuous change, and regular communication. For this and to carry out day-to-day management, people with appropriate skill-set may be required to be deputed.

10.10.10. Have the right questions been asked?

Assessment of requirements, understanding of processes, and appreciation of interdependencies as well as preparation and scoping are essential for success of a DT project. All these can be achieved only with proper communication for which asking right questions is the best way so as to get proper answers that would help in the planning, execution, and monitoring processes

****

APPENDICES

Scan the QR Code to have a look at the detailed Appendices

ABOUT THE BOOK

The Handbook on Implementation of Digital Transformation for Enterprises is meant for business management professionals to get a comprehensive overview about the digital transformation journey. By drawing from case studies, the handbook presents insights about the digital transformation process in a stepwise manner. From presenting the key concepts of digital technologies in today's world, to reviewing the best implementation practices, the book highlights the approaches, techniques, challenges, and opportunities to empower implementers to overcome the pitfalls which are ubiquitous to the digital transformation process.

ACKNOWLEDGEMENTS

The authors have undertaken the journey of bringing out this book with the objective of presenting a practitioner-focused resource to manage and lead digital transformation processes successfully. Drawing heavily from our experiences across countries, industries, and businesses, this book is an attempt at giving back to the community an opportunity to embrace the digital ways to navigate the future. As a part of our vocational service to the next generation, we aim at bringing to the table a more holistic understanding of the technology and its workings.

Individually, I, Soumitra, would like to thank my family members for supporting me in this journey and giving me the encouragement. My thanks are due to my peers in various projects and programs of work for their dedication and sincerity to accomplish the tech implementations on time and budget, and to my clients across the world for the opportunity to serve them on various transformation programs of work.

And I, Rajan, am grateful to almighty for having given me opportunities to work, experiment, experience and learn through successes and failures in a variety of projects, programs, and portfolios. The unstinted support and encouragement from my wife and my family members have seen me through the process of completion of this book, for which I am indebted to them.

We have included many use cases from various organizations and professionals, picking them from different sources as examples and learning events to elucidate the concepts and contents. We assure them that it is intended only for academic purpose, and we are thankful to all such organizations and people.

Soumyo Das, Researcher at Emylon Business School, France, and Tulsidharan Vishwanathan, Co-Founder at Vitti Research Foundation deserve special mention for their insights and contributions to the book. We would like to thank Blue Hill Publishers for the unstinted support in getting out the publication, and Usnish, Rahul and Dipayan for their valuable inputs and support.

We thank our well-wishers and ecosystem partners and hope that our effort reaches those who deserve it the most.

Soumitra Poddar
Kolkata

Rajan K Prasad
New Delhi

Printed in Great Britain
by Amazon

17451247R00135